Collecting Local History

Collecting Local History

James Mackay

LONGMAN
London and New York

Longman Group Limited
Longman House, Burnt Mill, Harlow
Essex CM20 2JE, England
Associated companies throughout the world

*Published in the United States of America
by Longman Inc., New York*

© Longman Group Limited 1984

First published 1984

British Library Cataloguing in Publication Data

Mackay, James
  Collecting local history.
  1. Local history – Fieldwork
  2. Great Britain – History, Local
  I. Title
  941'.007'23   DA1
  ISBN 0–582–40613–7   **68502208**

Library of Congress Cataloging in Publication Data   **PQ**

Mackay, James A. (James Alexander), 1936–
  Collecting local history.

  Bibliography: p.
  Includes index.
  1. Great Britain – History, Local – Collectibles – Cata-
logs.   2. Collectibles – Great Britain – Catalogs.
  I. Title.
DA22.A1M34   1984   790.1'32'0941   83–18732
  ISBN 0–582–40613–7 (pbk.)

Set in 10/11 pt Times Linotron 202
Printed in Singapore by
Huntsmen Offset Printing (Pte) Ltd

Contents

Foreword

Many books exist covering every aspect of collecting and collectables but none has ever attempted to survey the entire range of collectables from the local angle. The idea for this book came to me some years ago when I visited Hilary Guard of Douglas, Isle of Man and inspected his remarkable collections of picture postcards, cheques, banknotes, coins, medals, tokens, badges, crested china, glass bottles and stoneware ginger beers, nautical mementoes and railwayana. The common denominator of this incredible range of different subjects was the place where they were issued or used, for everything pertained to the Isle of Man. Seeing the Guard collection made me realize how much more interesting and meaningful a collection could be if it was confined to a single town, district, county or region. Instead of collecting certain subjects, like potlids, stevengraphs or horse brasses to the exclusion of all else, how much more fascinating to integrate the different media to develop the story of one locality. By pursuing this approach to collecting one can see how craftsmen, working in different media, tackled similar problems of portrayal or the depiction of scenery and landmarks. This method of collecting adds an entirely new dimension to the study of all kinds of subjects, from ephemera to militaria, from the applied arts to industrial archaeology, and from this we can learn much more about the socio-economic and political history of our own neighbourhood. Moreover, in many respects the local collector has the advantage of getting to know his subject intimately and, being on the spot, can acquire material for his collection more readily.

In compiling this book I have had the ready assistance of a number of fellow collectors: William Carson and Robert MacGavin of Ayr, Hilary Guard of Douglas and Stephen Murray of Carlisle. I have visited numerous local museums and libraries in search of ideas and material and to their staff I extend my thanks. I am particularly indebted to Dr Larch Garrad of the Manx Museum, Miss Sue Kirby of the Carlisle Museum and my old friend and mentor Alfred H.

Truckell, MBE, lately retired from the curatorship of the Dumfries Museum. I should also like to thank Mrs Vera Webster (Vera Trinder Ltd), Kathleen Wowk (Stanley Gibbons Ltd) and Noel Dinwiddie.

James A. Mackay
Dumfries, 1984

larly antiques, stamps and coins. Inevitably this led to a shortage of the better quality material and as demand continued to grow prices rose sharply. This stimulated the trend towards more recent material. In the world of antiques, for example, the dateline of 1830 which had long been regarded as the watershed between antique and non-antique was steadily advanced. Legally and fiscally, an antique is now defined as an object more than 100 years old. In practice, however, antique dealers have long since included anything from the reign of Queen Victoria (1837–1901) and have now extended this to include the Edwardian era (1901–10). Reputable art historians have played a prominent part in advancing the dateline even further. First art nouveau (1895–1910), then art deco (1915–30) and art moderne (1930–40) were subject to reappraisal by the pundits, made respectable by retrospective exhibitions at the Victoria and Albert and New York's Metropolitan Museums, not to mention a plethora of guides, catalogues and monographs. More recently the frontier of what is collectable on grounds of antiquity alone has been advanced to include the Second World War and the 'Utility' era, and now Postwar Austerity and Festival (of Britain) are labels being applied to the collectables of the late-1940s and 1950s. Stamps and coins are important categories of collectables which have traditionally relied on the new-issue market and this has even spread to 'antiques', with limited editions of artefacts reproducing traditional styles, using 'authentic' materials and craft techniques.

While there has therefore been a trend to broaden the time-span of collectables, there has also been a trend towards a much more liberal interpretation of what is collectable. To some extent this is linked to the chronological criterion. Nowadays virtually anything is collectable, not so much if it is old but if it is obsolete. The term 'bygones' has now been broadened to encompass things formerly in fashion or everyday use but which, due to changing habits or technology, are no longer manufactured or marketed. After a decent interval of a year or two, gathering dust in the attic or cellar, these objects emerge as suitable material for antiquarian study and collecting. 'Yesterday's junk – tomorrow's antiques' or 'trash into treasure' are catch-phrases which vividly convey the trend towards the collectability of the most mundane objects, often devoid of aesthetic appeal (e.g. old bricks and hunks of barbed wire) but providing endless fascination for those who get beyond the superficial sameness of the subject and discover the subtle nuances in design and composition.

These trends extending datelines down to the present time and broadening the scope of what is collectable suffer from a problem which has bedevilled collectors since time immemorial. This problem affects all forms of collectable in varying degrees, depending on the scope of the subject. The person who sets out to collect walking sticks or glass paperweights could, with endless patience and inexhaustible funds, eventually amass a collection amounting to several thousand items. Even though each item may differ from its neighbours in some way there are limits to the size, shape, colour, materials used and techniques of design and composition. The collector reaches a stage where he is rather overwhelmed by it all and doubt creeps in as to the purpose and meaning of the hobby. Or the collection of one class of object may become obsessive, compulsive, perhaps even fetishistic, and the collector may be driven relentlessly in pursuit of completeness to pay outrageous sums for relatively paltry items which just happen to fill a gap in the collection. The manic, addictive nature of over-specialization in one subject, or even a single period or aspect of a subject, is a pitfall which has entrapped many collectors. The specialist collector has been derided as someone who starts out by knowing more and more about less and less, and ends up knowing everything about nothing.

Specialization in collecting has its positive side as well. Without such single-minded dedication to the subject we would not have the wealth of specialist literature which is available today, or the range of specialist museums and specialized collections preserved in more general museums, an invaluable source of reference for further study. But most collectors can never hope to attain the ultimate accolade – a name which becomes a household word in collecting circles either in respect of the 'bible' of the subject or as an abbreviated title to the leading museum collection – and are more intent on deriving pleasure and profit from their hobby than on perpetuating their name.

Local collecting offers an attractive and practical alternative to the traditional forms of subject collecting, eliminating the bugbear of completeness and other unhealthy aspects of too narrow a specialization. Furthermore, by tackling collecting on a geographical basis alone, the collector adds an important dimension to his hobby – something that is denied the general one-subject collector (unless his specialization is confined to the products of a single, well-defined area, such as Tunbridge ware or Newcastle glass). The local dimension enables the collector to relate the collectable material to the town or district whence it came, and one class of object to another within the same locality. A collection of objects of different types and materials whose common denominator is the town, county or region where they were produced or used then becomes a major adjunct to a study of local socio-economic and political history and sharpens an awareness of the past.

The relics associated with our town or county can tell us far more than any amount of historical or topographical literature about the way our ancestors lived, worked and spent their leisure time, what industries flourished or declined and died out. The United Kingdom is probably better served than any other country in the world for local museums, but even now most of them are still trying to emulate all the national museums in London put together in the all-embracing but necessarily haphazard nature of their collections. Too often the random cosmopolitan nature of these collections reflects the tastes and the travels of the donors of the material. Most borough and county museums had their origins in the second half of the nineteenth century and were true to the Victorian ideals of classicism and a profound belief in the omnipotence of the British Empire. Just as British national outlook has shed much of the old imperial sentiment, local museums have shifted their interests from the world at large to regional or even parochial matters, but they still have a long way to go. Some of them now restrict their activities to the history and heritage of their own area; others, while still attempting to be omnivorous, are giving increased attention to local art and artifacts. Both rely on public-spirited individuals to come forward with material for preservation but the process of educating the public to think locally is slow and decidedly patchy. Inevitably, a great deal of invaluable material is pulped or incinerated every year, or otherwise dispersed.

On the positive side, however, general interest in collectables with a local slant is growing steadily. Established collectors of long standing are discovering the interdependence of the various collectable media. A collection of early nineteenth century railway tickets possesses considerable interest in itself but how much more fascinating is a collection which is confined to one line, say the Liverpool and Manchester Railway, and includes railway share certificates, Lancashire banknotes showing vignettes of the early locomotives, pottery mugs and rack-plates commemorating the opening of the line, local horse brasses with a similar theme, engraved glasses and pictorial tourist paperweights depicting the railway, stevengraphs and printed handkerchiefs, commemorative medals and local tradesmen's tokens, contractors' billheads and letterheads, posters and postcards and a whole host of miscellaneous memorabilia. Of course, the world's first passenger railway lines are a special case, but the same criteria can be applied to other aspects of British industrial history. Collectors in Birmingham or Sheffield, for example, would tend to concentrate on collectables associated with the metal industries of these cities, while collectors in the West Midlands might concentrate on the pottery and porcelain produced in that area. In both cases, however, it would not be sufficient to leave it at the end-products of industry. All the other forms of collectable material, particularly the various kinds of printed ephemera, would give the local collection infinitely greater meaning.

Even in the rural and relatively undeveloped areas it is surprising what a wealth and variety of collectable material exists. The

Appendix of this book lists the chief cities, counties and regions of the United Kingdom, with a numerically coded listing of the main categories of collectables. Few of the areas can claim a representation in all twenty-four categories listed, but a surprisingly high proportion of them can produce material in sixteen or more. Even Orkney and Shetland, which come at the bottom of the list, can each field ten categories of collectable, and I have no doubt that collectors concentrating on those areas would not be long in finding other categories which I have not listed.

The collectable material covers an astonishingly wide range. Apart from the end products of local industry certain types of collectable provide an excellent commentary on the history and development of the locality. Chief among these are picture postcards, maps and prints, posters, leaflets, tradesmen's billheads, trade cards and other ephemera. Cheques, banknotes, stock and share certificates and the trade tokens which circulated in lieu of small change tell us a great deal about the commercial development of our district. The larger, three-dimensional kinds of collectable, particularly the treen, metalware and ceramics, may either have been produced as tourist mementoes, publicizing local beauty spots, or as souvenirs of important occasions in local history or as a tribute to local celebrities. In both cases the tourist and commemorative wares reflect the attitudes of the past, and what our forefathers considered important at the time.

All of these objects may be collected purely for their own sake, but collectors, almost by definition, are inquisitive as well as acquisitive and an intelligent study of even one branch of collecting at a local level will lead the collector into all kinds of byways of local history and this, in turn, will produce innumerable links between one category and another. People who start out purely as collectors end up as local historians and vice versa. The objects of a bygone age and the history surrounding them are inextricably interwoven. The same applies to genealogy which is, after all, local history of a kind. One begins by researching a family tree and this may lead to concentration on one particular parish or county. The more the story unfolds the deeper becomes the interest in that locality. My wife is a New Zealander who began tracing her ancestry after she came to England, and eventually concentrated on the Matfield and Brenchley parishes of Kent. From this developed an interest in the history of that area in general and then, from the collectors's viewpoint, in the postal history in particular. This has since expanded to include not only old letters and postmarks of the area but picture postcards and printed ephemera and other material relating to those parishes.

At this juncture I should point out two of the pitfalls in local collecting which my wife has encountered. Since we do not live in

Kent her access to collectable material is very limited and she has to rely at second or third hand on dealers or other collectors of similar material. Secondly, Kent, as one of the Home Counties of England, ranks high in the popularity stakes and consequently material pertaining to it tends to be relatively expensive. The Home Counties have a high population density and include a large proportion in the higher socio-economic groups more likely to have a well-developed interest in collecting and the wherewithal to indulge that interest. Postal history material and picture postcards, maps and topographical prints from the Home Counties therefore tend to be much more expensive than comparable items from say Cumbria or County Down. This is particularly true when a well-established market for such material exists in a county town. Anything with a distinct local interest is subject to the normal laws of supply and demand and priced accordingly. Conversely some of my wife's best bargains have been picked up in other parts of the country where Kent-related material was not so highly rated.

No collector can derive the utmost from his hobby by pursuing it in splendid isolation. Since the vast bulk of the literature on collectables has been written on a thematic basis, there is a limit to how much one can glean from this source. When one wishes to get beyond the basic details of a subject and learn how it pertains to one's own district there are several lines of research to follow. First and foremost is the local public library, which will have a local collection of books, pamphlets, tracts, directories, newspapers and periodicals – an absolute goldmine for the student seeking further information which fills out the background to material in his collection. County or regional archives, invariably located in county towns, are a fruitful source of material of all kinds, from the records of old-established businesses to family correspondence, diaries and estate papers, which are often relevant to local collectables. Local museums are an invaluable adjunct to the collector, often providing assistance with identification, attribution and provenance of material and enabling comparison with items in the museum collections. Curators have a vested interest in helping the local collector since many of their acquisitions come from this source, but private collectors and museums are both pursuing the same quest for local knowledge and their co-operation with each other is often highly rewarding.

Antiquarian societies and field clubs began in the mid-nineteenth century and originally their activities reflected Victorian interests in classical antiquities, archaeology and the natural sciences, such as geology, botany and ornithology. Many of them still have a traditional bias, but in recent years they have widened their scope considerably in line with the development of interest in the newer collectables and the bygones of the recent past. The gap between the traditional and the modern has been bridged by industrial archaeology, a convenient portmanteau term which is discussed in the next chapter. The archaeological connotation lends respectability to a study of the industrial and commercial past which, till little more than a decade ago, was almost totally neglected. All aspects of local history are now explored by these societies, most of which are organized on a county or regional basis. Details of meetings, their venues and frequency, are available from the public library or museum. In many cases the local museum owes its origins to the public-spirited actions of the antiquarian society and there is generally a very close connection between them to this day.

Apart from the lectures, which range from pre-history to the changing urban and rural scene of the present day, these clubs offer, through their meetings and excursions, the opportunity for collectors to meet one another, discuss different viewpoints and dispose of duplicate material by sale or exchange. An important feature of these societies is their publications which range from regular newsletters and bulletins to the more formal proceedings or transactions (published annually or half-yearly). These provide the student with the opportunity to place his researches in a permanent form; and over the years the volumes of transactions add up to a considerable amount of local history material which is probably not available in any other form.

In recent years separate societies have been established in most parts of the country catering to collectors rather than historians. The Antique Collectors Club, of 5 Church Street, Woodbridge, Suffolk, acts as a co-ordinating body for these local clubs. The A.C.C.'s monthly magazine contains details of these clubs, with the names and addresses of secretaries and short reports of meetings. The magazine also gives wide coverage to small advertisements which are an excellent medium for making contact with like-minded collectors in one's own area. Significantly, the collecting section in the weekly *Exchange and Mart* carries a steadily increasing number of advertisements of a county or regional nature.

No survey of the local collecting scene would be complete without some reference to the trade in local collectables. Antique shops have proliferated in the past twenty years but I must admit that they are not primarily a good source for material of a purely local nature. The bulk of their stock in trade has a national or international appeal. Concessions to local interest, such as a folio of maps and prints, the occasional tray of tokens and medals or the odd shoebox of picture postcards, are naturally priced according to the law of supply and demand, so do not expect any bargains. Nevertheless the occasional unconsidered trifle does slip by and collectors are incurable optimists, so the antique shops should never be overlooked. The collector specializing in an area where tourism is, or was, important will need to be constantly on the lookout for picture postcards, crested china, Mauchline ware and other material which was produced for visitors to holiday resorts to take or send to friends and relatives at home. Sometimes there is a regional bias in this. A high proportion of the collectables pertaining to the Isle of Man consist of the tourist souvenirs of yesteryear and, as such, tend to turn up in the antique shops of Lancashire, Cumbria and the southwest of Scotland, traditionally the areas from which the island derived most of its visitors in years gone by.

By and large, however, much more fruitful sources of material are the collectors' fairs and itinerant dealers' bourses which are now regularly held in most towns. These events are publicized in the local press and usually take place in a community hall or a hotel. The more professional bourses and fairs are designed chiefly as a means of bringing dealers into contact with potential vendors of material and provide a convenient method of going on buying trips with the minimum of overheads. Theoretically this is a two-way traffic, enabling the dealers to offload stock in the area of greatest demand, but this seldom yields any bargains to the collector. Of greater benefit to all concerned are the amateur events, many of which are organized by the local collectors' club, and it is here that the collector can dispose of his surplus material at a fair price, or swap duplicate items with like-minded individuals. The junkyards and junk shops which used to be such a happy hunting ground are a thing of the past, and the street trader with his barrow or stall in the Saturday market has all but disappeared too, but the large collectors' markets, mostly in and around London, are always worth a visit. Unless your interests are confined to the collectables of the metropolis and the Home Counties, however, you will require endless patience and stamina to work your way systematically through the markets in the Portobello Road and Camden Passage, but these are just the places where material from the less fashionable counties can often be picked up – if not at bargain prices, at least substantially lower than the prevailing market at home.

Industrial archaeology

It is said that the late Professor Arthur Redford of Manchester University coined the term 'industrial archaeology' in the 1940s to describe the physical remains of past industrial activity, but as a subject of general interest, particularly to collectors, it has only developed within the past two decades. Interest in the artefacts of industry may be said to have begun as far back as 1850 when plans were laid for the Great Exhibition the following year in London, and this interest in the history and development of technology was subsequently fostered by the Science Museum, the first of its kind anywhere in the world. In 1854 the Royal Scottish Museum was founded specifically as 'The Industrial Museum of Scotland', and though it has since diversified into all branches of the fine, applied and decorative arts as well as the sciences, it remains to this day a splendid repository of Scotland's industrial and technological heritage.

Railwayana

In other parts of the United Kingdom museums at national, regional and county level were not slow in appreciating the antiquarian value of the objects associated with local trades and industries. The Newcomen Society, founded in 1919, was concerned from its inception with the study and preservation of examples of industrial development. Britain's Industrial Revolution started in the middle of the eighteenth century and peaked a century later. It has been argued that British industry began to decline about 1880 but even as late as the Second World War there were still abundant examples of factories and other industrial buildings which dated from the early years of the Industrial Revolution and which were still in use for their original purpose. This industrial expansion had gone hand in hand with a phenomenal growth in communications – first improved roads and bridges in the 1780s and 1790s, then extensive canal and inland waterway systems which were still in progress of development in the 1830s when they were rapidly overtaken by the railways. The peak of the 'railway mania' was in the late 1840s and early 1850s. Most of the lines now in existence were first laid down in that period, and many others were then in operation but have long since been terminated, first by rationalization and regrouping and latterly by savage retrenchment under the so-called Beeching Axe. In 1964–65 alone thousands of miles of track were scrapped, entire lines were closed and countless stations and signal boxes disappeared. This Draconian measure was coupled with a modernization programme which led to the withdrawal of the last steam locomotive in 1966 and the launching of the Corporate Identity Programme in 1965, transforming the appearance not only of the locomotives and rolling stock but even the uniforms of the railway personnel, the crockery and cutlery, the notepaper, tickets, labels and even the most trivial items of ephemera.

The railways, which had had a major influence on the development of our society, were, in their heyday, all-pervasive. Their disappearance gave rise to a mood of nostalgia out of which was borne the preservation movement which, in turn, led to a much wider interest in railway relics. The preservation, and, in some cases, the restoration, of disused branch lines and light or narrow-gauge railways began in the 1950s with the transformation of the Talyllyn Railway from a narrow-gauge line serving the slate quarries of North Wales into a passenger-carrying line forming a major tourist attraction for the area. This example has since been followed by numerous others, as far afield as Taunton and Dymchurch in the south, Ravenglass in the northwest and Strathspey in Scotland. These preserved lines provide the public with the opportunity to savour the steamy, sooty and smelly atmosphere of rail travel as it was in its heyday. More importantly, they set an example which museums of industrial archaeology have since followed enthusiastically. It is no longer sufficient to have static displays; the essence of a good industrial museum is that it is, in fact, a reconstruction of some aspect of the industrial past in full working order, and the best examples are those where the machinery is actually seen to be working.

From the collector's viewpoint, however, the railways stimulated interest in the collectables associated with industrial archaeology. Massive retrenchment and a radical change of image left British Rail with enormous amounts of surplus or scrap material. At first this was sold off wholesale to scrap dealers but from the outset railway enthusiasts badgered the regional offices for souvenirs of the closed lines. At first this activity was conducted on an informal basis and

Pre-decimal currency L.N.E.R. tickets (John H. Atkinson)

undoubtedly the 'early birds' acquired some priceless material for next to nothing. Gradually British Rail woke up to the fact that there was a second market, if not exactly an antiquarian interest, in their surplus material and therefore put this business on a proper footing, establishing collectors' shops and scrapyards at their regional headquarters, the best-known and probably the most comprehensive being Collector's Corner adjacent to Euston Station. This has encouraged the development of specialist dealers and auctions in railwayana, periodic fairs and swap-meets. Railway material, once regarded as the specialist interest of the dedicated few, is now a subject of general interest to virtually everyone who collects bygones and therefore may be found in flea markets and collectors' fairs.

Railwayana is not only the best-known form of industrial archaeology but also that best suited to the requirements of the local collector. Since so much of the material connected with the railways was identifiable, either because it bore the stamp or insignia of a railway company, or the actual name of a station, depot, junction or signal box, it can often be pin-pointed to an actual locality. Some idea of the scope of this may be gained from the fact that, when the Post Office negotiated the establishment of the parcel post in 1883, it had to come to an agreement with no fewer than eighty-one railway companies, ranging alphabetically from the Aylesbury & Buckingham to the Wrexham, Mold & Connah's Quay. Apart from Orkney, Shetland and the Western Isles, every county and region of the United Kingdom has or had a railway connection and in many instances can boast of a railway which operated entirely within its boundaries. Over the years amalgamations and take-overs reduced the number of railway companies, but in a period spanning almost a century, from 1825 till 1922, almost 200 railway companies, large and small, operated in the British Isles. Many were of brief duration, operating only long enough to leave their mark in the form of their insignia on seals and signs, uniform badges and buttons and a wide range of equipment which ran from brass oilcans to waiting-room and office furniture. Other railway companies never progressed beyond the drawing board but have left a rich legacy of promotional literature, prospectuses, stock and share certificates and other ephemera.

The era of the local railway companies came to an end in 1921–23 when the great majority of them were grouped into four large combines. The wisdom of operating the railways as a national utility had been demonstrated during the First World War when they had operated under Government control. When peace returned the Government was reluctant to lose the benefits of a co-ordinated railway system and the grouping of 1921–23 was a compromise which allowed the railways some measure of independence, competition and profits for their shareholders. During the Second World War the four companies – the London, Midland and Scottish, the London and North-Eastern, the Great Western and the Southern – were again under Government control and this paved the way towards complete nationalization in 1948 when British Railways (later known more simply as British Rail) was established. Each progressive stage towards complete centralization meant a corresponding diminution of local or regional autonomy, and consequently reduced the amount and variety of collectable material.

Apart from such categories as badges and buttons, tokens, medals, share certificates, commemorative or souvenir pottery and guides, timetables and tickets, which are discussed in the relevant chapters later in this book, there is a considerable amount of railway material with a purely local flavour. From the pre-grouping era, as the first century of railway history is usually known, comes a surprisingly large and diverse amount of collectables bearing the names, initials or emblems of the local railway companies. Among the items which have been recorded with some form of identification on them are guards' watches and whistles, station handbells, hand lamps and wall lamps, office seals and datestamps, undated brass telegraphic stamps, pens, inkwells, inkstands and writing sets, string boxes, cast-iron and leather paperweights and blotters, oilcans, buckets, signal padlocks, baggage checks and tolls of every kind. Few collectors could hope to obtain one of the teak-handled silver hammers, trowels or spades or the handsome carved oak miniature wheelbarrows associated with such ceremonies as cutting the first sod or

Pre-1922 G.N.R. station hand lamp made in Peterborough (John H. Atkinson)

driving home the last spike, although these choice items do come up at auction occasionally; but the more mundane, everyday tools and implements used by the railways often bore some indication of their ownership – sufficient to give them a place in the local collection.

The locomotives and rolling stock of the pre-grouping era provide a fertile source of locally orientated collectables. Steam whistles, brass heating control units from the carriages, light fittings, leather window straps, a vast range of cocks and gauges from the locomotive cab, even door knobs, handles and the elaborate finials on safety rails – all were cast, engraved or embossed with the company's name or insignia. Much of this material, particularly that dating before 1890, is quite elusive. By contrast, the various name- and number-plates which decorated locomotives and carriages have survived in considerable quantities, partly because rolling stock had a compara-tively long life (in some cases surviving until recent years in working condition), and partly because these items were often retained as mementoes when the stock was scrapped. The most highly prized material in this category consists of the locomotive nameplates. Practice in this regard varied considerably from company to company, but fortunately the smaller railways seem to have been the most enthusiastic when it came to giving their engines a name, and even the most humble tank engine often received this honour. These plates, cast in brass or iron and painted in the company colours, ranged from the prosaic types with lettering in a plain, functional style, to those which are a riot of art nouveau script entwined with floral ornament. Many of them incorporated the company badge which was itself often derived from the heraldic device of the towns or counties associated with it. Numberplates on the funnel, cabside or smokebox door tend to be fairly plain in appearance, in painted or enamelled iron with raised numerals either in brass or painted in a contrasting colour. Of greater interest to the local collector, however, are those small plates, usually cast or die-struck in brass, giving the maker's name and address, the date of manufacture and

L.N.E.R. name- and numberplate from a tube waggon built in 1947 (John H. Atkinson)

Brown enamelled station nameplate with contrasting white lettering and border (John H. Atkinson)

the works' serial number. These plates allude to the maker of the locomotive rather than the company that used it but if, at first glance, this seems to offer little scope for the local collector it should be borne in mind that the number of locomotive builders was enormous in the nineteenth century. Scotland had no fewer than thirty-eight, while counties such as Yorkshire and Lancashire could probably boast a similar number. Some of the larger companies eventually had their own locomotive engineering works and plates may be found combining the factory location with the railway company's name or initials.

Similar plates may be found in connection with the wagons, coaches and carriages but in general the collectables associated with the latter are more elegant. The most important items consist of crockery, cutlery and table linen decorated with the company's initials or emblems. Antimacassars similarly embellished are among the commonest items connected with the old railway companies, reflecting the fashion of the times when men smothered their hair in unguents and pomades.

Perhaps the largest and most attractive group of railway material comprises the signs, notices, carriage cards and panel prints, many of which survived long after the grouping of 1921–23. Furthermore, since many of these signs pertained to specific stations, this is one area of railwayana which offers a great deal of scope for the local collector down to the present time. Signs range from the quaint wooden boards carrying dire threats of transportation or penal servitude for life – the penalties formerly meted out to vandals who threw stones at passing trains – to the die-struck or cast-metal signs which adorned the permanent way. Many of the trackside plates included oval boundary marks containing the initials of the company, the small rectangular or circular plates bearing cryptic letters and numerals denoting gradients, speed restrictions and distances, and the instructional plates marked 'Whistle', 'Beware of Catch Points' or 'Shut off Steam'. Far more interesting, however, are the plates designed for the public. Many of them relate to trespass or the limitations of public right of way or access to the track, the restriction of certain foot-bridges and paths to railway personnel, or the limits of weight or speed on bridges over the railway lines. Not only do such signs include the company name, but may even show the name of the place where they were sited, or refer to local habits affected by the coming of the railway and long since forgotten. A familiar type of sign, dating from the 1840s, warned 'Men employed by farmers must not cross the main lines to fetch milk cans'.

Signs bearing the names of the stations range from the enormous enamelled sheet-metal signs used at the present day to the smaller cast-iron name plates with ornamental frames and raised lettering painted in a contrasting colour, used in the period prior to nationalization. Apart from the main station signs prominently displayed on the platforms there were smaller signs which were affixed to lampposts, gates and the backs of platform benches. Other signs, usually of enamelled sheet metal, appeared in station concourses, booking-halls, waiting-rooms and restaurants. They are just as important as the large platform signs and certainly easier to house – always an important consideration for the collector with a limited amount of accommodation.

Other transportation relics

Improvements in river navigation, the construction of weirs and locks, date from Tudor times, while the earliest canal systems in Britain were constructed in the seventeenth century. Most of the canals, the commercial and industrial arteries of their day, were cut in the closing years of the eighteenth century and the first three decades of the nineteenth century, opening up new opportunities in agriculture, mining, quarrying and the manufacturing industries. Much of the industrial development of England and Wales, the Central Lowlands of Scotland and the north-east and midlands of Ireland, was due to the inland waterways which offered a highly economic mode of transport in bulk. The Newry Canal (1730–44), the Manchester Ship Canal (1761–70) and later systems, such as the Leeds and Liverpool, the Shropshire Union, the Staffordshire and Worcester, the Kennet and Avon, the Forth and Clyde, and the Caledonian, have important county or regional associations. In addition to these major waterways, however, there were literally dozens of smaller systems, usually under 15 miles in length and primarily intended to augment existing river navigation for the carriage of minerals, fertilizers, agricultural and general produce. Few counties will not have had at least one canal system in existence during the half century (1780–1830) when inland waterways were at their peak. Many of these systems rapidly declined in face of the competition from the railways, or were deliberately taken over by the railway companies and either left to disintegrate or used as the basis for rail routes. The cutting through which the present-day railway line approaches Glasgow's Central Station was once the bed of the canal system which was to have linked the industrial heart of Central Scotland to the Clyde coast at Ardrossan. The connection between Glasgow and Ardrossan exists in the tenuous form of place-names. Eglinton Street, which runs alongside the railway line, is a reminder of Port Eglinton, the Glasgow terminus of the canal, named after the Earl of Eglinton who built the town of Ardrossan in 1806 and in whose memory the Eglinton Dock, built in 1886, was named.

Because of their demise before the coming of the railway era, the canals have left us little by way of collectable material, other than the share certificates, posters and other ephemera discussed in the next chapter. Significantly it is from those canals which later acquired a tourist interest that most of the three-dimensional memorabilia has survived. The 'water gypsies' who worked the canals of England and spent their lives in the narrow boats developed their own sub-culture, complete with folk art in the form of the highly decorated toleware buckets, pots and pans and the distinctive canal crockery, particularly the famous barge teapots with their miniature one-cup teapots mounted on the lids. Many of these items were decorated with the names of bargees and their wives and families, were exchanged as love tokens or commemorated weddings, births and other family events, reflecting the solidarity and rather introspective attitudes of a people whose way of life separated them from their fellow citizens. Maps and diagrams of the canals are an important and highly collectable subject, as attractive as the eighteenth and early nineteenth century prints and engravings of canal scenery. Before the rediscovery and rehabilitation of our long-neglected waterways in the past twenty years, certain canals retained their tourist potential. The Caledonian Canal, linking Inverness and Fort William, and the Crinan Canal which eliminated the long and hazardous voyage round the Mull of Kintyre, were relatively late on the scene but played a notable part in the development of tourism in the Highlands, especially after Queen Victoria visited the area and made Highland tours fashionable. Furthermore, they have enjoyed an unbroken history down to the present day and

Decorated toleware as used on nineteenth-century barges. The tall cans were used for drinking water and were kept on the left-hand side (looking forward from the tiller) and just forward of the cabin stove chimney pipe. The round tin would have been used for general food storage and the smallest can possibly for milk (Waterways Museum, Stoke Bruerne)

provide collectors in the Highland and Strathclyde regions with a wealth of material, ranging from tourist literature, postcards, tickets and posters to the models of the ships which plied these routes, such as the *Linnet* and the *Gondolier*. It should also be remembered that the world's first practical steamboat, the *Charlotte Dundas* (1802) was built for operation on the Forth and Clyde Canal and this vessel has been commemorated in various media.

If the canals had a somewhat chequered history, the river, lake and coastal shipping of the British Isles has fared much better, continuing to this day to play a valuable part in the country's communications and transport systems. Rivers assume an important role in the history of many counties and regions, though usually the same river is shared by several counties. As the navigation, dredging and maintenance of river banks and facilities was invariably vested in a river trust, transcending mere county interests, the scope for the local collector concentrating on a single county or town is less in this case than in the comparable railway or canal systems. An important exception to this is the River Clyde which, since regionalization in 1974–75, has run its entire course from its source in the Lowther Hills to its outlet and the vast convoluted stretches of its estuary, entirely within the aptly named Strathclyde region. Before 1974, however, the river's navigable regions would have impinged on the former counties of Lanark, Dumbarton, Renfrew, Bute, Ayr and Argyll, each of which was well represented in the tourist souvenirs of the Clyde coastal resorts and the nautical memorabilia of the small shipping companies that operated between the Clyde ports. Today most of these little companies have been swallowed up by the vast combine known as Caledonian-MacBrayne. In many respects the story of the Clyde and the history of steam navigation are synonymous, ever since Henry Bell's *Comet* took to the water off Helensburgh in 1812, though the Tyne and the Wear, the Severn and the Mersey, the Thames and the Avon have all contributed to the development of shipping.

Ship models represent the acme of the riparian or nautical material of regional interest, and range from the intricate builders' models, correct in every detail and mounted in glass cases, and the working scale models of naval architects, to the builders' half models, framed for mounting on a wall, the generally less-accurate commercially produced ship models and the efforts of countless old sea dogs and dedicated amateurs which amount to a form of nautical folk art. What the latter may lack in technical competence they generally make up in their naive charm and period flavour. Here again one can seldom attribute this material to a specific county or region, although it is in this respect that the island counties come into their own. Collectors of material pertaining to the Channel Islands, Orkney, Shetland, the Western Isles, Bute, the Isle of Man, the Isle of Wight and Anglesey will find a great deal of material pertaining to the steamship companies and ferry services in these areas. Apart from the ship models there are steering wheels, bells, binnacles, compasses and telegraphs which, with their brass and copper casings, have an innate decorative quality, apart from their association with particular ships. Painted wooden or leather buckets bearing the insignia of ships and shipping companies, ships' lanterns and navigation lamps with red and green bullseye lenses are much sought after. Like the railways, the shipping lines had their quota of crested cutlery and crockery, table napkins and cabin fittings. If anything, these coastal shipping lines, such as MacBrayne, the Caledonian and Isle of Man Steam Packet companies and the Holyhead and Kingstown packets, were more conscious of their corporate identity than the railways, since they tended to be more lavish in decorating everything with their insignia.

Local industries

Although we talk of an Industrial Revolution taking part in the mid-eighteenth century the process of industrialization evolved very gradually over a far longer period. Coal, iron and tin were mined in various parts of England and copper in Wales from Roman times, if not earlier, while pottery and glass were manufactured in Roman London. In this sense, industrial archaeology blends in with the more traditional aspects of this study. Industry revived in England after the Wars of the Roses and in succeeding generations benefited considerably from the influx of foreign craftsmen and technicians – Italians, Germans, Flemings and Huguenots – who introduced papermaking, glass, silkweaving and lacemaking, silversmithing and metalworking technology and established these industries in many parts of Britain. The location of these and other industries was due largely to the proximity of easily obtainable supplies of raw materials, the availability of wind and water power or fuel such as coal, timber or charcoal, convenient to existing urban markets and seaports, with an abundance of cheap labour and relatively good communications. There was a tendency for several industries to exist side by side, often dependent on each other as, for example, in the Thames Valley where an abundance of timber led to the development of the furniture industry and later to paper manufacture. Collieries often coexisted with brick and tileworks utilising the deposits of fireclay found in the mineworkings, and the mining of iron ore not only stimulated the growth of iron foundries in the same area but fostered the development of secondary industries such as metallurgy and engineering.

Few aspects of industrial archaeology, however, furnish the collector with material which is readily identifiable and thus coming within the scope of this survey, but there are several which may be found all over the country, and others which, being specific to certain areas, should attract the serious attention of collectors concentrating on those localities.

In the first category the outstanding example is bricks. Early English bricks dating from the fourteenth century are by no means uncommon and that they have stood the test of time is proven by the many buildings of that period still extant. These bricks were moulded by hand from local clay and then stacked in clumps mixed with small coal under piles of turf and earth. Proper kilns for firing the bricks at a high temperature were not developed till the end of the eighteenth century and even thereafter bricks were usually produced by hand, without any form of marking on them. They were flat on both sides but by the early nineteenth century a frog (the hollow depression which holds the mortar) was added to one or both sides and this was often impressed with the maker's name

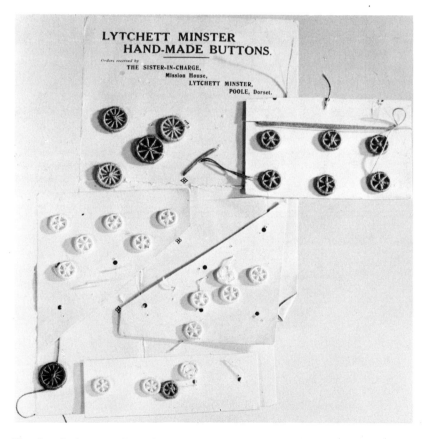

Handmade buttons from Dorset probably dating from the first decade of the twentieth century (The University of Reading, Institute of Agricultural History and Museum of English Rural Life)

Cast-iron cheese press from mid-nineteenth century, made by Pond & Son of Blandford, Dorset (The University of Reading, Institute of Agricultural History and Museum of English Rural Life)

and sometimes his address as well. This is an aspect of industrial archaeology which I literally stumbled upon, while strolling along the track of a disused railwayline near my home. I came across a brick bearing the name of a long-defunct colliery in a village where I had spent my childhood. Seeing that name again, once so familiar and now all but forgotten, immediately triggered off an interest which has developed ever since. My interest in old bricks contrasts with that of other enthusiasts. The whole world is their oyster and they will literally go to the ends of the earth in search of exotic specimens, such as the commemorative portrait bricks produced in America. My modest collection of little more than 200 specimens has been formed solely on the basis of what I have found in my home region of Dumfries and Galloway. It includes not only rare specimens of handmade bricks from Carsethorn and Kirkconnell near New Abbey, where James Maxwell introduced brickmaking to Scotland in the 1750s after a period spent as a Jacobite exile in France, but also the commercial bricks from the Buccleuch collieries at Kirkconnel (different spelling and different place, thirty miles distant) and Sanquhar. Since I also include bricks manufactured elsewhere but used in this region this part of the collection illustrates vividly how widely travelled bricks were. The incidence of early nineteenth-century bricks from the West Midlands and Lancashire found on sites along the Solway coast may be due to coastal shipping bringing cargoes of bricks in ballast before returning south with Galloway granite in their holds. From the humble brick, therefore, we may learn something of early trading patterns as well as local manufactures. Recently bricks were offered with the initials of Prince Charles and Lady Diana Spencer as a souvenir of their wedding, but commemorative bricks have been around for a long time. Some enterprising brickworks produced them for Queen Victoria's Diamond Jubilee and more recent examples included the 1953 Coronation and the Silver Jubilee in 1977.

Other examples of industrial artefacts bearing a name include bottles, metal signs and pottery and these are discussed in the relevant chapters. Some of the tools and implements associated with traditional industries were inscribed with names and addresses. The bobbins and shuttles used in the textile industry when it was still largely in the hands of the small operatives not only varied in size and shape from one district to another but frequently bore the name and address of the maker. Since handloom weaving was a widespread occupation before 1830 this is an aspect of industry which should appeal to most county collectors. Similarly, woodworking tools – mallets, spokeshaves, planes and chisels – often bear the name and mark of the manufacturer. Here again, there were numerous regional or even parochial variations which should provide considerable scope.

Selection of bricks, *from left to right*

Top row: Westbrick, a modern 'handmade' brick from Exeter; W. H.
             Wynn of Alvechurch, 1880; Furness Brick Co. Barrow, nine-
             teenth century

Middle row: Norton, Worcestershire, late nineteenth century; Ketley
             Brick Co. Brierley Hill, late nineteenth century; F. A. Hill,
             Redditch, 1900.

Bottom row: G. L. Stinson 'brick tax' brick, mid-eighteenth to mid-nine-
             teenth century; Holmer Works, Hereford, 1860s; Wheelook,
             Bromsgrove 1860 (Avoncroft Museum of Building – photo by
             Dr Peter Pollitt)

Most of the artefacts of industrial archaeology, however, are
unnamed, but are relevant to a local collection by virtue of their
connection with local industry. The tools, implements and equipment associated with these industries have long had appeal to collectors of bygones, mainly because of their rustic quaintness or
primitive appearance, but if they are linked to other aspects of the
commercial and industrial past, such as trade cards, bills and letterheads, discussed in the next chapter, their true significance will
become more apparent. One or other of the following activities will
have taken place in your area, and probably several: agriculture,
bleaching and dyeing, brewing, cider-making and distilling, chemi-
cals and tarworking, coal-mining, coopering, dairying, iron- and
brass-foundries, flax, jute, cotton or woollen mills, glassmaking,
grain mills and granaries, hosiery, glove- and hat-making, iron-
working, lacemaking, the leather trades, linen manufacture, papermaking, quarrying, salt-pans, tanning and wood-turning and
furniture-making. The tools of manufacture, the ephemera relating

to the administration of the industry, the marketing and distribution, and, in many cases, the end products can all be linked to other subjects, such as trade tokens, commemorative medals and pottery, picture postcards and advertising material to illustrate the birth and development, perhaps the decline and fall too, of the crafts and industries which made your area what it is today.

Ephemera

This term, derived from the Greek for 'day by day', is now used to denote anything printed for a short-term purpose. The essence of such material is its triviality but much of its charm lies in the fact that it was meant to be thrown away. Even the most ordinary scraps of printed matter take on a peculiar fascination if they are very old, for the good reason that such scraps have not survived in any quantity and thus have considerable rarity appeal. Often printed on hand-made paper, using artless typefaces and imbued with that cavalier approach to spelling which characterized provincial English before Dr Johnson tried to standardize orthography, these pieces of paper provide a window on the everyday world of bygone centuries, far more vivid than historical descriptions or even contemporary accounts and diaries which were often consciously written for posterity. The mundane printed matter is much more revealing about fashions, manners, morals and modes of thinking. This is particularly true of the advertisements of the seventeenth and eighteenth centuries, ranging from the simple, honest and forthright to the outrageous and extravagant. The former, with their bold woodcut illustrations and quaint mixture of different founts of type, have a surprising impact which the more subtle and sophisticated advertising practitioners of today would do well to study.

There are certain practical limits to the kind of ephemera one is likely to encounter. Paper itself was a major rarity in Britain before the fifteenth century and too expensive to have been used ephemerally to any extent before the late seventeenth century. Printing from movable type, widely practised in Europe before the end of the fifteenth century, was largely confined to London and the university cities of Oxford and Cambridge until the early seventeenth century. Before and during the Civil War (1642–49) there was a spate of tracts and broadsides, mostly of a political nature, but examples which may safely be attributed to specific localities are rare. Following the Restoration in 1660 printing in the provincial

towns and cities was more widespread but even as late as the 1730s
there were large areas of Britain which did not boast a single
printing press. Thereafter, however, printing made rapid strides and
within two decades had spread to every part of the country, except
the more rural and backward areas in the southwest of Ireland. This
spread of printing coincided with the first upsurge in literacy but
more than a century was to elapse before the British Isles could be
said to be literate at all levels of society.

The Iudgement of the Court of Warre upon the Charge laid
against Sir *Richard Cave*, for the delivery up of HEREFORD.

OXFORD, 26. *Iunij*. 1643.

 Hereas Sir Richard Cave *hath been accused to His* Majesty
for the betraying of the Towne of Hereford, *when Sir* William
Waller *came before that Towne : and that Accusation was
transmitted to the Councell of Warre, whereupon Witnesses
were examined upon Oath, and the Court of Warre several
Dayes heard the Depositions and the wholl Cause at large;
Upon the full hearing whereof the Court was fully satisfied, that Sir* Richard
Cave *was absolutely free from any imputation of any crime to be objected against
him for the betraying or delivering up that Towne or sending away the
men under his command from the Towne at the time when Sir* William Waller
*was before it, and that what he did therein was both by sufficient and full Warrant,
and by the advice and consent of the Commissioners of Army for that County who
were then present. And this Court hath thought it Iust and honourable in them to
Declare thus much under their hands, That as farre as in them lyeth they might
repare the Reputation of Sir* Richard Cave, *who hath very unjustly suffered by
this Accusation.*

RUPERT.	Forth.	
Grandison.	Hen: Percy.	
Tho: Wentworth.	Hen: Wentworth.	Ro: HEATH present
Joh: Byron.	Ioh: Belasyse.	by the Request of the
Will: Pennyman.	L: Kirke.	Prince his Hignesse and
Will: Ashbournham.	Henry Vaugham.	the Lord Generall.

Directed by the Councell of Warre to be Printed and Published,
and especially to be sent to HEREFORD.

Printed at Oxford by LEONARD LICHFIELD,
Printer to the University. 1643.

Civil War broadsheet of 1643 (W. J. Pemberton)

Newspapers and periodicals

The mechanization of paper manufacture from 1750 onwards brought printed matter before the public. Before that date printing was largely confined to more serious matters – books and documents of a permanent nature. Newspapers were very small by modern standards and, from 1712 onwards, subject to a tax which rose relentlessly to an alarming level during the Napoleonic Wars. Partly a lucrative source of revenue for the Government, it also served as a control on newspapers and periodicals and effectively curbed radical expression. It was this tax on paper, forced on the American colonies in 1765, which helped to precipitate the War of Independence a decade later. Ironically, the outbreak of that war led to a further halfpenny on the newspaper tax. By 1815 the tax had risen to 4d. per sheet, but the publishers partially offset this impost by making their sheets as large as the press platen could take, so that newspapers of the eighteenth and early nineteenth centuries became bigger and bigger. There were also taxes on advertising supplements and pamphlets. The pamphlet duties were abolished in 1833 since they were largely evaded and the cost of enforcing them was more than the revenue they produced. The newspaper tax was reduced to 2d. in 1836 and abolished in 1855. From then until 1870 only those newspapers transmitted by post required to show the tax stamp on the upper corner of the front page.

The fact that the sheets had to be stamped at Somerset House in London was a powerful disincentive to provincial newspaper publishing. The Irish were rather better off, since Dublin had had its own stamp office since 1712, but provincial offices in Britain were not established till 1837 when they opened in Edinburgh and Manchester. Local newspapers existed to a limited extent from the early years of the eighteenth century but most of them seem to have been short-lived. Nevertheless, they were sufficiently widespread by the 1780s that most county towns could claim at least one such periodical, usually a weekly. After the tax was substantially reduced, and provincial stamp offices opened, the volume of local newspapers rose sharply. Some idea of the scope of local newspapers and periodicals may be gained from the fact that between 1837 and 1855 almost 4,000 papers in Britain and 380 in Ireland have been recorded by Chandler and Dagnall (see Suggested Reading) as having had tax stamps with their own names. Newspapers were the principal medium of propagating political views and the local press was pretty evenly divided between Whig and Tory persuasions. The heyday of the local newspaper was from 1855 till the First World War. Not only did they reach their peak in this period in terms of numbers, but they were far meatier than their modern counterparts. Advertising was largely confined to the front page – a style which the *Inverness Courier* alone retains to this day – but the inside pages were crammed with lengthy articles on topical questions of national and even international importance. This aspect gradually died out as the popular national dailies gained ground towards the end of the nineteenth century but the matters of purely local interest continued to be reported at considerable length in the leisurely style of journalism then fashionable. These newspapers are an invaluable primary source of information on the locality, right down to parish and village level. Even quite small country towns published at least one weekly or twice-weekly paper so the range of material for the collector is very wide. Before the 1880s illustrations were virtually unknown in these local papers, other than a very elaborate masthead (often embellished with the national coat of arms) and stock engravings used as headings to each of the advertising sections. Under the influence of the *Illustrated London News, The Graphic* and other picture papers, pictorialism gradually crept in; first a line drawing or sketch here and there, then more elaborate process engraving. Half tone blocks reproducing photographs were adopted by the national press in the late 1890s and spread to the provincial press surprisingly quickly. By 1914 many of the local papers were illustrated photographically. From the 1920s onwards the editorial content became less and less as the volume of advertising grew. In the past decade the 'free-sheet' – given away to residents in certain areas and funded entirely by the advertisements – has spread to Britain. It is no less important than the conventional newspaper as a social document and potential source of material for the future socio-economic historian, for the insight it gives us about the consumer society at a local level.

Periodicals with a local flavour are of much more recent origin, if we ignore the magazines published in Edinburgh and Manchester and other provincial cities which assumed national status. Magazines devoted to current topics and aspects of life in a single county or other well-defined geographical entity date only from the turn of the century. The earlier breed of county magazines were designed to acquaint their readers with the history and cultural heritage, the fauna, flora and customs and traditions of the area, interspersed with reports on the activities of the 'county set'. Many of these early periodicals read like a popularized version of the proceedings of the local antiquarian society and field club, with a rather heavy didactic tone. Many of them were casualties of the Second World War and restrictions on paper quotas. When periodicals of this type were revived in the late 1950s they became much livelier, with greater emphasis on current events but still with the inevitable bias towards the landed families. In recent years rising costs and falling advertising revenues have considerably reduced their numbers and some exist only in the attenuated form of a quarterly or annual. Like the newspapers, these periodicals are invaluable reference material for the local historian and collector.

Business stationery

Among the most attractive, interesting and varied of all local collect-ables are the bills and letterheads, leaflets and trade cards produced by all kinds of businesses, large and small. Prior to the early eight-eenth century most business correspondence and allied material was entirely handwritten. One of my most prized pieces of ephemera is a doctor's bill for services rendered to various members of the same family over a period of twelve months. Not surprisingly, this bill is almost a metre in length, and provides a fascinating insight into the aches, pains and ailments that beset our ancestors and the pills, drugs, medication and treatment administered by way of a cure.

From the beginning of the eighteenth century printing creeps into these bills; at first confined to an assortment of different type faces, probably intended more to demonstrate the printer's versatility than to give the maximum impact to the tradesman's advertisement. By the late eighteenth century, however, small 'cuts' of pictorial devices, symbolizing aspects of trade, were beginning to embellish the headings and this was soon followed by individually designed and engraved vignettes, often showing the shop-front or the factory premises or some product which the tradesman wished to promote. Grocers were fond of country scenes, showing sheep and cattle grazing contentedly, but from the local collector's viewpoint the most interesting and valuable headings are those which actually show the shop-front or the façade of buildings which can be ident-ified. It is then possible to build up a collection of bills and business letterheads arranged numerically in street order, providing a record of the commercial activity in a town over the past two centuries. Such a collection can be enlivened by photographs of the same buildings as they are at the present time, showing how much (or how little) they have changed in the intervening years. The collection of local trade ephemera should be expanded to include trade cards, advertisement leaflets and posters, and integrated with other forms of collectable, such as trade tokens and firms' special cheques, discussed elsewhere in this book.

Even concentrating on the commercial ephemera of one average-sized country town may prove to be too large a subject, and it may be necessary to narrow the interests even further, to the shops and offices in a single street or district, or to certain types of businesses. A thematic approach can be adopted, if one concentrates on hotels, inns and public houses. Hotel bills are a particularly rich field, since

Two examples of individually engraved vignettes. The 'Tryner Lynn' was printed in lilac and the 'Phoenix Glass Bottle Works' black on white (Reproduced courtesy of *Finders Keepers*/*New Collecting Lines* magazines)

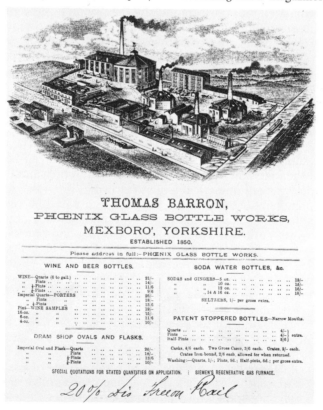

it was customary to show a view of the hotel on the heading of bills long after this custom had died out elsewhere, and this tradition also extended to the notepaper provided for the guests' use. Indeed, the latter often continues to this day to feature a view of the hotel or make some reference to local tourist attractions. The best of the pictorial hotel bills were produced between 1850 and 1890 when innovations like indoor plumbing, wash-basins with hot and cold water and electric lighting were considered sufficiently noteworthy to be highlighted in the headings. Prior to 1850, however, hotel bills may not have been so pictorial but they made up for this in the practice of itemising everything which could possibly be provided for guests' comfort and sustenance – and not just the guest, but his servants and his horses. Next to hotels and inns, the service trades provide the most varied and interesting ephemera. Plumbers, blacksmiths, milliners and dressmakers head the list of trades and professions which seem to have been singularly adept at advertising their skills and the latest products in the form of pictorial ornament in their bill- and letterheads. The finely engraved or lithographed bills died out gradually around the turn of the century, though a few continued to include a picture, reproduced by photographic halftone process, into the 1920s.

Trade cards and advertisements produced by or for shopkeepers, merchants, tradesmen and craftspeople of all kinds provide a rich and colourful field for the local ephemerist. As a form of self-publicity, these items were usually well designed according to the prevailing fashion, and gave far greater attention to pictorialism than the billheads. The advent of chromolithography in the mid-nineteenth century considerably enhanced these cards and leaflets but from 1910 onwards they tended to be less artistic as more scientific approaches to advertising were developed and letterpress printing ousted the more aesthetic lithography. The cards were usually quite small, ranging from playing-card to court-card size. Two developments from the early printed trade cards were the cigarette card, originally designed merely as a stiffener in the paper packs used in the late 1870s and 1880s, and the picture postcard discussed in the next chapter. The size of trade cards increased as the nineteenth century wore on and the larger ones, up to 20 cm long, were often used for window displays and shop decoration. Similar advertisements, printed on paper, were used as inserts in periodicals from about 1870 onwards, at a time when advertising printed in magazines was still largely devoid of pictorial character. While many of these advertising leaflets promoted nationally-known branded goods, others were printed for purely local consumption and either distributed as handbills or inserted in local newspapers. Grocers led the way in this medium, judging by surviving examples, and considerable attention was paid to providing attractive pictures of an appropriately seasonal nature at Christmas time when special lines in foodstuffs and alcoholic beverages were highlighted.

Envelopes for postal use, as we shall see in Chapter 6, did not become widely popular till after the reforms of 1839–40, but envelopes intended for non-postal use were widespread from 1800 onwards. The most notable use of envelopes at this early period was for medical prescriptions and these envelopes were invariably decorated with lavish engraving. Pictorial envelopes with advertising matter developed in the 1840s out of the official envelopes and wrappers designed by William Mulready for postal use. Though the Mulready envelopes were lampooned and ridiculed by the public, and withdrawn after a very short period (1840–1) in use, they inspired the commercial application of pictorial ornament to the front of envelopes used by firms and businesses. Examples before 1870 are decidedly scarce and it seems strange that there should have been a thirty-year gap between Mulready's florid symbolism and the commercial publicity envelopes. The best of them feature the latest products of companies and branded goods but even the most staid of business envelopes, with advertising confined to a few brief statements in discreet lettering, are of considerable interest. In many cases the commercial flavour was confined to an engraved or embossed crest on the flap. Again, these devices range from the self-effacing albino-embossed cartouche favoured by lawyers and other professional men to the more flamboyant pictorial engravings preferred by grocers. All of the railway and coastal shipping companies were enthusiastic users of such stationery and examples are much sought after. The fashion for decorating envelopes in this manner has waned in the past sixty years, its place being taken to some extent by firms' advertisements in meter franking (see Chapter 6). With the present growth of postage paid impressions, printed by the licensee direct on to envelopes, cards and wrappers, there is evidence of a revival in the advertising element in firms' stationery.

Pamphlets and leaflets

In an age when the media of mass communication were non-existent, the leaflet was the chief means of disseminating information. Rushed out, often at very short notice, by a local jobbing printer and distributed to passers-by or thrust under the front doors of houses by boys hired for the purpose, these handbills offered a crude but effective method of getting information to the public as quickly as possible. Such a medium, however, could only be practical at a limited level, but this is what gives these handbills their great interest to the local collector. Just as the area of distribution might

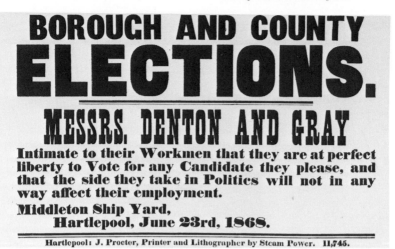

BOROUGH AND COUNTY
ELECTIONS.

MESSRS. DENTON AND GRAY
Intimate to their Workmen that they are at perfect liberty to Vote for any Candidate they please, and that the side they take in Politics will not in any way affect their employment.

**Middleton Ship Yard,
Hartlepool, June 23rd, 1868.**

Hartlepool: J. Procter, Printer and Lithographer by Steam Power. 11,745.

Notice for the Borough and County Elections, Hartlepool. The 1868 election was the last held under the old 'hustings' where the voting was done in public and the first at which most of the male adult working class population of the towns were entitled to vote. Hence the necessity for this declaration (Macmillan Publishers Ltd)

be confined to a single town, village or country district, so also the import of these bills usually has a pronounced local flavour. They are the most vivid relics of parish politics, often waxing vehement over the burning issues of the day, but particularly at a parochial level. The major political issues in general elections might often be reduced to matters which could be easily understood at grassroots level. So often this meant attacks and counter-attacks on the personalities of the candidates and at times this war of pamphleteering could be vicious and vitriolic. The heyday of the electioneering leaflet was undoubtedly the mid-nineteenth century, roughly the period between the passage of the Great Reform Act of 1832 and the Liberal campaign for Home Rule in Ireland in the 1880s. The personal or parochial element went out of national politics towards the close of the last century, but its place was taken by the growth of local government and the emergence of municipal and county councils whose members were subject to election. In many respects the literature of local elections is much more lively and interesting than the promotion of the party line at national level, especially since greater attention can be given to topics of a purely local nature.

Many of the handbills and flyposters which have survived are concerned with publicity for local events – literally everything from county horse shows and sheep-dog trials to the village hop on a

Election souvenir postcards
Top: R. L. Everett Esq. Once more voted M.P. for the Woodbridge
         Division of Suffolk. The full result of the voting was printed on
         the reverse of the card (*Reflections of a Bygone Age*)
Bottom: Successful candidate and wife (*Reflections of a Bygone Age*)

Saturday night. The elegant soirees, conversaziones and smokers' concerts of the late nineteenth century are recorded in the leaflets and programmes which have survived. Concerts and theatrical performances from an era when there was an infinitely wider range of live entertainment are remembered today by the rich variety of playbills. There was a time when every town of any size had a permanent theatre or music-hall, while repertory companies and strolling players took the Thespian arts into every village and hamlet in the land. Now, despite the inroads of television and bingo, there is a revival of live entertainment, both in workingmen's and political clubs, and also in local theatre groups and workshops, all of which add up to a formidable amount of current ephemera for the local collector. Fairs, exhibitions, tattoos and displays, touring advertising campaigns by all kinds of commercial and industrial concerns, and even the personal appearance of celebrities at the inauguration of new department stores, restaurants, civic centres and community projects also furnish a considerable amount of leaflets, pamphlets and brochures which are of ongoing interest to the local ephemerist.

Two playbills issued by the Theatre Royal, Norwich in 1830 (Jack Mitchley)

Tickets and passes

As the origin of the word shows; the ticket began life as something which was stuck on articles (from French *estiquier* – to stick – and *etiquette* – a sticker or label). It is not known at what stage it made the transition to having an independent existence as a small document, usually indicating the prepayment of a charge for transportation or admission, but tickets of this kind were in existence by the late eighteenth century. Mailcoach tickets issued by local stamp offices are among the earliest examples of this form of ephemera. Details of the places covered by the journey for which the ticket was issued were usually entered in manuscript. These coach tickets had become much more sophisticated by the 1820s, with a growing tendency to give the place names in a properly printed form. They were still made of paper, often in a large format, with a counterfoil retained by the ticket agent. Large paper tickets of this type were adopted by the railway companies in the late 1820s and continued to be widely used till about 1860. Joseph Edmondson, a clerk employed by the Newcastle and Carlisle Railway, invented the small pasteboard ticket about 1837 and this gradually spread throughout the railway network and remains in use to this day, although experiments with large tickets in thin card have been made in the past decade. Even in the age of British Rail, this is one form of railway memento which can be positively assigned to a particular area, because of the names printed on tickets. Before 1922–23, there is the added bonus of the names of the old railway companies, many of which had a purely local character. Since even the smallest and most insignificant of railway stations was furnished with a wide range of tickets of different classes and purposes and showing an almost infinite variety of destinations printed below its own name, this is a field with enormous scope for the local collector. I have in my own collection more than eighty different tickets which were in use at the tiny station of Gatehouse of Fleet at the time of its closure in the 1960s. A collection of tickets from all the stations on the line which once traversed Galloway from Dumfries to Stranraer, for example, would run into many thousands. Add to the conventional rail tickets the various kinds of platform ticket, the excursion and special tickets, and the tickets provided for the conveyance of dogs, bicycles, perambulators and luggage, and one can appreciate how vast this subject is, even at a fairly local level.

Despite the security and stringent regulations which have surrounded the issue of railway tickets ever since their inception it is amazing just how much of this material seems to have survived; collectors for more than a century have shown great cunning and ingenuity in finding ways and means of retaining their tickets at the end of the journey. By contrast, bus tickets have seldom been required to be surrendered to company ticket collectors and inspectors, but, conversely, seem to be much scarcer than rail tickets – probably because the level of interest in years gone by was very much lower. Nevertheless tickets bearing the names of local transport companies are of immense interest nowadays. My interest in this field was kindled some years ago when I purchased a trunk full of secondhand books whose previous owner had been in the habit of using old bus tickets as bookmarks. In this odd manner I acquired a collection of London and suburban bus tickets dating from the 1920s. Airline tickets are of far more recent vintage and offer much less scope for local interest, but the pioneer airlines were very small and operated a few short-distance routes, so that their tickets would almost certainly qualify for inclusion in a local collection. The heyday of the small independent airlines was the 1930s, when companies such as Highland Airways, Hillman Airways, West Coast Airlines, or Portsmouth, Southsea and Isle of Wight Aviation Ltd enjoyed a brief and hectic existence before being overtaken by the Second World War and the process of nationalization which led to the formation of British European Airways. Even in these times of the large national airlines there have been smaller operators, such as Dan-Air, Loganair, Air Aurigny, Air Anglia, Cambrian Airways and British Island Airways, operating on the remoter and less profitable routes, so that the scope for air tickets is not as sparse as might be imagined.

Other forms of transport of recent times provide a considerable amount of material for the ticket enthusiast. Hovercraft services have only existed for little more than two decades but by their very nature have tended to be local in character. Though this is now a favourite mode of travel across the English Channel, it should be noted that most services have been estuarial, such as the Rhyl-Wallasey and the Portsmouth-Ryde routes. Tickets for shipping range from the municipal ferries operated by many corporations and district councils to the coastal services of Sealink and Caledonian-MacBrayne, to say nothing of the countless shipping companies that preceded them and operated regular sailings all round the coasts of the British Isles. Indeed, coastal shipping offered the only reasonably safe and reliable method of long-distance public transport before the railway network was completed. The scope in sailing tickets with a local flavour is very considerable, especially in the period from 1820 to 1860.

Although transport tickets and the passes issued to directors and employees are the most popular category, one should not overlook tickets of admission to local sporting events and entertainment of all kinds, often coupled with souvenir programmes and other ephemera. Admission tickets of the nineteenth century were invariably relatively large (playing-card size being the average) and printed on stout pasteboard, often with ornate borders or scalloped edging. They were embossed, engraved or letterpress printed, often embellished with fancy ornament or small pictorial vignettes. Even though the tendency these days is for tickets in rolls of thinner carton or stout paper, devoid of inscriptions other than the price of admission and the serial number, there are still numerous examples of specially produced tickets that show that the art of the jobbing printer is alive and flourishing.

Miscellaneous ephemera

There are several other categories of ephemera, all eminently collectable for their own sakes, but which often have a pronounced local bias which should therefore recommend them to the town or county enthusiast. Some of these categories are inspired by the service industries, such as tourism, entertainment and catering. Probably the best known are coasters and dripmats used in bars and restaurants everywhere. Many of them, of course, advertise nation-wide brands of cigarettes, wines; spirits and beer, but a substantial number of beermats extol the merits of the local brew, a valuable weapon in the war waged between the independent breweries and the giants of the industry. Quite a few of these, in recent years, have also been commemorative in nature, celebrating centenaries and other anniversaries of the brewery and its ales. Some local breweries

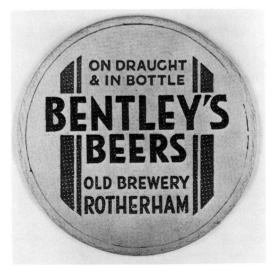

Selection of beer mats advertising local breweries

Left: Bentley's Beers, Rotherham, taken over by Hammond's United Breweries in 1956. This mat probably dates from the late 1940s although the lettering suggests it could be just pre-Second World War

Top: Jeffrey's of Edinburgh, closed in 1960; this mat was probably issued in the 1950s

Bottom: Truswell's Brewers Co Ltd, closed in 1955; this mat probably dates from the late 1940s to early 1950s (Bass Ltd, Burton-upon-Trent)

have also used beermats as a medium for publicizing tourist land-marks and beauty spots. Though the breweries have been the most enthusiastic users of these dripmats, ever since Robert Smith invented the wood-pulp throwaway mat in 1892, they have also been employed by restaurants. The dripmats used in catering tend to be much smaller, circular in shape and made of absorbent tissue. Because they are not as robust as, and generally less strident in design than, the beermats they have been largely ignored as a collectable until now, but their interest to the local collector is obvious. In addition, the American custom of attractively designed and printed paper tray-mats is rapidly gaining ground in the British Isles. The much greater area of these mats provides infinite scope for designs which are both attractive and informative. They are particularly popular in restaurants with historic pretensions, and are often rich in antiquarian interest and allusions. Nevertheless my most prized example in this genre is a mat used by a fast-food chain in London in 1977 giving the route map of the Silver Jubilee procession.

In the same year that Robert Smith devised the pulp beermat, Joseph Pusey of Philadelphia invented the match booklet (or paper book matches as he preferred to call them). Pusey envisaged book matches as an advertising gimmick to be given away and this is their primary function in the United States to this day. They were much slower to catch on in Britain, though they have been making steady progress since the 1920s. They are still not as widely used, however, in all walks of society and in every commercial undertaking, as their American counterparts, but they do provide local collectors with a

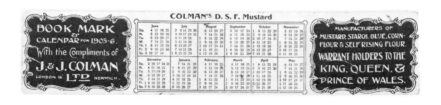

Bookmark issued by J & J. Colman Ltd. One side shows a calendar running from June 1905 to May 1906, the other side shows a view of the Colman Carrow Works in Norwich (Colman's of Norwich)

colourful memento of hotels, restaurants and cafes where they are mainly used. Apart from the catering and allied trades, I have only come across a solitary example of a commercial booklet from my little country town, and that was a giveaway by a dealer in musical instruments now long since gone into liquidation, his memory perpetuated probably by nothing more than these matches.

Bookmarks are another form of advertising giveaway, popular in the days when people actually read books. Nowadays they are far less common and largely confined to organizations and institutions of national importance, but a century ago they were widely used by all manner of businesses at a purely local level. This was a medium much favoured by the railways and shipping companies, and their bookmarks often gave details of sailings and rail timetables. At the turn of the century commercial bookmarks were popular with a photograph on one side and space for a message and the name and address of the recipient on the other, so that they could be transmitted by post as a miniature form of postcard. Bookmarks themselves were merely another form of the advertising trade cards mentioned earlier and illustrate how one collectable medium shades almost imperceptibly into another.

Bookmark currently available from Beach's Bookshop, Salisbury, which is housed in a fourteenth-century building (D. M. Beach – Ref. Anthony Pearce)

Menus originated in the early nineteenth century, combining the bill of fare in hotels and restaurants with pictorial embellishment of patriotic sentiment at the time of the Napoleonic Wars. Though the martial flavour disappeared after Waterloo, the pictorial element survived and for many years menus provided a graphic insight into the topical events of the period. In Britain, however, menus developed along more restrained lines. A favourite device was to include an engraved view at the top, either of the hotel or restaurant (so that the same engraving could be used on bills and notepaper) or a picture of some local beauty spot or tourist attraction. The earliest menus were printed on stout paper, relatively long and narrow so that the dishes could be set out in a single column. Embossed and cut card became fashionable about 1855 and chromolithography added a colourful touch a decade later. There were even souvenir menus for special occasions, printed in silk or extravagantly decorated with Victorian scrapwork. The 'book' type of menu, with a folding card cover, was established by 1890. Apart from the menus used by hotels and restaurants for everyday occasions there are the commemorative menus for banquets and Burns' suppers, for annual dinners of clubs and societies and all manner of institutions. These are generally more ornate, with lists of toasts and speakers, and provide an insight into tastes in food and drink over the years. Of course, menus were also produced by the railways and shipping lines but those with a local interest are decidedly elusive.

Labels and packaging are, for the most part, a product of the past hundred years, having received an enormous boost from the passage of the Trademark Act of 1875. This led to a vast expansion in branded goods of all kinds, and, in turn, this stimulated greater attention to the printing of distinctive labels and wrappers. There were, however, many examples of printed labels long before 1875. The best-known examples are the circular labels which appeared on the lids of pill boxes, and the equally ornate labels from medicine bottles. Patent medicines were the earliest form of branded consumer goods and examples are known from the late eighteenth century. Foodstuffs and other perishables were manufactured for local consumption and little attention was paid to their packaging, but, here again there were some notable exceptions. From the early years of the nineteenth century the soap manufacturers and the breweries were packaging their wares in a manner calculated to catch the eye of the customer. Tobacconists were also among the earliest traders to realize the importance of attractive packaging and they went to great lengths to achieve the right pictorial effect in their wrappers, many of which were beautifully engraved with scenic or allegorical subjects. Watchmakers had their own distinctive form of label, usually known as a watchpaper, and intended to keep the dust out of the working parts. This liner inside the lid of the pocket watch

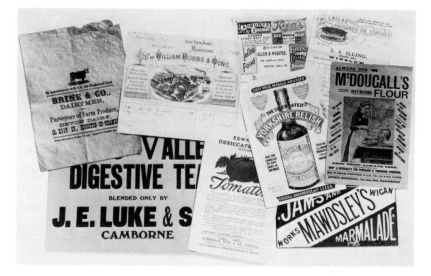

A selection of the type of labels and packaging used between 1890 and 1910 (Robert Opie Collection)

was invariably decorated with an advertisement for the watchmaker and since watchmaking, jewellery and engraving often went hand in hand, many of these papers were engraved by the watchmaker himself. They ranged from the fairly simple types, relying on a variety of typefaces for effect, to those which were fully pictorial with allegories symbolizing the passage of time as a favourite motif.

Apart from the breweries, whose beer and cider labels must run into thousands of different varieties, the distillers of gin and whisky had their own labels. This even extended in the 1880s and 1890s to individual public houses which liked to have their own brand of spirits. The whisky might be imported from the distillery in casks, but was then bottled locally for retail sale, and in this context the label was of paramount importance, long before the well-known proprietary brands began to dominate the market. Even today an estimated 3000 different brands of whisky are available in Scotland alone and many of these have a pronounced local interest, either distilled or blended in a particular locality which is reflected in the label. Mineral and aerated waters originated out of the health-giving properties of chalybeate wells and springs. It is not surprising, therefore, that the labels on bottles of mineral waters in the early nineteenth century combined the promotion of tourism in the spas and health resorts with extolling the virtues of the water. To the latter end lengthy quotations from eminent medical men were often inscribed on the label, as well as details about the depth of the well and the chemical analysis of the water. Just as the modern soft drink Coca Cola started life as a quasi-medicinal beverage, so also the aerated drinks manufactured all over Britain for a fairly local consumption often stressed the benefits to health. Some of the claims made in these labels were both all-embracing and extravagant, conveying the impression of a cure-all rather than a soft drink. After the First World War the local manufacture of soft drinks gradually died out, as the larger companies came to dominate the market. These local firms are remembered now by their trade cards and labels, and by the inscriptions moulded or embossed on their bottles, a subject discussed in greater detail in Chapter 11. Milk bottle tops are another form of packaging which had a very brief existence, from the 1920s when the churn-and-ladle era of milk distribution died out, till the 1970s when glass bottles were all but ousted by plastic or cardboard cartons. Even before the demise of the milk bottle, the standardization of bottles with a narrow rim suitable for a metal foil top meant the disappearance of the once familiar cardboard top. Every dairy had at least one variety and some of the more enterprising ones even produced special tops to celebrate jubilees and coronations. Quite a few tops combined advertising for nationally known branded goods, such as Horlicks or Ovaltine, with the name of the local dairy. It is the latter which gives the humble milk bottle top a hallowed place in any local collection.

A less likely subject for packaging at a local level is cigarettes, but before 1902 when most of the tobacco companies merged into one or other of the giant combines, cigar-making and cigarette manufacture were organized almost at a parochial level and practised by individual tobacconists. Some of them, like Alfred Dunhill of St James's, Benson and Hedges or Rothman of Pall Mall, eventually achieved national fame before becoming brand names perpetuated by the giant combines, but a century ago there were numerous small companies, little known outside their own limited areas and all but forgotten today, were it not for their cigarette packs and, in some cases, their cigarette cards. No fewer than 266 cigarette companies, as far afield as Aberdeen, Cornwall and Belfast, are known to have issued cigarette cards at some time or another.

Confectionery and baking are allied trades which are still carried on in the traditional manner, offering a welcome alternative to mass-produced branded goods. Modern hand-made chocolates and confectionery are expensive and rare, but forty years ago hand production was the norm and distribution tended to be fairly localized. Consequently the labels from tins and bottles of sweets and the wrappers from chocolate bars may be found in a very wide range, their designs limited only by the imagination of the manufacturer.

Jams, marmalades and preserves were also produced on a local basis and labelled accordingly. Other foodstuffs whose labels and wrappers have miraculously survived include cooked meats, sausages and dairy products. Tea and 'dried goods' were the province of so-called Italian warehousemen and they too have provided us with a large variety of distinctive labels and wrappers with a local character. Cakes, biscuits and shortbread were sold in tins on which were affixed paper wrappers, and some of the most ornate examples with a local flavour belong to this group. The relatively large area of cake boxes inspired large pictorial labels decorated with engravings and lithographs of local beauty spots. Long after transfer-printing and multicolour offset lithography directly applied to tins were widely used for nationwide brands local manufacturers continued to rely on the old-fashioned paper labels. They died out during or just after the First World War but have been revived successfully in recent years as improved techniques in food production have revolutionized packaging and permitted greater use of card and carton as materials in place of tins. Tins and tinware are now extremely popular as collectables in their own right, and are discussed in Chapter 13.

Associated with packaging and labels is the display material used

Examples of cigarette: packaging used around 1900 (Robert Opie Collection)

in window-dressing. Specially printed placards became fashionable around the middle of the nineteenth century, as the development of branded goods accelerated. These stout stand-up cards were the direct descendants of the dummy board figures which had graced alehouses and taverns since the seventeenth century. Today, these display pieces come under the heading of promotional material and tend to be universal in their application and standard in design, but from about 1870 till 1950, the heyday of the small business and the local manufacturer, these placards, often cut to shape, must have been produced in an enormous variety. Perhaps because they were bulkier and more cumbersome than paper posters they have not survived in such profusion but it is surprising how often these advertising aids of yesteryear come to light when high streets are redeveloped and old shops are pulled down.

Paper flags have had a relatively short life, from their inception on 26 June 1912 when the Queen Alexandra Rose Day was launched, to the late 1960s, by which time they had virtually been superseded by the self-adhesive 'patch' type of label now favoured by charities. From the First World War till the 1960s, however, countless charities and good causes were permitted to raise funds by means of the paper flag, given in return for a coin or two in the collecting-can. It has been estimated that over £15 million was raised by this means alone during the First World War and even after the war ended the flag-day was regarded as a powerful source of revenue for all sorts of charitable institutions. Few of the 'flags' given were actually in that form, but the general concept was the same: a piece of paper or card affixed to one's lapel by means of a pin. The 'flags' came in all shapes and were usually colourfully designed and printed. The majority of the causes in whose name they were issued were national, but within the broad framework of the Red Cross, the Boy Scouts or Guide Dogs for the Blind there was a considerable amount of latitude at one time and this resulted in countless local variants, bearing the name of the local branch. Instances of flagdays being licensed for purely local events are much rarer but not unknown. They were often issued in connection with a local disaster, a shipwreck or a mining explosion, and consequently have immense social interest and historical value.

Sources and preservation of ephemera

Given the nature of ephemera as something which was never meant to be preserved it is amazing how much of this material has survived. My interest in ephemera began years ago, largely as a spin-off from collecting postal history material. I would frequently purchase large cartons crammed full of old correspondence salvaged from legal accumulations, the dissolution of country estates or the redevelopment of shop sites. Much of this 'junk' came from waste-paper merchants who must have pulped material of this sort by the ton at one time. Now that primary sources for such large finds have virtually dried up, it is fortunate that public interest in, and awareness of, ephemera has grown considerably and this means that far less is cleared from attic or cellar and automatically consigned to the dustbin or the incinerator. Most antique dealers now take an active interest in ephemera and there are specialist dealers in London and many of the larger provincial cities, so that it is not so difficult for members of the public, with material for disposal, to contact dealers looking for ephemera of all kinds. Useful material turns up in the unlikeliest of places. Two or three years ago a crofter on one of the remoter islands of the Shetland group was repairing the roof of his cottage and literally stumbled on a cache of papers which had lain there for almost 120 years. It transpired that the cottage had been a post office for about twenty years, but this was closed about 1860. The sub-postmaster had systematically preserved all the notices and circulars sent to him since 1840 and when his office closed down he had stuffed all this paper into the roof space under the eaves, presumably for added insulation. Although the outer layers were beyond redemption the bulk of this material had survived in remarkably good condition. It eventually found its way to auction in Glasgow and was purchased by leading London dealers who appreciated the fact that no collection of postal documents of the mid-nineteenth century existed in such a complete state – not even in Post Office archives!

A few words on cleaning and care of ephemera may not come amiss. Dirt is the biggest problem and paper which has lain for generations in the attics or vaults of a country solicitor's premises will almost certainly have accumulated a great deal of dust, grime and atmospheric fall-out. Much of this dirt will come off readily with a fine soft brush or a jiffy cloth. The more persistent grime can then be removed by rubbing the surface gently with artists' gum rubber or white bread kneaded into a ball. Washing is not a course of action which I would recommend although, with experience, you will learn which kinds of paper may be boiled, which may be rinsed in cold water and which kinds should never come in contact with water at all. Foxing (speckled reddish brown spots caused by iron impurities in old paper) is a kind of fungus which can only be removed by a very weak solution of Chloramine T. This is a bleaching agent which can have an unpleasant side-effect so it is essential to rinse it off thoroughly afterwards. Labels with a starch or gum arabic fixative can usually be removed quite safely and effectively by immersion in lukewarm water, carefully rinsed, and then dried and flattened

Declaration of war and victory celebrations as recorded by two local newspapers in Norwich (*Eastern Evening News*)

between sheets of white blotting paper. Modern labels, however, are often held firmly in place by rubber or plastic fixatives and I must

confess that I know of no satisfactory method of removing them from bottles without damaging them. Such labels when affixed to card or paper wrappers are best left in place, the backing material being merely cut around.

Collectors use various methods for classifying and housing their material. There is a wide range of albums and guard-books available and though they may seem expensive their cost is relative to the value of the material you wish to preserve. A loose-leaf system is always preferable to a fixed-leaf system, since it allows for re-arrangement of the collection without having to dismount it. Additional binders for loose-leaf systems can easily be obtained as the collection expands. Many of the cover albums now marketed specifically for postcards are also ideal for cheques, banknotes and the smaller forms of ephemera. The smaller items may, alternatively, be placed in cellophane envelopes and stored upright in shoe boxes or the somewhat larger stout cardboard boxes which may be purchased from leading stationers. Box-files are ideal for billheads and other kinds of stationery. More expensive, but much more satisfactory, are lever-arch files combined with good quality album pages (Stanley Gibbons 'Senator' standard leaves are ideal for this purpose). The inner edge of the leaves can be folded back to make a double thickness approximately 2 cm wide and then punched so that the page fits the lever-arch file. The double thickness provides additional strength and enough stiffening at the margin to compensate for the thickness of the ephemera so that the file will not bulge unduly. Some collectors 'lay' their treasures on the pages of guard-books using flour and water paste which can easily be dissolved should it ever be necessary to remove the item. I prefer good old-fashioned stamp hinges, but only of the best quality peelable type which do not leave any mark should it be necessary to remove the item. On *no account* should adhesive tapes (Sellotape, Scotch tape, etc.) be used since the rubber fixative will stain the ephemera and the album page. Sticky rubber-based tape should never be used to repair tears. Thin gummed tissue, marketed for repairing sheet music, is ideally suited to the repair of posters and other ephemera but should be used sparingly. Transparent photographic mounting corners are a neat and effective method of mounting the thicker items, such as cards and tickets.

Old newspapers pose a number of problems. First of all, their size is a headache for most collectors, but they can be filed in the large folios used by artists for storing paintings, and kept flat. The dedicated collector may find a draughtsman's cabinet the answer; with its large shallow drawers it is ideal not only for newspapers but large maps, prints and posters. There are also many types of clear PVC or plastic sleeve available these days for the protection of individual newspapers, although I should point out the danger of offset from the printed surface on to some kinds of plastic sleeve. Newspapers should be lightly ironed flat (using a *warm* iron) after any loose dirt or dust has been brushed or rubbed off, before being placed in the PVC sleeves. The latter provide the additional advantage that one can stick a self-adhesive label on the top right hand corner of the sleeve and then annotate the sleeve with the details of the paper, its name, date, and place of publication. The main problem with newspapers, however, is the fragile nature of their composition. The older newspapers are, paradoxically, more likely to survive in pristine condition than their modern counterparts because rag paper was used. A century ago cheap Canadian wood-pulp paper was imported for newspaper production and this unfortunately does not stand up to the passage of time too well, especially if it is exposed to heat or sunlight. Most people will be all too familiar with newspapers which, even after a short space of time, show the telltale signs of atmospheric 'burn' – a distinctive browning followed by brittleness and eventually complete disintegration. The more modern the newspaper the more necessary it becomes to protect it from exposure to sunlight and atmospheric pollution.

Pictorial notepaper and picture postcards

Probably the most popular medium for the collector specializing in one area, the picture postcard has been in existence for less than a century, but it had numerous antecedents, most of which provide considerable scope for local collecting.

Popular prints, crudely pulled from woodblocks and sold 'penny plain, tuppence coloured' are known to have been produced in Germany, Italy and the Low Countries from the middle of the fifteenth century. A century later etched copper plates greatly refined this folk art and extended the range of subject which could be depicted. At first the designer was also engraver, printer and printseller, but by the early seventeenth century these skills were becoming more specialized. Popular prints were introduced into Britain from Holland in the sixteenth century and for a considerable time after that the vast majority of prints sold in England were of Dutch or German origin. The indigenous industry began about 1603 when Sudbury and Humble established their printshop at the sign of the White Horse in Cornhill. Sir Robert Peake and Sons had a printshop a little later next door to the Sun tavern in Holborn. Both firms commissioned engravings by the leading landscape and genre artists of the day. As the English print industry expanded, it continued to rely heavily on European talent. In the period immediately before the outbreak of the Civil War (1642) Wenceslas Hollar from Bohemia was the most fashionable engraver of panoramic scenes, best remembered to this day for his fine views of London.

This medium, which is discussed further in Chapter 7, was aimed at the upper classes who had the money and taste to appreciate such fine works of art. At the other end of the spectrum, however, the spread of popular prints to the labouring classes reflected the steady rise in prosperity of all classes in Britain from 1700 onwards. The prints aimed at this end of the market were much cruder than the scenic views, and had a vigorous earthy character lampooning and satirizing the public figures and the controversial issues of the day.

These prints, by Hogarth, Rowlandson, Gillray and others, were in the same tradition as the crudely illustrated tracts and broadsides which had been so popular during and after the Civil War. The vogue for cartoons and caricatures touched the bawdy sub-conscious in the British public – a rich vein which runs through the satirical envelopes of the 1840s and continues to this day in the seaside or comic postcard.

The Parisian engraver Demaison in 1777 conceived the notion of sending cartes-de-visite by post. These visiting cards had been in existence for over a century. At first people would write their names and addresses on the plain backs of playing cards, but by 1750 the roles had been reversed and specially printed calling cards were being produced with finely engraved scenes, both landscapes and architectural features, on the reverse. Had Demaison succeeded with his plan to transmit these pictorial cartes-de-visite through the post, the postcard would have been invented a century earlier than it actually was. The scheme was turned down, however, on the grounds that the transmission of private messages in so public a manner 'might stimulate the malignity of servants who could thus penetrate family secrets.'

About the same time, however, the Northumbrian engraver Thomas Bewick was making his reputation as an engraver of country scenes and wildlife. Bewick started his career as a woodblock engraver specializing in the small decorative vignettes which were then being widely used in advertisements and trade cards. He worked closely with jobbing printers whose craft was minuscule for the most part, and in this manner he mastered the art of engraving in a very limited space. Bewick was only one of countless engravers similarly engaged up and down the country on letterheads and bill-heads. Bewick's genius rose far above mere competence and he is justly remembered for his lively realism in the depiction of animals, domesticated, wild and exotic. Bewick's reputation and influence extended far beyond his native Northumberland and his example undoubtedly helped to raise the standard in the engraving of pictorial vignettes in commercial stationery at the beginning of the nineteenth century.

This influence was slow to affect non-commercial stationery, because of the iniquitous postal charges of the time. Letters were not charged by weight, as they are nowadays, but by the number of sheets of paper used and the distance conveyed. Since it cost, in 1837, the equivalent of a labourer's wages for three days' work to send a single-sheet letter from London to Edinburgh, that very select group of the public that actually sent letters had to be very careful to make the fullest use of what paper was used. This had two immediate effects. It prevented the use of envelopes (which automatically counted as a second sheet, thus doubling the postage

charged) and it induced letter writers to use every square centimetre
of space on the sheet, which had to be folded and sealed in such a
way that the back of it served as the wrapper for the letter. This
discouraged the spread of pictorialism which, for upwards of half a
century, was virtually confined to commercial stationery.

The postal reforms of 1839–40 however, revolutionized the
fashion of letter writing. Envelopes not only came into use overnight
but, from the very beginning of uniform penny postage prepaid by
stamps or stationery, the envelopes and wrappers sold by the Post
Office were frankly and fully pictorial. Rowland Hill placed much
more faith in the pictorial stationery designed by William Mulready
than he did on the small pieces of paper 'just big enough to bear
the stamp' which he had thrown in, more or less as an afterthought.
Mulready's pompous design, showing Britannia and the British lion
sending winged messengers with letters to the far-flung outposts of
Empire, was lampooned by *Punch*, ridiculed by the public and
vigorously parodied by Richard Doyle, Phiz (Hablot Knight
Brown), John Leech and many others. Packets of these Mulready
caricatures were sold by Ackerman's, Fore's and other leading
printsellers of the period. At first these parodies closely followed
Mulready's design, but soon they were branching out into all manner
of topical or thematic motifs of their own. Pictorial envelopes of this
sort, for example, were published as a form of Christmas greeting
and foreshadowed the introduction of the first Christmas cards in
1843. Others had musical or sporting themes, or were sold in sets
with scenic motifs. R. W. Hume of Leith and James Valentine of
Dundee were in the forefront of this movement, publishing comic
envelopes whose ribald humour was, in some respects, not as subtle
as the later seaside postcards. These comic envelopes were originally
sold for a penny each, but prices soon tumbled to sixpence a dozen.
On a less frivolous note, pictorial envelopes were also published in
the 1840s and 1850s for St Valentine's Day, Easter and other
seasonal greetings, thus, like the Christmas envelopes, foreshad-
owing the greetings cards. Another important class of pictorial
envelope took on a much more serious character and was widely
used as a propaganda medium. The abolition of slavery, the brotherhood of man, the abolition of war, universal suffrage and the aims
of the Chartist movement all found expression in the envelopes.
Both Hume and Valentine also led the way in the publication of
envelopes with assorted views engraved thereon. These scenic
envelopes are scarce today and much sought after. They arose out
of the earlier musical and sporting envelopes, and incorporated
scenes appropriate to these subjects, but later they concentrated
solely on landmarks and landscapes.

Pictorial envelopes were a fashion which waned in the 1860s,
although they continued to be popular for some years later in

America, Europe and Australasia. Indeed, they never really died out since they were taken up by the postal administrations of certain countries for tourist-oriented postal stationery at the turn of the century and this has continued fitfully to this day. Many towns in New Zealand encourage the use of pictorial envelopes extolling the scenery and industry of their neighbourhoods. Though not official, in the sense that stamped postal stationery is, these envelopes are now avidly collected. Pictorialism on envelopes tended to be frowned on by the British Post Office and it gradually died out, although it lingered on in the form of commercial stationery, mentioned in the previous chapter.

This was far from the end of pictorial stationery. The pictures merely moved from the envelope to its contents. The exquisitely engraved vignettes that graced the top half of sheets of notepaper differed in most respects from the pictures which had appeared on the envelopes. They were in existence even before 1840, though they are rare in that pre-reform period. They were devoid of the robust vulgarity which was so characteristic of the envelopes and very few of them exhibited the propaganda material found on the later envelopes. Patriotic sentiment during the Crimean War (1853–56) and Irish nationalism of a non-political quality seem to have been the limit of the propaganda element in pictorial notepaper. Instead these letter sheets concentrated almost entirely on scenery and landmarks. The earliest examples were quite small, and approximated to the vignettes found on tradesmen's letterheads of the period. By the 1850s, however, the engravings were increasing in size and eventually occupied about half of the space on the front of the sheet. At this time the average sheet of notepaper was demi-octavo in size, but the much larger quarto format was also popular. In the latter case the decoration might take the form of a triptych – a large engraving flanked by two smaller vignettes in floral or rococo cartouches. The vast majority of examples were clearly captioned, not only with the name of the scene depicted, but also with the name and address of the engraver and printer and even the exact date of publication.

In this medium the Scots again led the way, the earliest pictorial notepaper being claimed by George Stewart of Edinburgh. This claim has been disputed by the Edinburgh firm of Lizars who utilized engravings which they had previously prepared for cheques and banknotes. Be that as it may, the Scottish firms of Stewart, Hume, Valentine and Lizars were very prominent in this field, often engraving, lithographing and publishing notepaper for parts of the British Isles far removed from Scotland. In England the leading firm engaged in this business was Rock & Company of London who instituted the system of serially numbering their vignettes. One example in my collection, dated 6 April 1864, has the serial number

4982 which would seem to indicate a fairly prolific output in the course of a quarter of a century. Other publishers included Newman & Company of Watling Street, London and Marcus Ward of Belfast, the latter specializing at that time in Irish scenes. By the early 1880s, when Newman had moved to premises in Southwark Bridge Road, their vignettes were also being numbered, though the highest serial I have recorded is 1041 (Penarth, near Cardiff, No. 2). This sheet is dated July 1881, one of a set of at least four published on that date, which disproves the widely held theory that pictorial notepaper died out a decade earlier. Certainly they reached their zenith in the 1860s and examples after 1870 are decidedly scarce.

These letter sheets appear to have been produced and marketed in the same manner as the modern postcards. Every tourist resort had at least one stationer who sold them singly or in sets and it is evident, from the messages written on them, that they were purchased specifically to send to friends and relatives as a tourist souvenir. Since the tourist industry grew steadily in the 1870s and 1880s it is a mystery why pictorial notepaper went into such a decline in that period. Perhaps changes in postal rates provide the explanation. In October 1870 Britain introduced the printed paper rate of a halfpenny per item. This applied to newspapers transmitted by post and also to postcards. The latter were the official Post Office issue with an imprinted stamp and though they were devoid of pictorial matter they probably caught on very rapidly because they were half the cost of a letter. Since pictorial notepaper had to be sent in an envelope and was treated at the letter rate of a penny the competition from the postcards must have been too much for the notepaper to survive. Significantly the only examples of pictorial notepaper to survive well into the 1880s and beyond were those provided by hotels, mainly to advertise themselves and their amenities. The wheel had thus come full circle, since hotel notepaper, like other commercial stationery, had been the forerunner of pictorial notepaper. Hotel notepaper continued to be finely engraved until the turn of the century when lithography deteriorated in quality, and was then superseded by the much cheaper halftone process which, unfortunately, produced poorer results. Pictorial notepaper is still an attractive feature of many hotels overseas but sadly plays little part in the hotels of the British Isles at the present day, although here and there I have observed a few notable exceptions. There was a very short-lived vogue in the 1920s for pictorial letter-cards (similar to the Post Office issue, with perforated margins) showing views of hotels and local beauty spots, but this charming custom was a casualty of the Depression and has never been revived.

Picture postcards

Professor Emmanuel Herrmann of the Wiener-Neustadt Military Academy is generally regarded as 'the father of the postcard' since it was he who induced the Austrian Post Office to issue them in 1869; but, like most major inventions, the picture is not quite so simple and other people played a part in the formulation of this great idea. Credit for dreaming up the postcard should go to John P. Charlton of Philadelphia who obtained a patent in 1861 for a private postal card. Charlton sold his copyright to his fellow citizen H. L. Lipman who subsequently published plain pasteboard cards with a slight decorative border and the inscription 'Lipman's postal card, patent applied for'. Lipman cards were widely distributed in the United States and continued to be sold until 1873 when the U.S. Post Office introduced its own postcards. These cards were sold unstamped and required an adhesive stamp to frank them. It is thought that Dr Heinrich von Stephan, the Postmaster General of Prussia, may have had a Lipman card in mind when he advocated the issue of postcards in 1865. F. S. C. Lundy, writing in 1889, claimed that his father had published postcards at Leith in the early 1860s advertising his services as an artists' colourman. Mr Lundy would seem to have taken trade cards of the period a stage farther by actually sending them through the post. If so, he would have gained nothing from the exercise, since there was no rate lower than a penny at that time. It should be noted, however, that Leith was one of the towns in which a circular delivery company operated in direct contravention of the Postmaster General's monopoly and it may be that the Lundy advertisement cards were transmitted by the delivery company at a farthing or a halfpenny a time – considerably less than the prevailing Post Office rate. Von Stephan's suggestion was made at a postal conference held in Karlsruhe, Württemberg, but it failed to rouse enthusiasm among his fellow postmasters and was hardly discussed. The concept was revived four years later by Professor Herrmann who advocated its use in an article in the *Neue Freie Presse* in January 1869.

Herrmann's idea was taken up by the Austrian Post Office which issued the first *Correspondenz Karte* on 1 October 1869. The cards were printed in black on straw-coloured carton, with a 2-kreuzer yellow stamp impressed. Although the Austrian postal administration had doubts about the scheme, on the grounds that the public would never permit their privacy to be invaded in this manner, the cards proved to be a runaway success, and over 1.5 million were sold in the first month alone. This development was keenly observed in other parts of Europe. Britain and Switzerland both adopted postcards exactly one year later. The British cards were not only half the price of a letter postage stamp – a halfpenny – but were actually sold for that sum, so that the card itself was free. The stationers protested vehemently at this unfair competition and this led the Post Office to raise the cost in 1872 to 6½d. for a packet of twelve cards. The protests of the stationers were largely academic since the Post Office had a monopoly of postcards. Only the official issue, with a halfpenny stamp impressed in violet (later changed to brown and then to green), could be sent at the reduced rate. Occasionally the public tried to get away with sending private postcards bearing an *adhesive* halfpenny stamp (intended for circulars) but this was frowned upon and the offending item surcharged a penny – a halfpenny to bring it up to the letter rate at which it was grudgingly permitted, plus another halfpenny by way of a fine. Faced with obstructiveness of this kind it is hardly surprising that the postcard in Britain lagged far behind its European counterparts.

The first *picture* postcards were produced in October 1870 in France. Léon Besnardeau, a stationer in the little town of Sillé-le-Guillaume, produced special cards decorated with military and patriotic motifs as a memento of the fighting during the Franco-German War then at its height. In 1910, when he celebrated his eightieth birthday, Besnardeau published his claim to have invented the picture postcard, although his production was of a purely private nature, without official sanction. France, however, could also claim to have issued the first official picture postcards, in 1889, as souvenirs of the Exposition Universelle that year. The earliest official cards depicted the Eiffel Tower which had made its début as the focal point of the Exhibition. The following year Britain issued a card commemorating the Jubilee of Uniform Penny Postage. This card was sold for sixpence but only paid a halfpenny postage, the balance being credited to the Rowland Hill Benevolent Fund for Post Office Widows and Orphans. Incidentally, at the same time, a pictorial envelope in the best tradition of William Mulready was issued at a price of a shilling (a penny postage and elevenpence to charity). Its vignettes contrasted the state of the Post Office in 1840 with the progress made by 1890. Inevitably this envelope was soon parodied by Harry Furniss and used as a propaganda weapon in the battle of postal employees for better wages and working conditions. In 1891 Britain again issued an official card, for the Naval Exhibition, and this had a larger pictorial element than the card of 1890. Meanwhile the German publishers were permitted to issue unstamped cards and this rapidly became a medium for the beautiful chromolithography of the period. The German cards are popularly known to this day as 'Grüss Aus' cards, from the first two words of conventional greeting on the picture side, followed by the name of the place depicted. At first the pictures were grouped across one corner, but gradually they spread across the obverse of the card, reducing the space used for the message until it had little more than a narrow band at the foot of the picture. The reverse of the card was reserved for the name and address of the recipient. These cards were internationally sanctioned by the Universal Postal Union in 1892 but two years elapsed before the British Post Office gave way.

From September 1894 private picture postcards were permitted in the United Kingdom. Prior to that date increasing use had been made by commercial firms of the official stamped cards which subsequently had various forms of printing (including illustrations) added to the obverse. This was an unsatisfactory state of affairs, and these early pictorial cards compare very poorly with their colourful Continental cousins. The earliest private picture postcards were court size, conforming to the Post Office regulations of the time. Furthermore, the reverse had to be kept exclusively for the name and address of the recipient, and a substantial portion of the obverse was therefore required for the message. Consequently the earliest British picture postcards have fairly small pictures, often mere line engravings in the manner of the earlier notepaper. Significantly, George Stewart of Edinburgh was the first to issue these postcards after the ban was lifted. For five years postcard publishers had to get by in the cramped confines of the court size (115 × 89 mm) and it was not until 1 November 1899 that the Post Office agreed to the plea of Adolph Tuck (of Raphael Tuck Ltd.) and relaxed the regulation on size, to enable British cards to attain the same dimensions as European and American cards (140 × 89 mm). The extra inch in width made all the difference to the pictorial treatment possible. For a further three years the reverse remained exclusively for the name and address but in 1902 the German publisher, F. Hartmann, who had established a branch in England, persuaded the Post Office to allow both message and address to appear on the reverse, separated by a vertical line. Cards of the pre-1902 era are known as 'undivided backs' and those after that date are 'divided backs'. At first this concession could only be used on postcards transmitted within the British Isles but later they could be sent overseas, as other countries relaxed their rules too.

These changes in the rules coincided with enormous strides in the technical perfection of printing. James Valentine of Dundee pioneered the use of collotype in 1895, permitting much finer reproduction of pictures, while the extension of the photographic halftone process the following year immediately brought the postcard within the realm of the street photographer. This ushered in a golden era of local postcards. Just as this medium appealed to everyone, regardless of class, and was universally used in the same casual manner that we nowadays use the telephone, the publishers of postcards vied with each other to produce newer, more interesting and more exciting cards. The postal services were at their peak of efficiency and most towns received three deliveries of mail every weekday (including an evening delivery) and even one or two deliveries on Sundays, so that it was not uncommon for someone to write a card to a friend who would receive it the same day and still have time to pen a suitable reply for delivery first post the following morning. That this method of quick and cheap communication was widely used is borne out by a collection of cards I bought some years ago. It had been formed by a young couple in their courting days, when both of them were in domestic service but in separate establishments. Most of their assignations were arranged by postcard, often at what would seem to us today as exceedingly short notice – and yet the Post Office never let them down!

The ease with which cards were sent and received sparked off a craze for postcard collecting. The handsomely bound album, laid prominently on a table in the parlour for the delectation and edification of visitors, became as indispensable to the Edwardian household as the television set is to ours. Many of the postcards one encounters have messages on them which indicate that they were avidly exchanged between collectors. The latest issue was eagerly sought out, and the publishers responded by capturing every transient occasion, every incident no matter how trivial, on cards. Whenever a tramcar was derailed, a ship ran aground or heavy rain flooded a street, the cameraman would be there with his cumbersome equipment ready to snap the scene and within a matter of hours it would be available as the latest postcard. No other medium ever trapped the trivia of this passing world so swiftly or so effectively as the picture postcard. The local publishers, the men on the spot, were at their best in the production of what collectors now know familiarly as ASS (Animated Street Scenes). These cards may not have had the technical refinements and polish of the cards produced by the giant publishers of the industry, but they made up for this in the sense of immediacy in their scenic cards. Usually at least one urchin has moved his head as the camera shutter clicked, but from my viewpoint this merely adds to their charm, a fleeting moment frozen in eternity like a fly in amber.

Millions of postcards were sent and received during the dark days of the First World War, when they undoubtedly did much to boost morale at home and in the battlefields. But the doubling of the postcard rate to a penny in February 1918, and a further increase to 1½d. not long afterwards, effectively sounded the death-knell of the postcard as a popular vehicle of communication. Though the rate was reduced in 1922 to a penny it was still more than many could afford in the long depressed years of the Twenties and Thirties. Of course, postcards have survived to this day, despite escalating postal charges, but they will never again enjoy the degree of popularity which they had in the period from 1900 till 1918. This is regarded by collectors as the Golden Age of postcards. To be sure, there were many later improvements in the quality of production, notably in the use of multicolour photography, but modern cards lack the naive charm which endears the Edwardian and early Georgian cards to their collectors. On the local front, in particular, the changes in fashion after 1918 forced out the smaller publishers and henceforward postcard production was left in the hands of the nationwide manufacturers.

Interest in postcards as collectables dates from about 1958 when the first handbooks and periodicals devoted to the subject were published. Since then deltiology, to give it its pseudo-scientific name, has grown enormously, at a far greater rate than numismatics and almost outstripping philately as the premier acquisitive hobby. There are now several excellent catalogues which provide a useful guide to values according to the subject, artist and period of issue. Much remains to be researched, notably in the field of publishers. A great deal of sterling work has been done by individuals and also by the postcard clubs. Occasionally wholesale stockbooks and publishers' lists come to light, giving chapter and verse on the output of a publisher at a certain period, but most of the research into individual publishers has been compiled by collectors pooling their resources and recording items in their collections. The second edition of the Stanley Gibbons Postcard Catalogue (1981) has given a lead in this direction, by publishing a section devoted to a few publishers chosen at random, giving an outline of their activities, followed by a check-list of their cards, in the period up to 1918. Of the 8,000 cards believed to have been published by the International Art Company, some 2,000 are listed according to their serial numbers (501–2550). The vast majority of these are comic cards without topographical significance, but another section lists all the cards known to have been published by LL (Louis Levy) covering the London area in the pre-1918 period. These cards run from 1 (St Paul's Cathedral) to 420 (Trafalgar Square and St Martin's Church). Admittedly London is a large subject in any medium, but the fact that 420 different cards were produced by one firm out of the many that flourished in that period shows the immensity of the subject.

One collector of my acquaintance has amassed over 4,000 postcards showing views of the Isle of Man. Naturally he takes an interest in cards of all periods from the 1890s to the present day, but it illustrates the problem one encounters when considering one of the more popular tourist haunts. Every nationwide publisher would have had an extensive series of Manx cards on his list, while the island was large enough to support a number of indigenous publishers. It is in the latter respect that the greatest amount of research remains to be done. The collector who concentrates on a single county, or even one town or area within that county, and studies the postcards 'in depth', can still make a major contribution to our knowledge of local cards.

Here again Tonie and Valmai Holt, the editors of the Gibbons catalogue, have set an example in the latest edition. Following the publication of the first edition they sought the assistance of postcard clubs all over the country with a view to including a local publishers' section in the second edition. Evidently the response was so overwhelming that this project was found to be unmanageable within the framework of the present catalogue. A major new section has been promised for future editions, though my guess is that it will entail a separate volume to do adequate justice to the subject. As a start, however, the compilers listed the known publishers of cards in and around Canterbury. There were no fewer than twenty-two local publishers operating in Canterbury at one time or another, while a staggering sixty-three non-local publishers included Canterbury views in their repertoire. Of these, Louis Levy is believed to have published at least eighty-six different designs. It will be seen that collecting all the cards of Canterbury could be a lifetime's work, and the same is probably true of other towns of comparable size and importance.

As an example of the sort of treatment which, ideally, every small, local publisher should eventually receive, the catalogue has taken Sydney Smith (1884–1958), a photographer-cum-publisher who worked in the Yorkshire town of Pickering. It is thought that his first cards were a series of three published in 1909 to record the laying of the foundation stone of the local Liberal club. Over the ensuing thirty years Smith produced cards for all manner of events, from the funerals of prominent citizens to the local celebrations of coronations and the Silver Jubilee of 1935, visits from members of the royal family and political figures, Lord Howard opening the sewage works (1933) and inspecting the Air Raid Precautions unit (1940). Exceptional blizzards, hailstorms and floods provided Smith with abundant material – no fewer than thirty-three cards for the 1927 floods and thirty-two for the 1930 inundation. Fires and other accidents were faithfully recorded in postcards as well as the more mundane matters such as the annual Wesley Day and Remembrance Day observances. Mr and Mrs Holt make the observation that local enthusiasts, seeking the elusive missing link to complete a series, would pay high sums, whereas people with no local interest would tend to disregard such cards and not rate them highly at all. Fortunately, the fact that cards were meant to be sent through the post usually resulted in their widespread dissemination and many of these local event postcards are likely to turn up in other parts of the country. A few years ago the dedicated local collector would always make a point of visiting flea markets and junk shops wherever he happened to be on business or holiday, in the hope of finding some

Postcard of the local fishing industry. Grimsby cod fishermen of the late nineteenth century (Humberside Libraries)

of the lacunae at little cost. Nowadays, however, the dealers are organized into fair circuits and tend to sort their stocks with an eye on the local collector market in whichever town they happen to be, with the inevitable increase in prices. One consolation is that dealers cannot be omniscient and even allowing for some increase in price on account of local interest, they may not always appreciate the significance or rarity of a particular item.

The Holts have appealed for details of cards, series, artists and publishers classified on a local basis so I decided to try and help with information on my own town, Dumfries. Apart from the fact that I have quite a large collection of local cards (which I had been amassing for the whole of Scotland since my school-days) I was fortunate to have, as my next door neighbour, Noel Dinwiddie, managing director of Robert Dinwiddie Ltd, stationer, printer and publisher. The company was formed in 1846 as J. Maxwell & Son as stationers, printers and newsagents. In 1887 Robert Dinwiddie went to work for the company as an office boy and thirty years later took over the firm from the Misses Maxwell. The name of the company was changed in 1920 to Robert Dinwiddie & Co. Ltd and continued to operate as printers, booksellers and stationers. Subsequently the firm added a subsidiary, Farm Records Ltd, specializing in the production of ledgers, stationery and office equipment for the rural community. Another development was the Typewriter Shop, which branched out into all kinds of office equipment. Between the world wars Dinwiddie's also ran a travel business specializing in holiday cruises. Over the years the company has been responsible for a great deal of printed matter, ranging from the usual ephemera associated with jobbing printing – tickets, menus, posters, labels and packaging – to a substantial output of books, mainly of local interest, but also including publications for organizations and institutions as diverse as the Royal Horticultural Society, the Pobjoy Mint of Sutton and the Royal Yacht *Britannia*!

Production of postcards seems to have begun in the late 1890s, one of the earliest showing the commemoration in Dumfries of Queen Victoria's Diamond Jubilee in 1897. After such a promising start, however, the firm largely ignored local occasions. Among the few later cards tied to specific events I have only recorded the capture of a suspected German spy at Newton Stewart (1915), invalided servicemen at the Burns anniversary celebrations (1918), the Silver Jubilee celebrations (1935), the unveiling of the memorial to John Paul Jones at Arbigland (1953) and the centenary of the death of Dr Henry Duncan, founder of the savings bank movement (1946). One may also include a card produced in connection with the Dumfries Health Exhibition (1938) which advertised the company and showed its 'holiday cruise and hygienic office' stands at the exhibition. No records of postcard production have survived but Noel Dinwiddie recently presented his collection of the firm's postcards to the local library. Mr Dinwiddie, now in his eighties, recalls that when he was a boy his uncles Robert and William Dinwiddie travelled all over Dumfries and Galloway with a pony and trap, laden with a whole-plate camera and tripod. Out of these forays into the remoter parts of south-west Scotland the Dinwiddie brothers eventually obtained the photographs which formed the basis for over 3,000 picture postcards, ranging from Gretna Green to Portpatrick and Stranraer. The vast majority of these postcards were published between 1900 and 1920 and consequently bear the imprint of J. Maxwell or J. Maxwell & Son. Relatively few cards were inscribed R. Dinwiddie & Co. and most of the later cards are either anonymous, or bear the name and address of the retail outlet in each village, often preceded by the formula 'Published by . . .' This creates the misleading impression that the village stores in Penpont or the sub-postmaster at Gatehouse had been responsible for the design and production of the cards they sold when, in fact, they were merely the sole distributor for those particular cards.

Local cards bearing the names and addresses of the village stationer or post office are not without considerable interest on this account, since they often provide valuable clues to the ownership of shops at a particular period, especially if the postcard is date-stamped or otherwise dated. I have found such inscriptions to be of

MADEIRA WALK
BRIGHTON

Postcard of Madeira Walk, Brighton, postmarked 1921; typical Edwardian scene painted by A. R. Quinton (from the collection of Tonie and Valmai Holt)

great assistance in my researches into local postal history, in cases where the name of the postmaster might otherwise be unknown.

By concentrating on the postcards depicting the towns, villages and rural scenery of a single county or district, the collector should get a good cross-section of both local and nationwide publishers. Many of the latter were originally German, since Saxony was the world's leading centre of postcard production, and names like Hartmann and Hildesheimer, Stengel and Schwerdtfeger are deltiological household names, vieing with Valentine of Dundee, Tuck of London and Judges of Hastings. Many of the Edwardian postcards bore an inscription alluding to their Saxon origins, but after the outbreak of the First World War the gorgeous chromolithographs of the Golden Age gave way to drap sepia monochrome cards which proclaimed defiantly that they were 'British Throughout' or professed to be 'A Real British Photograph'. Not until the advent of modern multicolour photographic processes did British postcards regain their pre-war polychrome character. In the 1950s and 1960s there was something of a renaissance in multicolour postcards, the chief exponent of this being J. Arthur Dixon of Yorkshire and the Isle of Wight and nowadays all but a few local cards are produced in full colour. By studying the cards pertaining to a single town over the past ninety years one can trace the developments in the technique of production, as well as the subtle or dramatic changes which have taken place in our urban scenery. This undoubtedly explains the particular popularity of Animated Street Scenes. The clothing of the people reflects their times, while the presence or absence of horse-drawn vehicles, the later motor cars in all the numerous and varied styles, the pattern of shopfronts, the many changes in the names on the fascia boards, the presence or absence of posters and the subject of their announcements can all tell us a very great deal about the town at the time when the card was published. If you arrange your cards as I do, street by street, subject by subject in chronological sequence, they present a vivid panorama of the progress and development of the town over the most dramatic century in all of human history.

Philately

To most people philately means the study and collecting of the postage stamps issued by Government postal administrations, and it comes as a surprise to them to learn that the subject also encompasses a great many stamps issued by private concerns. Sometimes they flouted the traditional monopoly of letter-carrying enjoyed by Postmasters General since the seventeenth century; at other times their activities were condoned or tolerated by the authorities. Since the postal monopoly was confined to letters, and has never applied to parcels (even though the Post Office has operated its own parcel post for over a century), it follows that railway companies, haulage companies and freight lines were perfectly entitled to issue their own stamps to indicate the prepayment of the freight charges on parcels. At certain times, and in certain modes of transport, the Post Office has allowed the carriage even of letters, subject to certain regulations, and as a result many different issues of stamps have been made by private companies for the purpose. Finally, there are several categories of label, produced under the auspices of the Post Office which, because they bear the name of a post office, can be studied and collected on a town or county basis. Moreover, even the Post Office issues of stamps have been subjected to security endorsement in the form of the initials of firms, and these too can be collected on a local basis. Below, each of these categories is examined in some detail.

Express and parcel companies' stamps

More than 140 years after the birth of the Penny Black the arguments continue to rage over who should have the title of 'father of the adhesive postage stamp'. Sir Rowland Hill is generally recognized as the originator of stamps, but claims on behalf of James

Chalmers of Dundee and Laurence Koschier of Zagreb are still occasionally advanced. None of these may be entitled to rank as first, but it all depends on how we define a postage stamp. In *The Romance of the Postage Stamp* (1962) Gustav Schwenk makes the extraordinary and highly intriguing claim: 'In 1811 . . . a Scottish shipping line used adhesive stamps for its private postal service, though unfortunately little is known about these. They were probably inspired by the brilliant idea of the 24-year-old Prime Minister, William Pitt, who for the purposes of his hat tax introduced stamps which had to be stuck into the hats.' I have searched all available records in vain for anything that might substantiate this story; nor have I been able to trace the source of this statement. On one score at least Mr Schwenk was correct. Adhesive stamps denoting the payment of the hat tax did exist – but this method of prepaying taxes had existed even earlier. Adhesive stamps prepaying the duty on patent medicines had existed since 1802 and even earlier there had been similar stamps denoting the tax on dice, playing cards and gloves, while small rectangular adhesive labels were used from the 1690s onwards as a means of securing the staples which, in turn, affixed the thick embossed stamps to legal documents of vellum or parchment.

Certainly, within a decade of the alleged Scottish shipping line, adhesive stamps were being used by Messrs C. & R. Elliott who operated a parcel company from an office in Sackville Street (now O'Connell Street) opposite the General Post Office in Dublin. A red oval adhesive stamp bearing the company's name and address, and rated at 6s. 6d. (32½p), is known on the wrapper of a parcel sent from Dublin to Ludlow, Shropshire in 1821. Most of the known parcel stamps, however, seem to have been issued after 1840, inspired no doubt by the stamps issued by the Post Office. Among the earliest of the companies using its own distinctive stamps was the London Parcels Delivery Company which had two types of stamps from the mid-1840s, a prepaid stamp printed in black on orange paper, and an unpaid stamp printed on white paper, with legend 'Carriage to Pay'.

The Robson Lowe *Encyclopaedia of British Empire Postage Stamps* (1952) states that the parcel post remained in private hands until the services were nationalized in 1883 and continues 'Most of the stamps were withdrawn from use about 1883, but some services continued to use them, presumably by arrangement with the G.P.O.' In August 1883 the Post Office instituted its own parcel post in direct competition with the railways and the freight companies, but in no sense did the Post Office 'nationalize' any service which existed at or prior to that date. The Post Office had to rely on the co-operation of the railway companies for the carriage of parcels nationwide, since they alone, at that time, had a network of communications suitable for the purpose. The statement that most of the parcel company stamps were withdrawn in 1883 is also untrue. They continued to issue their own stamps so long as they stayed in business and, of course, there are many varieties in existence to this day. These inaccurate statements reflect the relative state of ignorance of this fascinating sideline of philately barely thirty years ago. In the intervening years, however, the issues of the express and parcel companies have been avidly studied by members of the Cinderella Stamp Club (which was formed specifically to cater to the 'cinderellas' of philately), the Railway Philatelic Group and other bodies concentrating on the philately of certain areas.

In addition to firms such as Pickford's, the Atlas Express Company of Liverpool, or Sutton's of Manchester there were smaller parcel delivery companies in Bradford, Newcastle and Portsmouth, and express companies which handled parcels and other goods rapidly in London, Liverpool and Manchester. It is likely that similar express and parcel companies existed in other cities, such as Birmingham, Edinburgh and Glasgow, but no stamps issued by them have so far come to light. In a way, this reflects the fashions in philately. At the time when such stamps were current Victorian philatelists were concerned only with Government issues and consequently seldom took the trouble to preserve examples of these unofficial labels. The modern equivalent of these carriers are the great mail order houses, such as the British Mail Order Corporation, Geest, and Littlewoods who either use their own distinctive labels on goods transported by postal and rail service in addition to their own systems, or use the labels of National Carriers, British Road Services, Roadline or Selnec (an acronym from South East Lancashire North East Cheshire Parcels Delivery Company). Individual mail order companies seldom indicate their names on these 'stamps' though names, addresses, trademarks and even advertisements of these companies appear in the address labels which, nowadays, often incorporate a Postage Paid impression, and these are, themselves, eminently collectable.

Tramway stamps

From about 1880 till the end of the First World War tramways, electric traction companies and light railways operated in and around the larger towns and cities of the British Isles. They were the first effective form of public transport, developing at a time when the urbanization of Britain was accelerating. Some of these tram routes extended for twenty miles or more out into the surrounding countryside and were ideal for the commuter traffic at the turn of the century. They were superseded to some extent by trolley buses, but eventually motor buses ousted them and they have all but disappeared. Only the promenade trams at Blackpool and the 'toastracks' in Douglas, Isle of Man have survived to this day. In their heyday these tramcars not only carried passengers but freight and mails as well. From the mid-1880s many of them even had a posting-box affixed near the doorway so that letters could be posted en route. This custom was suspended during the First World War, fitfully revived in the Twenties and finally abolished in 1939, although Blackpool revived this charming tradition in 1981 as a tourist attraction, complete with distinctive postmark.

Many of these tramways issued their own stamps for use on parcels conveyed over the company lines. Among the best known of the tramway stamps were those issued by the Manchester Carriage & Tramways Company (1890–1900), the Potteries Electric Traction Company (*c*.1900), the Dublin United Tramways and the Lucan Steam Company of Dublin, the Blessington Steam Tramway and Leeds City Tramways. Tramways were an economic mode of transport in the smaller islands of the British Isles and special stamps are known to have been issued by several of them, notably the Guernsey Electric Railway (which, despite its name, was actually a tramway system), the Guernsey Steam Tramway, the Jersey Western Railway and the Isle of Man Electric Railway. Many of the tramways elsewhere in the British Isles certainly issued stamps but so far examples have proved to be very elusive. Only a single example is recorded of the 4d. stamp issued by the Lanarkshire Tramways in 1905 and barely a handful of the 2d. stamp issued by the Edinburgh and District Tramways about the same date. No stamps have so far been recorded from the Gateshead & District Tramways Company, the Tynemouth & District Electric Traction Company, or the Jarrow & District Electric Traction Company which amalgamated in 1913 to form the Northern General Transport Company. Its stamps are known only from 1928 onwards, though they must have existed prior to that date. Clearly this is a subject which awaits research by dedicated enthusiasts on the spot.

Bus stamps

If doubts have been expressed over the identity, let alone the authenticity, of the Scottish shipping line mentioned by Gustav Schwenk, there is no doubt regarding the earliest road transport stamps which originated in Scotland in April 1829. In that month Scott, Sawers & Company of Edinburgh inaugurated a parcels service between that city and Stirling. The parcels were conveyed aboard the *Tally Ho* passenger coach and an insurance scheme was operated in respect of parcels worth £5 or more. The adhesive parcel stamps were very simple in design, being merely inscribed 'S. S. & Coy . . . PAID', typeset in black on thick white ungummed paper which had to be pasted to the parcel. Although the stage-coaches were rapidly ousted by the railways as official mail carriers a considerable amount of parcel traffic continued to be conveyed by coach, especially in the remoter districts which were late in receiving the benefits of a rail connection.

Many of the bus companies that flourished in the first half of this century could trace their origins to carters who carried parcels and the occasional passenger by pony and trap, often as a feeder service from a railhead into the surrounding countryside, or linking one town with another. These carters were greatly encouraged by the Post Office which awarded contracts for the conveyance of letters and later parcels by private individuals. Not only did the Post Office payments help to subsidize services in areas which might otherwise have gone without, but by enforcing strict regulations concerning the size of carts and gigs, the maintenance of horses and equipment and the carriage of passengers and non-postal freight, the Post Office raised the standards of these services. Many of them followed the example of the Post Office in the early years of this century and became motorized, although horse-drawn coaches survived in the Scottish Highlands and Islands until the 1920s. Unfortunately, very little is known about the parcel services operated by these small companies and no stamps have been recorded, though the possibility that they exist cannot be ruled out.

From the mid-1870s onwards, many borough councils and civic corporations began organizing transport systems, using horse-drawn trams and buses, followed by the heyday of the electric tramways at the turn of century and then adopting motor buses before the First World War. The conductors on these buses were responsible for handling parcels, and carried a small stock of stamps ready to be affixed to packages handed to them for transmission. Numerous private bus companies operated in the inter-war years and competition between them could be fierce at times. They competed not only for passenger traffic but for lucrative freight contracts and provided special stamps in many cases for this purpose. Since the passage of the Transport Act of 1968 and the reorganization of most bus services into giant passenger transport authorities the number of different services has dropped sharply, but there are still many small independent operators, especially in the remoter areas, and the majority of these continue to issue their own distinctive stamps.

Bus stamps, by and large, are utilitarian in design, seldom running to anything so frivolous as a pictorial device, far less the full-blown pictorialism usually associated with stamps. But they possess considerable interest for all that, and have the merit (not shared by many 'official' stamps these days) of being produced strictly for the prepayment of parcel postage and not with any designs on the wallets or purses of stamp collectors. Many of these stamps were printed in coils or rolls by such firms as Williamson of Ashton or the Bell Punch Company of London and consequently look more like tickets than stamps. Indeed, some of them are actually inscribed PARCEL TICKET, although they are, in fact, stamps in the true sense. Others are printed in violet from T.I.M. (Ticket Issuing Machines Ltd) devices, similar to those used by many bus conductors for producing tickets, and have a similar appearance. Curiously enough, both the British and Irish postal administrations used similar machines to produce gummed labels for their parcel services, and Ireland continues to use this system to this day. The more attractive bus stamps, however, are those which were prepared by the local jobbing printer, relying on the sometimes limited resources of such firms in the way of producing multiple designs, gumming and perforation. Though often primitive in appearance they are usually quite informative, often serially numbered, with the names of termini or routes, or even the class of parcel or freight. Some companies issued separate stamps for parcels, luggage, newspapers, agricultural produce and even milk churns! Because the vast majority of the smaller companies operated within their own county area these stamps should be of interest to the county collector.

Among those bus companies which are known to have issued stamps at one time or another are Alexander's (Glasgow), Brown's (Dorking), the Cream Bus Service (Stamford), Gibson's (Dumfries), the Green Bus Company (Rugeley), Highland Omnibuses, the Highley Bus Service (Worcestershire), Jersey Motor Transport, Johnson & Son (Buckinghamshire), MacBrayne's (Scottish Highlands and Islands) and Store and Morgan joint services (Doncaster-Goole area). Among the borough or corporation transport services whose buses had distinctive stamps may be mentioned Bury, Colchester, Lincoln, Maidstone, Wigan and Wolverhampton. These bus stamps continue to this day and, indeed, have proliferated in recent years due to inflation which has spawned frequent changes in parcel rates, and the imposition of Value Added Tax which often appears on the stamp as a separate sum. Again, changes in the rate of V.A.T. from time to time have precipitated changes in the design of the stamps.

Telegraph and telephone stamps

The telegraph system of the British Isles was nationalized in 1870 and operated thereafter by the Post Office, until 1981 when it was hived off to form a separate corporation known as British Telecom. For a generation before 1870, however, the telegraph service was in the hands of a number of private companies. The Electric Telegraph Company began operating in 1846 over lines erected by some of the railway companies. In 1851, at the Great Exhibition, London, the company produced a special telegram form with an embossed stamp and this is considered to be the first telegraph stamp. Later adhesive stamps were used by this and other companies but few have survived in genuinely used condition since it was the custom, then as now, for the telegraph service to retain the forms which then went through the company's channels and ended up as security scrap, to be pulped or shredded. When the companies sold their interests to the Post Office in 1870, however, the unsold remainders of their stamps came on the philatelic market. These remainders can often be distinguished from the genuinely used stamps by the absence of the serial numbers which the companies impressed on them at the time of issue. One of the most frequently encountered sets of stamps was that prepared for use by Bonelli's Telegraph Company in 1868. The company was bought out by the Post Office before it commenced business, and its stamps are therefore unknown in actual use, but still quite plentiful as mint remainders. Stamps are known from the British and Irish Magnetic Telegraph Company (1857–60), the British Telegraph Company (c.1855–57), the Electric Telegraph Company (1855–61), the English and Irish Magnetic Telegraph Company (1853), the London District Telegraph (1862–65), the Submarine Telegraph Company (date unknown), the United Kingdom Telegraph Company (1862–63) and the Universal Private Telegraph Company (1864–68). It will be noted that most of these companies had names which implied a nationwide service. Doubtless this was their intention long-term, but, for the most part, their areas of operation were quite small. The 'Universal', for example, confined its activities to a line between Glasgow and Helensburgh, a distance of under 20 miles!

By contrast with the prosaic character of most bus stamps, the telegraph stamps were exceedingly ornate and often verbose. The Electric Telegraph stamps even included a lengthy disclaimer: 'The Electric Telegraph Company will not be responsible for Mistakes in transmission of unrepeated Messages from whatever cause they may arise. Nor will the Company be responsible for Mistakes in the transmission of a repeated Message nor for delay in the transmission or delivery, nor for non-transmission or non-delivery of any Message whether repeated or unrepeated, to any extent above £5, unless it be insured. Send the annexed message according to the above conditions.' Below this was a space for the sender to append his signature. The same company also had an elaborate series of stamps for the personal use of directors of the company; examples bearing the names of G. P. Bidder, Thomas Brassey, Captain Huish and Lord Alfred Paget are known. The South Eastern Railway also issued telegraph stamps, in September 1860. Incidentally this company's first telegraph office was at Aldershot, for the convenience of the military.

The National Telephone Company issued its own stamps in 1884 to prepay the charges of casual customers, and also long-distance calls of subscribers who got their local calls free at that time. The stamps portrayed the chairman of the company, Col. Robert Raynsford-Jackson and were withdrawn in 1891 because the Post Office objected to this. These stamps were used nationwide, but would merit inclusion in a Glasgow local collection since they were printed by Maclure, Macdonald and Company of that city. The telephone service was nationalized in 1912.

Railway newspaper and parcel stamps

From the outset a considerable revenue was earned by the railways through the carriage of freight. In default of a Post Office parcels service they carried parcels swiftly and efficiently, offering an automatic form of registration and compensation against loss, and despite the multitude of railways parcels could be transmitted from one end of the country to the other, since each company agreed to convey parcels originating elsewhere, the share in the proceeds being arranged through the central Railway Clearing House. Here again Robson Lowe is in error in saying that, prior to the Post Office undertaking the parcel post in 1890 (it was 1883 actually), the railways issued their own stamps. In most cases parcel stamps are now known to have been in use long after 1883, since the railways continued to operate their own parcel services, frequently undercutting the Post Office service. Their stamps survived the reorganization of 1922–23, but after that date the designs used by the 'Big Four' were much plainer and more functional. Even to this day British Rail uses parcel stamps of a sort, through its Red Star service. Altogether some sixty-five companies in England and Wales, seventeen in Scotland and eight in Ireland are known to have issued parcel stamps between 1855 and 1922. Most of these stamps were inscribed 'Prepaid Parcel' or 'Prepaid Newspaper Parcel', but there were some unusual types inscribed 'Milk Parcel' (Furness Railway), 'Corn Samples' (Great Eastern), 'Farm and Agricultural Produce' (Great Western), 'Local Prepaid Parcel on Corn or Coal Business' (Midland), 'Sugar Sample' (Glasgow & South Western), 'Book Parcel' (Caledonian) and 'Periodicals' (North British).

Perhaps the oddest of them all was the 'Market Basket' stamp issued by the Midland Great Western, an Irish railway. This stamp was affixed to a market basket which had to be padlocked (sender and recipient having duplicate keys), and handed over to the station-master half an hour before the departure of the train. This enabled people in the remoter areas to shop by train, since the basket went to the retailer who complied with the order inside, filled the basket, locked it and returned it to the original consignor. A weight not exceeding 112 lb could be conveyed up to fifty miles for 1s. 3d. and over 100 miles for 2s. 6d.

The Highland Railway issued stamps for use between certain specified stations, in the same manner as the railway tickets, and these are known with inscriptions signifying Perth-Inverness, any station west of Dingwall, Thurso-Stromness, Wick-Lybster, Golspie-Helmsdale, Bonar Bridge-Golspie, Helmsdale-Thurso-Wick, North of Inverness and on board the company's steamer to Orkney. There was even a joint label for use on parcels conveyed over the Highland, Sutherland, Duke of Sutherland and Caithness railways.

Some of the railway parcel stamps were very large, up to 4 inches square being recorded. They were usually ornate, decorated with the company arms and often embellished with tiny vignettes of locomotives, wagons and parcel vans.

Railway letter stamps

Prior to 1891 it was illegal for the railway companies to carry letters other than the Royal Mails entrusted to them in sealed bags, but the public were not slow in appreciating that messages could be sent quickly by train and so long as someone collected them at their destination the time in transit from sender to recipient was far shorter than the normal postal service. Newspaper reporters, in particular, were in the habit of using the railways. The loophole was to send the letter as a railway parcel, tied up with string and franked by a newspaper parcel stamp. The Post Office were well aware of the fact the Postmaster General's monopoly was being flouted but were powerless to suppress this apparent abuse. After the inauguration of the parcel post in 1883 the Post Office was increasingly beholden to the railways for the efficient working of this service and in 1891 was forced, as part of a renegotiation of the terms of the parcel post, to concede a railway letter service. From 1 February 1891 the railways were permitted to convey letters so long as they bore a Post Office penny stamp and, additionally, a special 2d. railway letter stamp. Senders took these letters to their nearest railway station and the letters were then sent forward to the nearest station of the address where they either lay until collected, or were then handed over to the post office for delivery in the normal way.

Part of the agreement insisted that the railway letter stamps had to be uniform in colour and appearance and a standard design was devised for this purpose. Most companies abided by this ruling, but notable exceptions included the Freshwater, Yarmouth and Newport, the Great Northern, the Lynton and Barnstaple, the Wirral, the Lancashire, Derbyshire and East Coast, the Shropshire and Montgomeryshire and the Londonderry & Lough Swilly railways. Even those companies which followed the regulation and issued green stamps in the approved style exercised their individuality in such matters as printers and printing process as well as minor features of the design. Moreover, the name of the company appeared on its stamps. Between 1891 and 1922 some ninety-one railways in England and Wales, fifteen in Scotland and thirty-five in Ireland issued these stamps. All of them were of 2d. denomination – except the Londonderry & Lough Swilly which perversely issued penny stamps. The Post Office only permitted the latter so long as they were used in pairs. The rate remained at 2d. until January 1920 when it was raised to 3d. and then, only nine months later, it was increased to 4d. This led to a large number of provisional surcharges and hurriedly revised designs, so that there was quite a spate of new issues in the last year or two before the railways were swallowed up in the regrouping which came into effect at the beginning of 1923. After that date the major railway companies ceased to issue distinctive letter stamps, but frequently used their parcel stamps instead. As the latter invariably bore the name of the station of issue, the range of collectable stamps is almost infinite. The present system operated by British Rail is called Railex and relies on machine or handstruck markings rather than adhesive labels.

This is by no means the end of the story of railway letter stamps. The Talyllyn Railway, a narrow gauge light railway hauling slates from a quarry in North Wales, escaped the big mergers of 1922–23 and nationalization in 1948 because of its insignificance and the fact that it did not, at that time, carry passengers. This line was rescued from oblivion in the 1950s and became the first of the preserved lines which are now such an important tourist attraction. Now almost a score of railways in the British Isles are being operated by preservation societies and about half of them regularly issue railway letter stamps. The Talyllyn pioneered this in 1957, followed in the late 1960s by the Ffestiniog and Ravenglass & Eskdale. In 1970 British Rail jumped on the band wagon by issuing stamps for the Vale of Rheidol light railway and in 1971–72 the Isle of Man Steam Railway and the Manx Electric Railway followed suit. In addition commemorative issues of railway letter stamps have been produced by British Rail (celebrating the Advanced Passenger Train) and by the railway societies in Ireland for use on souvenir mail carried by rail. This branch of philately now has a large following, and supports a considerable literature in its own right.

Circular delivery company stamps

Mention has already been made of the fact that the Post Office had no rate of postage lower than a penny until October 1870 when it was forced to grant a printed paper and postcard rate of a halfpenny. This concession was in direct response to the illegal competition provided by a number of private companies which had been established from 1865 onwards expressly for the delivery of circulars. It was realized that circulars could be delivered quickly at a fraction of the official costs, especially if confined to the larger urban areas. The prime mover in this enterprise was Robert Brydone, an Edinburgh businessman. The stamps used by his network of circular delivery companies were printed by his father, James E. N. Brydone. The first of these services was established in 1865, being grafted on to the existing Edinburgh and Leith Parcels Delivery Company. The stamps of both circular and parcels companies showed the conjoined arms of Edinburgh and Leith and differed only in their inscriptions and denominations. The circular stamps were issued in values of a farthing and a halfpenny – thus considerably undercutting the Post Office rate. The service was an immediate success and inspired Brydone to establish the London Circular and Pamphlet Delivery Company the following year. In 1867 he instituted similar services in Aberdeen, Glasgow and Liverpool, and expanded his London activities into three separate companies, the London, the London and Districts and the Metropolitan. He had just established the grandiose National Delivery Company when the Post Office pounced. Proceedings were taken against Brydone in May 1868 and resulted in a decision in favour of the Post Office. Brydone appealed but this was dismissed the following month. Stamps were then in preparation for use in Birmingham, Manchester and Dundee but were never issued though sheets exist with stamps of the nine different companies side by side, in various colours. Although Robert Brydone lost his case, and his circular delivery companies were suppressed after such short duration, they did prod officialdom into providing cheaper postage. One other company, operated by Clark of Edinburgh, also issued stamps in 1866. Though undenominated, they were sold for a farthing.

Recent announcements in Parliament envisage a relaxation of the Government's postal monopoly to permit the carriage of urgent letters by private companies so we may be on the verge of a renaissance in delivery company stamps.

College stamps

The origins of the university posts are lost in the mists of antiquity, but it was a traditional privilege of the universities all over Europe from the Middle Ages onwards that they should operate their own postal services. This was all well and good in an age when there was little or no competition from the State postal systems, but by the mid-nineteenth century the college posts were an anachronism which the Postmaster General barely tolerated. In fairness to the Oxford and Cambridge colleges which operated this system, the vast majority of the letters were transmitted from one college to another or within the college precincts, the college porters acting as messengers. Letters were sent unstamped but from 1871 till 1885 adhesive stamps were issued for this purpose by Keble (1871), Merton (1876), Lincoln (1877), Hertford (1875), Exeter (1882), All Souls (1884), St John's (1884) and Balliol (1885) at Oxford; and at Queens' (1883), St John's (1884) and Selwyn (1882) at Cambridge. In December 1885 the Postmaster General suppressed them, though Keble, which had instigated the stamps in the first place, continued to defy the authorities by issuing stamped envelopes and postcards till 1886 and then got round the ban by selling envelopes with the college crest on the flap at 8d a dozen, using the crest to 'frank' the letters contained in these envelopes. This dodge continued for many years. In 1971 Keble celebrated the centenary of its stamps by issuing an adhesive label and this was transmitted, complete with 'postmark' through the university postal system, apparently with the tacit agreement of the Post Office.

The college stamps, of course, will only be of interest to collectors in Oxfordshire and Cambridgeshire and nothing comparable has been recorded from any other part of the British Isles. These stamps were usually printed locally by such firms as Spiers & Sons or Emberlin's in Oxford, while all the Cambridge issues were lithographed by W. P. Spalding. Lincoln College alone went outside Oxford, getting its stamps engraved and intaglio printed by Alan Wyon of London. In every case, the college arms were depicted. Usually the college name was given, except in the case of Lincoln which was the only stamp to state a value – 'Message One Penny'. The Balliol stamps had no inscription at all and from the fact that they were never issued I wonder whether what purports to be a Balliol stamp – a red shield on a plain white ground – was merely the first stage in production, the intention being to add inscriptions in the borders in a second colour. These Balliol stamps were unusual in that they were produced in vertical strips of seventeen, the end stamps being inverted in relation to the others.

Airmail stamps

The United Kingdom is one of the very few countries which has never issued an official airmail stamp thus inscribed, though certain values in the definitive series are intended for airmail. To some extent, however, this lack has been remedied by several independent airlines which, in times past, issued stamps to prepay the postage on letters carried over their routes. To this day British Airways (and its predecessor, British European Airways) have or had distinctive stamps for this purpose. These air letters may be posted at any airport and will be forwarded through the normal postal channels at the post office nearest to the airport of arrival, or may be collected by the addressee at the airport, in the same manner as a railway letter.

Distinctive stamps were produced in the 1930s by International Airlines (August-September 1933) Provincial Airways (November 1933) and Portsmouth, Southsea and Isle of Wight Aviation (February 1934). Oddly enough, the lead in this matter was taken by a railway company, the Great Western which inaugurated an air service between Cardiff and Plymouth in April 1933. At first the railway newspaper parcel 3d. stamps were used but latterly a distinctive stamp showing a biplane was provided. The service lost a great deal of money and was terminated in September 1933. North of the Border, Scottish Airways, based on Aberdeen, and Highland Airways, serving Inverness, Wick and the northern isles, issued colourful labels, more for publicity reasons than as actual stamps, although they are invariably found on flown covers and cards from May 1934 onwards. North Eastern Airways, operating between Perth and London via Doncaster and other towns in the east of England, issued a blue label showing a De Havilland Dragon Rapide. Various versions exist with overprints to mark the inauguration of different routes or stages. An air service was operated between Bideford, Barnstaple and Lundy and the latter issued airmail stamps as part of its prolific series of local stamps, discussed later in this chapter. The earliest Lundy air stamps were printed in continuous rolls like tickets – which, indeed, they were in every sense – but later issues were printed in more conventional form, perforated all round. In 1923 the *Daily Mail* sponsored a contest for the longest distance accomplished in one flight by motor-assisted glider using one gallon of fuel. The contest was staged at Lympne and a small quantity of mail was carried to Hastingleigh by a glider of the Air Navigation and Engineering Company. Special labels bearing the names of the take-off and landing points were issued for use on flown covers.

Experiments with mail-carrying rockets date from 1928, when Friedrich Schmiedl carried out tests with letter-carrying projectiles

Two examples of UK Airway Letter Service inaugural flights covers (Mark A. Greening)

in Austria. The early research in this field was almost entirely German, and in 1934 Gerhard Zucker came to Britain to conduct mail-carrying experiments. Special stamps for this rocket mail were produced in connection with an airmail exhibition in London, but the rocket flight was postponed and the stamps not actually used on flown mail. Britain's first actual rocket flight carrying mail took place in June 1934 at Rottingdean on the Sussex Downs and the exhibition labels were suitably overprinted for the occasion. At the end of July Zucker went to the Outer Hebrides and attempted to send mail from the island of Scarp to the island of Harris. Two stamps inscribed 'Western Isles Rocket Post' were issued. The experiment failed when the rocket exploded on take-off and many of the covers were charred and subsequently received an explanatory cachet at Harris post office. Zucker later overprinted some of the Western Isles stamps for use in a rocket experiment to carry mail between Lymington, Hampshire and the Isle of Wight but again the attempt was a failure.

Since the Second World War interest in mail-carrying rockets has revived in Britain. The vast majority of these rocket flights have been conducted by the Paisley Rocketeers Society, founded in 1936. In the three years prior to the outbreak of the Second World War the society successfully launched sixty-one rockets, of which fourteen actually carried mail bearing adhesive stamps which were printed by hand. The society was revived in 1946 and has continued with its experiments to this day. Since 1969, following a Home Office ban on the use of explosives, the rockets have been powered by aquajet and some quite remarkable mail-carrying flights have been achieved by this means. Perhaps the best known were the 'transatlantic' flights, to and from the island of Seil, off the coast of Argyll in 1966, as part of the celebrations marking the 30th anniversary of the society. Other flights have been staged in aid of charity and have taken place in many different parts of Scotland. The flown flimsies, special labels, cachets and stamps form a colourful and interesting collection covering one of the little known aspects of modern aviation development. A number of experiments have taken place in recent years on the Sussex Downs and special stamps have been provided for use on the flown flimsies. In 1982 the British Space Modelling Association was founded to co-ordinate the activities of the rocket research societies in many part of the country.

Local carriage labels

This term was devised by the Philatelic Traders' Society and the British Philatelic Federation to denote labels issued by various offshore islands round the British coasts. These labels purported to prepay postage on mail to and from the mainland, in cases where the Post Office did not provide a service. These stamps had a curious origin. In October 1925 Martin C. Harman, a London businessman, purchased Lundy, an island in the Bristol Channel. At that time the island had a post office and was regularly served by mail cutters from Instow on the Devon coast. At the end of 1927 the mail contract expired and Mr Harman did not renew it. Furthermore he informed the Post Office that he wished the sub-office to be closed. From 1 January 1928 the Post Office had nothing further to do with the island. Mail continued to go to Instow but Harman himself was solely responsible for its carriage. Until November 1929 he conveyed the mails in both directions free of charge, but in the previous summer he conceived the idea of issuing his own stamps, ostensibly as the easiest and most equitable method of exacting payment for the services he provided, but in light of later developments it seems that Harman had ambitions to become the King of an independent Lundy. The Lundy stamps which were launched in November 1929 were inscribed, not in pence, but in puffins, a 'money of account' derived from the island's commonest bird. The Post Office tolerated the Lundy stamps so long as they conformed to the regulations and did not appear on the front of the envelopes. When Harman went so far as to commission his own coins (see Chapter 8), he fell foul of the Coinage Offences Act of 1870 and was prosecuted before the magistrates of Bideford. He denied the right of the magistrates to try the case, as an infringement of Lundy's sovereignty since the island was more than three miles from the mainland. His notion of territorial waters, however, was not upheld and he lost his case. This did not affect the stamps which continued until the Harman family disposed of the island in 1969. Since then the present owners, the National Trust, have revived the custom. There is a substantial volume of mail to and from the island and its stamps are affixed to mail in both directions. The stamps are attractively designed and printed by the leading security printers in Britain and have followed a modest policy on new issues.

Unfortunately the same cannot always be said of some of the other local carriage labels. In the 1960s they proliferated for such islands as Sanda and Davaar off the coast of Kintyre, Pabay off the coast of Skye and Stroma in the Pentland Firth. Stamps purporting to emanate from the island of Soay off the south Skye coast were shown to be bogus when this writer contacted the owner of the island who was totally unaware that his island had had this benefit conferred upon it by a London stamp dealer. In more recent years, although these issues have suffered considerable criticism and adverse publicity in the lay and philatelic press, issues have been produced by the Government of Staffa (*sic*), an uninhabited rock off the coast of Mull best remembered as the setting for Mendelssohn's 'Hebridean Overture'. Undoubtedly the promoters of the Staffa 'stamps' went over the top with labels embossed on gold foil sold at astronomical sums. Much of this material was aimed at collectors in America, but the US Supreme Court pronounced in 1981 that they were not stamps in the sense of having been issued by a recognized Government for a properly constituted postal service. Since this decision meant that the 'stamps' could not avoid import duties, the Supreme Court effectively curbed a very lucrative business. Other issues which are questionable include those inscribed Gugh Island, Eynhallow (Orkney) and Bernera (Lewis). Gugh and Eynhallow are uninhabited islets while Bernera has a perfectly good sub-post office and is linked to the Lewis mainland by a causeway.

One would not object to the issues for these remote rocks were it not for the fact that they are promoted, by and large, by people with little or no connection with the places concerned. The true test would be that the public should be able to visit the islands and purchase the stamps over the post office counter for use on outgoing mail, but in very few cases is this facility provided. In other cases, where a limited postal facility is provided, only token supplies of stamps are available, the bulk of the issue being handled by mainland entrepreneurs, usually in or around London. The stamps themselves seldom have any bearing on the islands concerned, but depict all manner of subjects from Old Master paintings to the Apollo moon landings and the wedding of Prince Charles and Princess Diana. The only stamps of which I have personal knowledge of their authentic use are some of the earliest issues from Pabay, Stroma, Davaar and Sanda, the stamps produced by the Scottish National Trust for the island of St Kilda, the stamps produced by the Manx Museum for use on the Calf of Man, the stamps used at Tanera in the Summer Isles off the coast of Wester Ross and the stamps of Herm, Jethou and Lihou in the Channel Islands before the establishment of the Guernsey and Jersey postal administrations in 1969. Bogus labels purporting to come from the Principality of Thomond (roughly where Shannon Airport stands today) were in circulation in the 1960s, before the promoter was successfully prosecuted by the Irish authorites. Since then Ireland's sole contribution to the local carriage label business was a stamp from Long Island (Inis Fada) near Schull, County Cork, in 1973.

Parcel labels

When the Post Office inaugurated its parcel post in August 1883 it provided every post office in the British Isles with distinctive labels, bearing the royal coat of arms and the name of the post office. Apart from a brief experiment in 1884–85 with anonymous labels, these named labels continued in use until the end of the First World War, when they were superseded by midget anonymous labels. By that time the larger offices were equipped with facsimile label rubber datestamps but to this day the smaller offices continue to use the unnamed midget labels. From the local collector's viewpoint, the thirty-five years from 1883 to 1918 provide tremendous scope. In that period there existed over 30,000 post offices in the British Isles, including a substantial number which flourished only briefly in that period and are remembered today solely on account of their parcel labels. Over the years the style and design of the labels underwent numerous changes. The late C. F. Dendy Marshall, who first classified these labels in 1926, listed sixteen major types for England and Wales, fourteen for London alone, thirteen for Scotland and ten for Ireland, but, including sub-types and minor variants, the number of variations runs to over 500. Not every type was in use at every office in each county by any means, but from six to ten different types per office would be a good average. The types reflected changes in the parcel service, to include registration, express and insurance fees, as these facilities were gradually introduced. An important feature of these labels, and one of the principal reasons for their adoption, was the X List, a list maintained at every post office giving brief details of the parcel and its address. This enabled the Post Office to work out which parcels were transmitted by rail at some stage in their journey. These had to be accounted for separately since the railway companies were entitled to 55 per cent of the postage, whether they were conveyed by rail all the way or only for a portion of their journey. The X List system gradually fell into abeyance after the outbreak of the First World War, when the railways were temporarily taken under Government control. This, in turn, did away with the necessity to have separate labels for each office and they were phased out in 1918, although the smaller offices, which did not have a rubber parcel date stamp, were allowed to use them till stocks ran out. The fact that some offices were still using these pre-1918 labels as late as 1946 is an indication of how few parcels they sent over the intervening years. The labels had spaces for the attachment of the postage stamps and a panel on the right for the office datestamp. These labels are therefore of considerable interest to stamp and postmark collectors.

Registration labels

Everyone is familiar with those blue and white horizontal labels used on registered mail. They bear a prominent 'R' to denote registration, with the name of the post office and a serial number. Their interest to the local collector has been sadly diminished of late, since it is now policy to issue labels bearing the name of the head office only, but until the mid-1970s every post office had its own labels, and even town sub-offices could be identified by the suffix number after the head office name. Labels as a means of identifying registered packets originated in Germany and Sweden in the 1870s and were widely used by the 1890s, although the United Kingdom did not adopt them until February 1907. Like parcel labels, many different types were produced over the years, England, Scotland and Ireland at first having their own distinctive types. They provide an even greater variety than parcel labels since many of them were distributed to large companies and Government offices and these may be identified by initials or suffix numbers after or below the head office name.

Commemorative labels and publicity stickers

Nowadays the Post Office issues commemorative stamps every other month and there is little need for the public to provide their own commemorative labels, but before the policy on new issues was liberalized in the 1960s it was not uncommon for current events and organizations celebrating anniversaries to resort to adhesive pictorial labels. These had no franking validity but were designed to adorn souvenir mail. Such labels are sometimes known as poster stamps, since they performed the same function as posters in publicizing events, but resembled stamps. Special labels are believed to have been produced for the use of the commissioners of the Great Exhibition in 1851 although only impressions printed directly on to their envelopes are actually known. From the early 1860s, however, pictorial labels were a feature of many exhibitions and reached their peak in 1924–25 when many of the stand-holders at the British Empire Exhibition, Wembley, published their own labels. Exhibition labels have declined in recent years although, paradoxically, they have proliferated for philatelic exhibitions, and even been augmented by issues of miniature or souvenir sheets reproducing postage stamps of the past, by permission of the Post Office.

In 1864 a large red label portraying William Shakespeare was issued with the inscription 'Shakespeare Penny Memorial'. This was the first label ever issued to raise money for charity. Christmas seals, sold to raise money for anti-TB campaigns, were invented by Einar Holboell of Denmark in 1904 and have since spread to many countries. Most of the charity labels have a nationwide character but quite a few are known to have been confined to purely local charities and these come within the scope of the local collector.

Strike post stamps

The postal services in the British Isles have suffered from industrial trouble over the past two decades. At the beginning of 1962 the Union of Post Office Workers was engaged on a 'work-to-rule' which severely disrupted the mails and induced an organization called the People's League for the Defence of Freedom to offer an alternative service. On 8 January the League announced that an Urgent Mail Delivery Service would commence three days later. On 11 January eighty-seven letters were despatched from the League's office in Baker Street, London but five hours later the service closed down, following receipt of a letter from the Postmaster General pointing out that his monopoly was being infringed. As there was no objection to parcels, however, the League continued to handle them and on 17 January issued stamps for this purpose. The first issue was overprinted by a rubber handstamp with the names of the seven depots then in operation: Baker Street, Birmingham, Brighton, Cardiff, Glasgow, King's Cross and Manchester. A second issue appeared on 25 January machine-overprinted in red ink with the names of twelve depots, including the preceding (but with York Way replacing King's Cross) and the addition of Colchester, Edinburgh, Exeter, Liverpool and Newcastle. The U.P.W. ended its industrial action on 31 January and the People's League immediately ceased operations. The service formed an interesting chapter in British postal history and the stamps are now regarded as a legitimate part of any serious collection of Great Britain. In 1964 the U.P.W. again resorted to a 'work-to-rule' campaign and services were inevitably disrupted. On this occasion the League issued a uniform series of stamps' modelled on the railway letter stamps of 1891–1922. This service was even more short-lived and there were no regional overprints.

Industrial trouble broke out anew early in 1971 and ended in an all-out postal strike which continued until 8 March. For the first time in three centuries the Post Office monopoly on the carriage of letters was waived and private companies and individuals were permitted to establish private postal services for the duration of the strike. Over 200 services eventually operated in the United Kingdom during the six weeks of the dispute and the vast majority of them issued their own stamps. Many of them were quite frankly philatelic in inspiration, often being organized by stamp dealers who were sometimes accused of exploiting the situation. To be fair, however, they at least would have a better idea than most about the running of a postal service. Towards the end of this period several of these services combined to offer the mutual transmission of mail, and it has to be admitted that the services were, on the whole, efficient and well run. The stamps ranged from the strictly utilitarian to the exotic and colourful. Many of them injected a note of political satire lampooning the Post Office or the union leader, Tom Jackson. Others were obviously inspired by historic issues of stamps; but most relied on local scenes, maps and heraldry for their subjects. The situation was made more interesting because decimal currency was introduced on 14 February, thus necessitating sets of stamps in the obsolescent £.s.d. and the new £.p currencies. Few counties in Britain were without at least one of these services and, together with press cuttings, photographs, posters, leaflets, souvenir covers and folders, quite an interesting and unusual collection can be formed of these stamps on a local basis.

Official postage stamps

No fewer than five entirely separate postal administrations now operate in the British Isles where, until 1922, only one existed. In that year the postal service of the provisional government of Ireland was instituted, soon to be followed by the Irish Free State and latterly the Republic of Ireland. In 1969 the British Post Office became a public corporation and the crown dependencies of the Isle of Man and the Channel Islands were given the option of establishing separate postal authorities. The Isle of Man declined but both Guernsey and Jersey commenced their own operation at that time. Both Guernsey and Jersey had a previous history of their own stamps, emergency issues having been produced in both bailiwicks during the Nazi occupation of the Second World War. Most of the wartime stamps featured the arms of the bailiwicks, but Jersey also had a set of six pictorial stamps designed by the local painter Edmund Blampied. In 1958 Guernsey, Jersey and the Isle of Man, along with Scotland, Northern Ireland and Wales, began issuing regional stamps. These were – and still are – valid for postage anywhere in the United Kingdom, but give the smaller countries of the United Kingdom a measure of individual identity. England, for some curious reason, has always been left out of this. The regional stamps of Guernsey and Jersey ceased in October 1969 when the independent stamps were launched. In 1973 the Isle of Man had second thoughts and established its own postal authority in July of that year. Guernsey, Jersey and the Isle of Man have all produced very attractive stamps, postage due labels, stamped stationery and other philatelic material since attaining postal independence. From time to time there have been discussions between the States of Guernsey and the local authorities in Alderney, with a view to granting autonomy to the latter's postal service. Distinctive stamps for use in Alderney were introduced in 1983.

Revenue stamps

Adhesive stamps prepaying fiscal duties of various kinds have been
in existence since the early 1800s, while stamps directly embossed
or printed on documents date from the late seventeenth century.
Most of the adhesive revenue stamps were national in character but
there have been several classes which applied to certain localities.
In late-Victorian times gaol and fine stamps were issued with overprints denoting the town or district in which they were issued. Scotland, Ireland, the Isle of Man, Guernsey and Jersey all had their
own revenue stamps, and since the crown dependencies were entitled
to arrange their fiscal and monetary affairs themselves the range of
stamps they issued was much larger and more varied than that used
in the United Kingdom. Distinctive revenue stamps in Scotland and
Northern Ireland no longer exist but the offshore islands have
continued to issue them, and the Isle of Man in particular has had
attractive pictorial designs in recent years. The current issue is
particularly noteworthy since it reproduces details of Manx coinage,
ancient and modern.

Perfins

This is a term coined by collectors to denote postage stamps which
have been perforated with initials as a security measure, to prevent
pilferage or misuse. Even before the puncturing of stamps was
permitted in 1868, however, several firms and organizations applied
an overprint or an underprint to stamps. The Oxford Union Society
was the first to do so, applying its initials across the face of stamps
from 1859 onwards. This was quite unofficial, but in 1867 the Post
Office began offering underprinting of firms' names as a service.
These underprints were made on the backs of stamps before
gumming. Including the Oxford Union Society only five organizations availed themselves of this service: J. & C. Boyd & Co., W. H.
Smith and Son, Copestake, Moore & Crampton (later Copestake,
Hughes, Crampton & Co.) and the Great Eastern Railway, all based
in London. This privilege was withdrawn in 1882, by which time the
perforation of stamps was well established.

Until recently stamp collectors tended to regard these punctured
stamps as imperfect or damaged and either threw them away or
totally ignored them. Then collectors of railwayana woke up to the
fact that the stamps used on company business were invariably
perforated with the railway's initials. Furthermore it was discovered
that many government departments had used perforated stamps
down till 1904 when the crowned 'Official Paid' stationery was intro-

duced, and quite a few continued to use such stamps even after that date. Nowadays, with the increasing specialization in philately and a tendency to concentrate on smaller areas, serious research has taken place into these perfins and several county or regional philatelic societies have published lists of the firms and organizations known to have used them. They were widely used from the 1880s till the 1960s but usage has decreased as other methods, such as meter franking and postage paid impressions, have replaced them. Ideally they should be collected on entire envelopes or cards, which have a clear postmark as well as the name and address or initials of the issuer on the left hand side or on the flap, so that identification can be positively made.

Organizing a local stamp collection

Philately being the largest and most widespread of the acquisitive hobbies, there can be few towns in the British Isles that do not boast at least one stamp club. In the areas of greater population density these clubs are usually organized into county federations which hold regular exhibitions and conventions. Apart from this regionalization, there has been a phenomenal growth in local study circles and specialist groups, mainly concerned with postal history and discussed more fully in the next chapter, but naturally taking an interest in all aspects of philately at a local level. In addition there are national organizations, such as the Cinderella Stamp Club (devoted to local stamps, revenue stamps, commemorative labels and all other sidelines of philately), the British Air Mail Society, the Railway Philatelic Group, the Great Britain Philatelic Society, the Irish Philatelic Study Circle, Alba (devoted to Scottish philately) and specialist societies dealing with the philately of the offshore islands. All of these organizations publish periodicals and sponsor publication of catalogues and handbooks. They hold regular meetings and club auctions or circulate packets of material for sale and exchange.

Postal history

Stamp collecting as a pastime has been in existence since the 1840s, but the serious study of the postal services and the collecting of the ephemera associated with them are of much more recent origin. A few collectors in the 1880s were forming sideline collections of post-marks, but this was usually pursued at a jejune level. The marks were cut square, regardless of the stamps, and the pieces pasted in albums or notebooks. Some Victorian vandals, with more time on their hands than sense in their heads, actually took the trouble to trim their specimens into neat circles, following the outline of the impression – again disregarding the stamps which were, for the most part, the common or garden Penny Lilacs and Halfpenny Vermilions of the period. A more scientific approach did not develop until the 1920s, when collectors like C. F. Dendy Marshall, George Brumell and John Hendy, curator of the Post Office Record Room, began exploring the background to postmarks, and delved into the history of the postal services. Even as recently as twenty years ago postmark collecting was still an esoteric interest which a few philatelists engaged in as a sideline to their main interests, and postmarks were still being cut out rather than kept intact. Many old-time postcard albums were pillaged and their contents destroyed so that the collector could get a nice cut square postmark. This has all changed, fortunately, and as postmark collecting and the study of postal history have grown, the tendency is to keep envelopes, entires and postcards intact so that the transit marks, endorsements and details of sender and recipient are preserved as an entity. Matters which the earlier collectors ignored, such as unusual combinations of adhesives used to frank the envelope, or mysterious manuscript markings denoting accountancy charges, are now closely studied and their significance fully appreciated.

Postal history is far older than philately, dating back four or five thousand years to the cuneiform clay tablets of Sumeria and the papyrus writings of Egypt. For all practical purposes, however,

British postal history does not go back much before the beginning of the sixteenth century. Most of the letters dating from Tudor times are now in museums or archives, but occasionally the dispersal of the accumulated papers from country solicitors' offices yield a few estate letters of that period. Such letters would have been transmitted by private messenger, a trusted servant perhaps, and are consequently very rare. Seventeenth-century letters are much more plentiful, especially in and around London which had a comparatively high level of literacy and a well-developed commercial and business sector. The monopoly of letter transmission, vested in the Crown and exercised by generations of Postmasters General, arose initially from the fact that only letters of state were transmitted by official messengers. State posts were often set up for specific purposes. Thus a postal network linking London to Scotland and Ireland was established temporarily in 1481 by Edward IV for the conduct of military campaigns. After the accession of Henry VII in 1485 and the gradual return to peace in Britain postal development was very slow. In 1516 Henry VIII appointed Sir Brian Tuke as Master of the King's Posts but the service he organized was almost exclusively for the use of the king and his court. By the end of the sixteenth century however, there was a considerable traffic in correspondence between England and the Continent, much of this in the hands of the messengers employed by the merchant companies. In 1591 Queen Elizabeth decreed that overseas mail had to be entrusted to the state system, and appointed a Postmaster General for Foreign Parts. Under James I the need for regular communication between Edinburgh and London was recognized and a network of posts was established. This was opened to the general public in 1635 but progress was retarded by the Civil War (1642–49) and it was not until 1657 that the Commonwealth was able to re-establish a service covering the entire kingdom. At the Restoration the postal service was farmed out as a monopoly. Colonel Sir Henry Bishop, who held the farm of the posts for a fixed rent in the early years of the reign of Charles II, was responsible for the first handstruck postal marking in the British Isles. 'A stamp is invented', stated the *Mercurius Publicus,* 'that is putt upon every letter shewing the day of the moneth that every letter comes to this office, so that no letter Carryer may dare to detayne a letter from post to post; which before was usual.' The earliest examples of the Bishop mark are recorded from April 1661 and consisted of a circle divided into two segments containing the abbreviated form of the month and numerals for the day. These marks were at first confined to London but extended to Dublin by 1672 and Edinburgh in 1693.

None of these marks bore the name of the city and, indeed, marks thus inscribed were not used in the three capitals of the United Kingdom till 1857. The post offices in provincial towns had no marks at all until the closing years of the seventeenth century when a few Irish towns, such as Strabane, Mullingar and Waterford, got straight-line name stamps. Letters from the Worplesdon, Farnham and Chichester area have been found from 1681 with a curious mark, dubbed the 'hot cross bun'. The noted postal historian, R. M. Willcocks, considers that this mark, which is not unlike the rudimentary town plan of Chichester at that time, may have been intended to distinguish letters coming from the Chichester post-route. The earliest true town stamps date from 1697 when both Bristol and Exeter got variants of the Bishop mark. Instead of a circle, the date appeared within the arms of the initial letters of these towns. The first English town to have its name in full, however, was Chester, which used a stamp with a large initial 'C' enclosing the remaining letters arranged in two lines: HES/TER. Several towns in the early 1700s had straight-line stamps with an 'X' after their name to indicate usage on Cross Post letters (i.e. those going from one provincial town to another without going via London). From 1701 several towns, such as Stone, Bolton and Coventry, had stamps with their name alone, and this was the pattern which spread throughout the British Isles as the century wore on. Scotland was a late user of such marks. The earliest, used at Duns (1731) and Dumfries (1732), may have been influenced by towns such as Berwick and Carlisle just over the Border which had used such name stamps for several years by that date.

From 1784 till 1789 many English post towns had a mileage mark, a stamp in which numerals denoted the distance in miles from London. When many of these mileages were found to be inaccurate the stamps were scrapped, but a new system was introduced in 1801, using different types of stamp, and this continued till the end of 1828 when it was abolished. Scotland was a late user of such stamps. Dumfries had an English-style mileage mark from 1801, but the rest of the country did not adopt mileage marks until 1808. They, too, were scrapped in 1828, but some offices continued to use them for many years thereafter, and some even survived into the era of Uniform Penny Postage when the computation of postage by distance was abolished.

A penny post was established in London in 1680 by a merchant named William Dockwra. To Dockwra goes the credit for inventing the first postage stamps in England, albeit handstruck ones, denoting the prepayment of the charges. He also devised time stamps which were used to show the actual hour of posting – a system which the Post Office was not to revive fully until 1895! Such enterprise was met with the usual response. Less than two years after the service began it was suppressed by the Government. Dockwra was vindicated, however, when his service was run by the Post Office and he himself was appointed Controller. An Act of 1765 permitted the establishment of penny posts in provincial towns but none took advantage of this until October 1773 when Dublin instituted a local service. Possibly in the same year, but certainly by May 1774, a penny post started in Edinburgh. This was a private venture, organized by Peter Williamson, but it survived till 1792–93 when it was taken over by the Post Office, Williamson receiving a pension of £25 per annum for his troubles. About the same time penny posts started in Birmingham, Bristol and Manchester, to be followed by Glasgow (1800) and Liverpool (1801). By that time the London service was a twopenny post and postal charges beyond these local services were exorbitant, the minimum rate being fourpence. This encouraged the expansion of local penny posts in the aftermath of the Napoleonic wars and by 1839, when Rowland Hill and Robert Wallace were spearheading the movement for postal reform, most urban areas and many rural districts had penny posts of their own. From this it was but a logical step towards uniform penny postage, extending the benefits of cheap postage throughout the country regardless of the distance a letter was carried.

Although many of the receiving houses (as sub-post offices were originally called) established in the late 1830s had stamps bearing their name, with the words 'Penny Post', many of the earlier establishments merely used a stamp containing a numeral which identified them in the local penny post network. These numeral stamps survived the reforms of 1839–40 but by 1845 it was customary to issue even the smallest offices with an undated stamp bearing its name. The more important sub offices and all post towns had a date stamp with movable date slugs. From 1840 the post towns also had a brass canceller for defacing the new-fangled adhesive stamps. The Maltese Cross, as it is popularly though erroneously called, was superseded in 1844 by a system of numeral obliterators. Each post town was allocated a number in alphabetical order, and separate sets of obliterators were issued in London, England and Wales, Scotland and Ireland. Stamps which combined the date stamp and the obliterator, were issued to some offices experimentally in the early 1850s and gradually extended to most post towns by the 1860s. These duplex or double stamps continued in some cases to the end of the century, or even later, but they were superseded by combined date and obliterating stamps, known as 'squared circles' in England and Wales (1879 onwards), while Scotland had circular stamps showing the office number at the foot and Ireland had similar stamps without the number. These stamps continued in use well into this century, although a new type, with thick obliterating arcs at the sides, was adopted in 1894, shortly before the Post Office permitted 'time in clear' in the postmarks. Many of these combined stamps are in use to this day, in the smaller offices which still cancel mail by hand, though a more modern type with thin side arcs was adopted in 1949.

Machine cancellation dates from 1857 when Sir Rowland Hill's son, Pearson, devised a treadle machine. This was not so much a machine dispensing with the human element as a form of mechanized assistance to hand stamping. Machines in the true sense were developed in the 1860s by Charles Rideout and J. G. Azemar but they were unsatisfactory. German machines of the Höster patent were used in London from 1882 till 1891, but in 1886 electrically-driven American machines were imported and after a lengthy period of trials in London they were distributed to the major post offices. Hand-operated Krag machines of Norwegian manufacture were also purchased and were widely used in the years up to the Second World War but since then they have been usually confined to the smaller offices, as a transitional system from handstamping to the use of electrically-driven Universal machines.

The receiving houses and smaller sub-offices did not cancel mail, but in the period up to 1860 they applied their office stamp to the backs of outgoing mail. In Scotland alone, between 1854 and the end of 1859, these offices were permitted to cancel outgoing mail with their undated name stamps and these so-called Scots Locals have long been immensely popular with collectors – even as far afield as the United States. In 1860 the undated stamps were withdrawn. A few of the more important receiving offices, as they were now called, were given a date stamp but as a rule the smaller sub offices only got a date stamp if they were elevated to the status of a minor money order office or, from 1870 onwards, became a telegraphic office. Otherwise there was little or no need for an office stamp. The only time that these small offices would have needed one was when a letter was handed in for registration, but it was the practice then for the receiver or sub postmaster to annotate the receipt given to the sender in manuscript and the letter was sent forward to the head office for cancellation.

In 1881 the postal order system was introduced. This was much more flexible than the earlier and rather cumbersome money order service and the handling of postal orders was extended to many of the smaller offices. Since a proper date stamp was needed to mark these orders at the point of issue those smaller sub-offices which were appointed to handle postal orders were given a rubber date stamp. The decision to extend the system to some of these small offices came in 1885, at a time when rubber stamps were being tried experimentally as a much cheaper substitute to the brass and steel stamps then generally used. The introduction of the parcel post in 1883 also gave rise to a need for date stamps, though this was not so important as the postal orders and many small offices continued to annotate their parcel labels in manuscript long after they had been given a rubber date stamp for postal order work. By the mid-1890s, however, offices with a rubber stamp were invariably using them on parcel labels, but these date stamps were rarely used in any other postal context at that time. They are occasionally found on the back of redirected or mis-sent items but very seldom on registered letters which continued to be processed by the parent office. The postal order system was gradually extended, and more and more of the minor offices consequently got rubber date stamps. As they were upgraded to telegraph offices these offices got steel single-ring date stamps and ceased using rubber stamps. In 1904 it was decided that all sub offices, no matter how small, should be allowed to sell and cash postal orders, and there was then a spate of issues of rubber dates stamps, so that the situation of 1859, in which every office had its own stamp, was attained once more.

The following year even the smallest sub-offices in the country areas were permitted to postmark outgoing letters and postcards. Their rubber stamps (or steel single-ring stamps, if they were telegraph offices) were applied at the side of the adhesive stamp which was cancelled at the parent office in transit. Two or three years later the regulation was changed and the rural sub-offices were allowed to cancel outgoing mail with their rubber or single-ring steel stamps, while the canceller of the parent office appeared at the side. Before the First World War the use of the parent office postmark was phased out. Many of the smaller offices continued to use a rubber datestamp until the mid-1930s but all of those which were still permitted to cancel mail were then given a steel combined date and obliterating stamp. Town sub offices were given steel single-ring stamps, since they only required them for registered mail, parcel labels where used, and miscellaneous counter work.

Although machine cancellers were used in the larger provincial towns from 1906 onwards, and gradually extended to most head offices by the mid-1930s, a high proportion of mail up to 1960 was still handstamped at the local office of collection and this provided a very rich variety of material for the postmark collector. Since then the closure of many country sub-offices, and the gradual centralisation, concentration and automation of mail handling and processing, have considerably reduced the range and variety of postal markings. A typical example of this is provided by the Isle of Wight. Prior to 10 October 1977 mail was cancelled by machine in Newport, Ryde, Sandown, Shanklin, Ventnor, Bembridge and Freshwater, while the thirty-four smaller rural offices cancelled outgoing mail by hand. On that date mail concentration was introduced and this meant that letters, postcards and packets were taken to the sorting office in Newport for sorting and cancellation, only first class local mail posted in the letter boxes at the post offices immediately prior to letter deliveries continuing to be cancelled in the various salaried sub offices on the island. This local mail was cancelled by hand – a somewhat retrograde step, but there was

A selection of postmarks from the Isle of Wight, ranging from the two-line postmark of 1720 to those of the present-day. Many of these postmarks are typical of those used in other areas of the country. (James Mackay)

obviously little need for machines to be retained at these offices when so little mail had to be cancelled there. Machine cancellation was confined to Newport, but even it lost its identity since the cancelling dies were merely inscribed 'Isle of Wight'. Steel and rubber stamps similarly inscribed were also used in the Newport sorting office, and included the special First Day of Issue handstamps. The handstamps used at the post office counters throughout the island, however, were unaffected by these changes, and steel single-ring date stamps for counter work and registered mail, and rubber parcel date stamps, continue to bear the names of the individual offices, including the town sub offices, to this day. In 1981 concentration of mail was taken a stage farther when Portsmouth became the chief office for the Isle of Wight. The loss of even the limited identity of the Isle of Wight on the island's mail was too much for the inhabitants, but the Post Office, bowing to public pressure, decided that the cancelling dies used at Portsmouth should be amended to read 'Portsmouth & Isle of Wight'. These cancellations now appear on mail posted in a wide area around the Solent whether actually emanating from either Portsmouth or the Isle of Wight.

A similar story could be told for many parts of the United Kingdom. All of the mail posted in the Grampian region, from Buckie and Banff in the north to Stonehaven in the south, and inland to Braemar, is now concentrated on Aberdeen which is a Mechanised Letter Office (MLO), submitting even the most rustic correspondence from the remotest glens to the indignity of phosphor dots, ident letters and postcodes. An ominous portent of things to come is the fact that all post offices and addresses in the west of Scotland, as far north as the Butt of Lewis, now have a postcode with the prefix PA of Paisley, and it would appear that eventually all but the small amount of local first class mail will be processed at one giant sorting and cancelling centre. This may be highly efficient and cost-effective but it tends to diminish the scope of local postal history. It is in the remoter districts, especially the small islands scattered round the Scottish coast, that the traditional methods will continue to the last. In many parts of England and Wales, however, we have already entered the era of generic postmarks, such as that used at Portsmouth. Slogan and machine cancellations are already in use inscribed Medway or Thanet (Kent), Lancashire, Gloucestershire, Clwyd, Gwent, Mid-Wales, South Devon, South Humberside or West Yorkshire, though sometimes a code number is used to identify the particular town in those areas where the cancellation was applied.

Despite this process of centralization there will still be a great deal of material for the local collector. The British Post Office shows no sign of altering its policy regarding the individual naming of every post office, right down to the lowliest town sub-office – a practice which can seldom be found to the same extent in other countries – and with a little patience, persistence and leg-work the dedicated collector can make a collection of the current postmarks of his locality. You do not have to send expensive registered letters every time you want the counter date stamps. Every time you post a letter or parcel, fill out a certificate of posting which the counter clerk will date-stamp for you. Until recently this service cost a penny but it is now provided free. Every time you buy a postal order, get the counter clerk to date-stamp the counterfoil for you; this, too, is permitted according to postal regulations. I have found, though, that it is handy to be able to quote the relevant page of the *Post Office Guide* since many counter clerks seem reluctant to comply with this regulation either through ignorance or laziness. This appears under the heading of 'Counterfoils' in the Postal Order section on page 558 of the current edition. When you purchase stamps or stationery you are entitled to a receipt for this. Usually this is a service used by office girls to keep their petty cash accounts straight, but the general public are entitled to it if they so wish – even for a single stamp if need be; and, of course, it duly receives a specimen of the counter date stamp.

Slogan postmarks have been in general use in the United Kingdom since 1917, when they were used to promote the national war bonds campaign. Collectors in Kent and Essex, however, may wish to aim for examples of the world's very first slogan postmarks, handstruck marks applied to mail as long ago as the 1670s advertising 'Essex Post Goes and Coms Every Day' or 'The Post for all Kent Goes Every Night from the Round House in Love Lane & Comes Every Morning', but these are exceedingly rare and fetch thousands of pounds at auction. Slogans were national in character, although used in conjunction with the town dies of the respective post offices, and this system continues to the present day, with the ubiquitous 'Postcode' slogan. Slogans used at only one office include a few provided at exhibitions such as the Wembley Exhibition of 1924–25, or other events, such as the Olympic Games (1948) and the Festival of Britain (1951). But slogans used in a town to celebrate an anniversary or other local event date only from 1956 when Rochdale celebrated its centenary in this way. Thereafter 'one-town' slogans have steadily increased in number and frequency. In 1963 the Post Office permitted local publicity slogans, advertising the scenic delights or the industrial potential of towns and districts. Hastings was the first to take the opportunity, issuing a slogan in April 1963 showing Happy Harold and the caption 'We're ready for your invasion at HASTINGS'. Local publicity slogans have been extensively used ever since, and there have even been cases where a seaside resort, such as Ventnor, Isle of Wight, has advertised itself on the slogan dies used elsewhere – in this instance, in Birmingham, in 1972–73. Many of these local publicity slogans are based on, or used in conjunction with, posters, publicity labels, postcards and tourist leaflets, and one can form an interesting collection of slogan postmarks linked to allied material.

Apart from the permanent postmarks used at the post offices in each town or county, there are many categories of mark of a more temporary nature, or provided for some special service. Special event postmarks have been in use at temporary post offices since the London Exhibition of 1862, although most of the nineteenth century examples will take some finding, since they were often confined to telegrams and registered packets and even many of the later examples, down to about 1955, are elusive because collector interest was minimal at that time. The commonest examples are those which were used to cancel the postcards sent by the thousands of visitors who flocked to the great exhibitions held in London, Edinburgh, Glasgow and Dublin in the Edwardian era. The scarcest of the comparatively recent examples include the postmarks used on delegates' mail at political party conferences in Llandudno, Douglas and other resorts in the 1950s and early 1960s. In the case of many of the less important events, the Post Office provided a skeleton date stamp – one whose inscription was made up of movable type. As some conferences and congresses had very long names it was often necessary to abbreviate the inscriptions or include only the initials, a situation which has only rendered these postmarks more obscure. The hand stamps used on special occasions were generally plain in design, but pictorialism crept into the design of a series of stamps used at the exhibitions held at the Guildhall and the Science Museum, South Kensington to mark the golden jubilee of Uniform Penny Postage in 1890, and occasionally from then onwards a pictorial device was incorporated in the design. This was still used conservatively until the late 1950s, but since then the majority of 'specials' have been pictorial in character. Since 1966 many specials have been used in conjunction with special posting boxes rather than temporary post offices, and this facility has considerably increased the frequency and range of these pictorial postmarks. There can be few towns which have not had a special pictorial hand stamp at some time during the past eighteen years. Many of these attractive postmarks have been used in conjunction with local events and historic anniversaries. Increasingly these stamps have been sponsored by firms celebrating their centenaries or other anniversaries, and not just important events in parochial or county history. Anyone may sponsor a special hand stamp, and details will be readily given by your local head postmaster. The ultimate in special handstamps occurred on Friday 2 April 1982 when Emily Edge and Victor Roberts of Cannock, Stafforshire celebrated their Golden Wedding anniversary with a special postmark; what a charming idea – and another 'first' for the postmark collector.

Details of forthcoming special handstamps and slogan cancellations are published in the Post Office's fortnightly *Postmark Bulletin*, available on subscription from the Philatelic Bureau in Edinburgh. Provided one sends stamped addressed envelopes at the minimum second class rate, plus a fee of 3p, to the postmaster of the town concerned, these postmarks can be obtained quite easily with the minimum of bother. Many hand stamps are sponsored by individuals and organizations who also publish special covers and these are regularly intimated in the Post Office's monthly *Philatelic Bulletin* and in the philatelic periodicals.

There will be few counties which have not, at some time or another, had the services of a travelling post office, or accommodated a military camp, either a semi-permanent wartime establishment or a peacetime volunteer or territorial camp, or had a wartime RAF post office located on an airfield, all equipped with postal facilities and consequently providing mementoes in postmark form. Coastal towns and counties may even have used a special mark on ship letters or, more recently, paquebot mail. Railway and sea mail and forces postal history are subjects which have a wide following, with a wealth of periodical literature, catalogues and guides, but by collecting everything pertaining to a single county or other limited geographical area one may get a good cross-section of all these ancillary services. Few areas may be as well served as the Isle of Man which, in addition to the full range of ordinary postmarks, special event handstamps and slogans, can boast of having had military (Peel Camp), RAF (Jurby), prisoner of war mail (Knockaloe), internment mail (in both world wars), ship letter and paquebot mail, railway mail and airmail, censor marks, strike posts, local posts and first-day covers. The island has its own postal history society which anyone, whether resident or not, can join, and it has an abundant literature, including an excellent book by Dr Tim Whitney who even sponsored a special postmark in 1981 to mark its publication!

Most collectors concentrate on the postal markings issued by the Post Office and ignore the red meter franks used by firms and organizations. This is a great pity since these marks are every bit as much a part of local postal history as any other. Meter franking originated in Norway and New Zealand and spread to the United Kingdom in 1922, offering a more efficient and secure method of handling business mail than the traditional adhesive stamps. A further advantage of meter franking was the use of the firm's own slogan and this facility has undoubtedly played a major role in the history of advertising over the past sixty years. Increasingly I note that collectors are giving meter marks the attention they deserve. To this I would also add the postage paid impressions which have been widely used since 1966 and allow firms to print a device on envelopes, cards and wrappers in conjunction with their name, address, trademark and advertisement. Although some of these impressions bear the cryptic legend PHQ (Postal Headquarters, London) so that they can be posted anywhere, the vast majority of them bear the name of individual towns, followed by the serial number of the licences. They are thus a legitimate part of postal history, proving that this aspect of socio-economic history need not be confined to the past, but is an ongoing situation. Everything is grist to the local collector's mill, whether it be a seventeenth century letter carried by private messenger, without any postal markings, or a meter-franked, postage paid impressed or phosphor-postcoded envelope retrieved from the office wastepaper basket this morning.

Every collector has his own method of housing, classifying and presenting his material. One leading collector has his whole-world collection of postmarks arranged neatly on file cards contained in trays in filing cabinets, but for most individuals, particularly those forming a purely local collection, the traditional album leaf, peg-fitting binder or lever-arch file systems are more convenient. I prefer album leaves punched and inserted in lever-arch files, since this is the system best suited to my needs, and is flexible in that I can use it also for ephemera, postcards and scripophily, so that these subjects can be interchanged or brought together if necessary. When I started collecting postal history as a schoolboy in the early 1950s, it was possible to buy ancient letters by the sackload for next to nothing and, as there was no hard and fast market in postal history material, and stamp dealers knew nothing about the relative values of different postmarks, I was encouraged to collect on a fairly broad scale, taking the whole of Scotland into consideration. Even now, I try to collect on a national rather than a regional basis, but the collector beginning today would do well to concentrate on a single county, or even one town, if he has any hope of ever attaining a reasonably complete coverage of the subject. Out of approximately 3,900 post offices which have ever existed in Scotland I now have examples of the postmarks from all but 250 and though I still turn up the occasional item to cross another name off my wants list, the search becomes harder and harder each year. The beginning collector today will face an even more daunting task, since about a third of all country sub offices that existed in 1945 have since closed.

My interest in postmarks was desultory and I merely dabbled in it as a sideline to philately until I was called up for National Service and was posted to the Outer Hebrides. At the railway bookstall in Oban, on the way to the Western Isles, I came across a slim volume entitled *The Postmark on a Letter* by R. K. Forster. Reading this on the steamer was little short of a conversion on the road to Damascus and I vividly recall going ashore at Castlebay, in Barra and making a beeline for the post office where the sub-postmaster kindly furnished me with specimens of all his postal markings. Had he complied with the regulations (of which I was then blissfully ignorant) and quite properly refused my request, I might never have taken this interest any farther, but thanks to his courteous, if amused response to my eccentricity, I got off to a flying start. Though I collect everything Scottish the postal history of the islands continues to be a speciality. My main collection, however, is devoted to the Dumfries and Galloway region where I now live and where I am likely to encounter the relevant material most readily. Redevelopment of commercial premises, the amalgamations of the old country banks and mergers in firms of solicitors have all yielded a fine harvest of material. The same story can be repeated in every part of the country and even now some rich finds of material are coming to light, despite wartime salvage drives and air raids which took a very heavy toll on the accumulated paperwork of the centuries.

Postmarks, as I have already said, are best collected on entire envelope or card, though I do not spurn the occasional 'cut-out' acquired from old-time collections and scrapbooks if I can find nothing better for the time being. Many collectors are content with a single example of a postmark but I prefer to take every conceivable variation in the time slugs shown in the date, since these relate to the times when the daily collections of mail were processed. As these schedules have changed enormously over the years it is possible to trace these changes by means of the time slugs in the date stamps. I include the earliest letters I can find, dating from the middle of the seventeenth century and carried privately. These are followed by entire letters of the early eighteenth century with the postal rate shown in manuscript, together with the name of the town – either 'Dumfries' in full or abbreviated to 'Dumf' or 'Dfs' – which preceded the advent of the first handstruck stamp in 1732. There follow the full range of handstruck straight-line and circular name stamps down to the end of the eighteenth century, the mileage marks from 1801 till 1828, the earliest date stamps of the pre-adhesive period and then the advent of the local penny posts, which I illustrate with sketch maps to show the location of the receiving houses and the postal routes.

With the introduction of Uniform Penny Postage in 1840 I include the handstruck paid marks which were optional till 1852, along with early examples of adhesive stamps used locally, beginning, of course, with the Penny Black of 1840. The experimental duplex stamps of the 1850s are followed by the double stamps and the combined numeral stamps later in the nineteenth century, then the modern hand stamps, counter stamps, charge and explanatory marks, machine cancellations and slogans, paid handstamps and machine markings, meter franks and postage paid impressions. Each of the town sub offices has its own section, showing both counter and parcel date stamps. In addition to the postmarks, which are mainly on entire covers or cards, I include old maps of the district showing postal routes, photographs of the post offices and press-cuttings about postal developments – even the retirement of veteran village postmen – receipts, labels and assorted ephemera associated with the postal services. As regards the ancillary services which have existed at some time or another I include items from the Galloway Sorting Tender and the later Travelling Post Office, though I am still hunting for an example of the mail which was damaged in a train fire at Newton Stewart in May 1957. I have not yet acquired an example of the very rare Dumfries Ship Letter mark, known to have been used in the early nineteenth century, though I do have a fine specimen of the equally elusive Stranraer Ship Letter mark of the same period. I have examples of the postmarks used at all the RAF post offices in the region, from Wig Bay and West Freugh in the far west to Tinwald Downs and Creca east of Dumfries, but I am still looking for an example of the postmark which was used at Chapel-cross Camp, a construction workers' camp which flourished briefly in the mid-1950s while the nuclear power station was being built. So often it is the items of the more recent past which are the hardest to find. Military material is comparatively scanty, although I have covers and cards from the pre-war territorial Burrowhead Camp, and some nice material pertaining to the Norwegian Army which was stationed in and around Dumfries during the Second World War. Dumfries was the venue of the Royal Highland Show on a number of occasions and I have registered covers posted at the temporary showground post offices. A strike post was organized in 1971 by the electrical firm of Gardiner and Ball and I have examples of their stamps on covers posted during that episode.

Research in Post Office Archives, London has given me details concerning the opening and closing dates of post offices, information regarding postmasters and letter carriers, and much else – all of which is used to annotate the pages and bring the local postal story to life.

Dumfries, with a population of 32,000, is an ideal size of town for the postal historian to research thoroughly. A market town, with some manufacturing industries but mainly serving the needs of a rural community, a minor seaport situated on a railway junction (though the westward Galloway line is now closed), an important tourist centre with a long and sometimes turbulent history, associations with both Robert the Bruce and Robert Burns, Dumfries is a good example of the average town in many respects, and its postal history is no exception. A few dedicated collectors have been known to tackle such subjects as the postal history of Glasgow, Birmingham or Manchester but to treat them adequately would leave little time for anything else, and a further degree of specialization may be necessary if one hopes to reach completion. I know of no one who has had the temerity to take on the whole of London, but there are collectors who have concentrated on single districts, such as Blackheath, Paddington or Woolwich. At the other extreme the postal history of a single village may not appear to offer much scope, but much depends on the village, which may have been a place of considerable importance in earlier centuries. Most people start out with the idea of collecting an entire county or region but as their collection develops they tend to concentrate on more specific localities, so that is probably the best method to adopt.

Apart from the national organizations devoted to the subject, such as the London-based Postal History Society, the Great Britain Postal History Group and the Society of Postal Historians, there are now specialist societies in many parts of the country, catering to the interests of students of East Anglia, London, the Channel Islands, the Isle of Man, Yorkshire, Wessex, Wales, Scotland, Ireland, Kent, Lancashire and Cheshire, as well as the various railway, airmail and forces postal history societies mentioned in the previous chapter. The British Postmark Society caters mainly to twentieth century postmarks, while the Meter Stamp Study Group and the Postal Mechanisation Society cover other aspects of interest to all postal historians. Details of these organizations may be found in the British Philatelic Federation directory and yearbook.

Maps and prints

Few countries have been so frequently and exhaustively surveyed as the British Isles. The Low Countries and Germany may claim the greatest cartographers on a global scale, from Mercator, Ortelius, Hondius and Blaeu to Moll in the early eighteenth century, but the British mapmakers showed an attention to detail and combined artistry with accuracy to produce some of the finest local maps anywhere in the world. Prior to 1900 the majority of maps were brilliantly decorated, using ornamental lettering and an abundance of tiny pictures and engraved vignettes to fill up the odd blank spaces. They were generally sold uncoloured and it was left to the bookseller or the customer to provide the colouring. The quality of colourwork therefore varies considerably but at its most sumptuous it is of unsurpassed brilliance, with rich deep colours and a lavish use of gilding in the borders and cartouches. These maps were published in atlases and folios, most of which survived intact until the late nineteenth century when the vogue for local collecting began. This explains why so many of these maps, dating in some cases from the late sixteenth century, have such bright colouring even to this day. Once the decorative qualities of these county maps were realized, however, the atlases were broken up and individual maps mounted and framed as wall ornaments. Very few of the atlases of the sixteenth and seventeenth centuries are now in complete condition, and fetch astronomical sums when they pass through the salerooms. In addition to the atlases it was customary for mapmakers to sell the sheets separately, often for little more than a few pence, to help defray the cost of producing the atlases. It is clear, therefore, that county maps have had a distinct appeal to the public from their very inception.

Unlike other works of art, for such these hand-coloured maps may be regarded, maps require no special knowledge or the cultivation of special taste to appreciate and understand them. Their geographical interest and the sometimes naive light they shed on people's lives and habits in bygone centuries explain their immense appeal to the collector. Nowadays no dealer in his right mind would break up one of these fine old atlases to sell the maps individually. He would be more likely to add individual maps to complete an atlas which lacked a few plates and whose binding was still reasonably sound, for a complete atlas is worth infinitely more than the aggregate of the individual maps. Of course, it sometimes happens that a 'breaker' turns up, that is to say, an atlas in such incomplete condition and with such poor binding that there could be no hope of reconstituting it. In this case the maps can be dismounted and sold off separately. The market in individual county maps is exceedingly brisk and dealers often have a waiting list for the more popular sheets. The appeal of these antique maps is not hard to find. Despite the enormous changes which have been wrought in the British landscape over the past four centuries the basic features, such as rivers, mountains, promontories and bays, remain much the same as they did in Tudor times. The names of towns, villages and other places may not be quite the same but they are usually recognizable; even the differences, mainly due to changes in spelling, have a peculiar fascination. In the earliest maps of Warwickshire, for example, Bromychm, Smethik, Solyhull and Coventre are more or less recognizable as Birmingham, Smethwick, Solihull and Coventry. It should be noted that Bromychm was printed in the same type as Solyhull, so one may suppose that the two places were of comparable size at the time. Two features which immediately strike us when we examine maps of the sixteenth and seventeenth centuries are the almost total absence of roads and the incredible fragmentation of counties. Many of them resemble the bantustans of South Africa, often scattered enclaves entirely surrounded by neighbouring counties. This fragmentary character reflected feudal landholdings, on which the British county system was based, and these anachronisms were not ironed out until the nineteenth century. A few of them survived till the 1970s. The Hundred of Maelor was a little bit of Flint (Wales) almost entirely surrounded by England (Cheshire and Shropshire) and detached from the rest of its county by the Welsh county of Denbighshire. Kirkintilloch and surrounding district was a detached portion of Dunbartonshire, cut off from the rest of the county, first of all by Lanarkshire and latterly by the county of the city of Glasgow.

Not surprisingly, certain maps are more popular than others, and reflect partly the density of population and their socio-economic gradings at the present day, and partly the vagaries of fashion. The most popular maps are those of the Home Counties – Middlesex, Hertfordshire, Essex, Kent and Surrey. The adjacent counties are also popular, by and large, but while there is a keen demand for maps of Sussex, Berkshire and Buckinghamshire, there is relatively little demand for maps of Bedfordshire and Huntingdonshire. The other popular counties are Devon, Cornwall, Lancashire, Yorkshire and Hampshire, probably reflecting a measure of local patriotism which is particularly strong in these areas. The Welsh counties and those of the English Midlands occupy a middle position, though Wiltshire and Brecon come near the bottom of the list, according to a sample poll of mapsellers. Maps of Scotland, Ireland, the Isle of Man and the Channel Islands tend to have a more limited appeal, though, even here, one may discern certain preferences. In Scotland the maps of Lanarkshire and the Lothians which included the largest cities, Glasgow and Edinburgh, are the most sought after, followed very closely by the maps of Orkney, Shetland and the Hebrides. In Ireland maps of Dublin and Cork are in the greatest demand. Below, the various cartographers and their local maps are examined in greater detail.

Christopher Saxton

Often described as the father of English mapmaking, Saxton was the first to publish an atlas encompassing the whole country. Very little is known of the man himself, beyond the fact that he was probably born at Dunningley, Yorkshire and died about 1608. He worked as a surveyor and was fortunate to secure the friendship of Thomas Seckford, a Master of the Requests to Queen Elizabeth. Seckford financed Saxton's county project and provided the necessary backing to allow him access to country estates and to towers and hill-tops from which vantage points he carried out his surveys. When he had completed his set of maps the finest engravers, mostly from the Low Countries, such as Hogenberg, Ryther, Scatter and Terwoort, were commissioned to execute the work. Saxton's maps were published individually between 1573 and 1579 and were issued both plain and coloured, the former being much the rarer. The Saxton maps were highly decorative, being lavishly embellished with coats of arms, tiny ships and sea monsters. The earliest editions were printed on paper with a watermark of small interlocking circles, but later editions had a crossed arrows watermark. With the exception of Yorkshire, which was printed on two joined sheets, all the maps were double-page size. For the sake of economy Saxton lumped several of the lesser counties together. Kent, Surrey, Sussex and Middlesex appear on the same map, which consequently makes it easily the most sought after of the entire series. Northamptonshire, Bedfordshire, Cambridgeshire, Huntingdonshire and Rutland were on the same sheet and other groupings were Warwickshire and Leicestershire, Oxfordshire, Buckinghamshire and Berkshire, Lincolnshire and

Nottinghamshire, Radnor, Brecon, Cardigan and Carmarthen, Merioneth and Montgomery, Denbigh and Flint, and Anglesey and Caernarvon. The remaining counties were printed individually. All of the maps were dated, except Northumberland which was probably issued in 1577. Each map was signed 'Christophorus Saxton descripsit'. Most of the maps also bore the names of the six engravers, significantly in larger script than Saxton's own name, for upon their skills so much of the success of these maps depended. As a rule the coastal counties are the best, with their splendid nautical ornament on the surrounding sea. By contrast the inland counties were the least felicitous, being usually overburdened with detail and largely devoid of the more fanciful flourishes.

Saxton's maps underwent several editions which can only be determined by the degree of the wear in the finer details and the subsequent retouches and re-entries made to strengthen the lines on the copper plates. In 1645 the Saxton atlas was re-issued by William Webb. Maps from this edition were generally dated 1642, except that of Oxfordshire, Buckinghamshire and Berkshire which bears the date 1634. The royal arms were changed and several town plans were included which do not appear in the Saxton originals. A third edition was published by Philip Lea in 1689–93 and apart from changes in the royal arms his maps were notable for the greater number of town plans and, most of all, for the inclusion of roads, a feature cribbed from the rival maps of John Ogilby (see below). Subsequent editions of Saxton were made by George Willdey (1720), Thomas Jefferys (1749) and Dicey & Company (1770). The Lea maps are the most plentiful of all these editions and while some maintain that the town plans are a useful feature it has to be admitted that they lack the charm and attraction of the armorial bearings of the earlier editions. There are numerous variations in these editions, and even between early (1689) and late (1693) versions by Lea, so that the Saxton maps alone provide a lot of material for serious study.

John Speed

Born in Cheshire in 1552, Speed was a tailor whose business prospered and gave him the time to devote much of his life to his consuming passion for cartography. In 1598–1600 he presented several maps to Queen Elizabeth and to the Merchant Taylors Company and this brought him to the attention of Sir Fulke Greville who agreed to subsidize him while he worked on his grandiose project, eventually published in 1611 as *The Theatre of the Empire of Great Britain*, now chiefly remembered on account of its sumptuous maps. While the *Theatre* was in progress Speed published the maps separately. Speed freely acknowledged his debt to Saxton and other contemporary mapmakers saying 'I have put my sickle into other mens corne', but at least he was honest enough to quote his sources and to take considerable pains to make corrections and improvements where necessary. His maps are a goldmine of detailed information, with descriptions and histories of each county on the back, as well as detailed lists of towns and villages. Copies of the maps with plain backs may have been proofs sold before 1611 and these are particularly sought after. The *Theatre* was published in 1611 by Sudbury & Humble, and the first edition is the most prized on account of the fact that good quality thick paper was used and the new printing plates gave a very rich, dark impression. The maps were reprinted in 1614–15, 1616 (with Latin text), 1627–31 (including maps of other parts of the world), 1646 (with imprint of William Humble alone), 1662 (by Robert Rea), 1676 (the commonest edition of all, by Bassett and Chiswell), 1713 (John Overton) and Dicey (1770). By the time of the Bassett and Chiswell edition the plates were showing distinct signs of wear and this became progressively worse. The Overton edition was scarcely redeemed by the presence of roads and it seems that there were few purchasers, for this edition is quite rare. The Dicey edition has poor, very pale impressions and is not rated highly on this account though the dedicated county collector will want to include the Dicey version of the Speed map for the sake of completeness. The Dicey edition did not attract much custom at the time and it, too, is quite elusive. Speed's maps covered the whole of England, Wales, Scotland and Ireland. Individual maps of the English and Welsh counties were included, but Ireland was represented by maps of its four historic provinces, Ulster, Munster, Leinster and Connaught, while Scotland was consigned to a single map. The maps of Scotland and Ireland were based on those published by Mercator in 1595.

John Norden

A contemporary of Saxton, he suffered from lack of capital and died in obscurity. Because he failed to win influential patronage he did not complete his projected series of maps and they were confined to the counties of southeast England: Essex, Hampshire, Hertfordshire, Kent, Middlesex, Surrey and Sussex. The original edition, published in 1580, is a major rarity, seldom encountered outside museum collections, but Norden's maps were reprinted by Peter Stent about 1660 and by John Overton ten years later. Ironically, though Norden received neither fame nor fortune in his own lifetime, his maps were used extensively by William Camden for his *Britannia*, published in 1607. Norden planned to back up his maps with detailed county guides, but only two ever saw the light of day: Middlesex (1593) and Hertfordshire (1598). To Norden goes the credit for inventing a system of conventional symbols, while his delineation of the roads was an early and major improvement on mapmaking up to that time.

William Camden

Born in London, Camden was educated at Christ's Hospital and Magdalen College. He returned to London in 1571 and devoted the rest of his life to the study of history and antiquities, becoming head-master of Westminster School in 1593. During the school holidays he travelled all over England gathering material for his history entitled simply *Britannia* which was originally published in 1586 without maps. The success of this edition encouraged him to publish a second and greatly expanded edition in 1607, together with a hand-some set of maps largely derived from Saxton although, as previously noted, he preferred those of Norden for the south-eastern counties. The map of Pembrokeshire was based on an original by George Owen, while the general maps of England and Wales, Scotland and Ireland were derived from Mercator. Camden secured the services of William Kip and William Hole who engraved thirty-four and twenty-one of the maps respectively. Though not as decorative as the Saxton maps, they were competently engraved, and have delightful cartouches. The coastal counties, in particular, are attractively decorated with ships and serpents.

The 1607 edition was printed with a Latin text on the reverse, which often shows through the paper, marring the overall effect. The second edition, in 1610, lacked the Latin text and though commoner than the first edition, is a more attractive series. A third edition of the maps accompanied the history in 1637 and is comparatively common. No further edition appeared till 1695 when Bishop Edmund Gibson published an English translation of the Latin text. The work was completely revised and the maps were supplied this time by Robert Morden. The atlas contained fifty maps of the English counties, one each for Scotland and Ireland and two for Wales, plus three general maps. In 1722 a second edition of the Morden maps appeared, the most notable feature of which, from my personal viewpoint, was that Scotland was now divided into two maps. The best use of the paper was not made, however, since about half of Scotland overlaps the two maps – with quite a few discrepancies in the two versions of the central belt. These maps were, in fact, by Andrew Johnston, while similar maps of Wales were supplied by an unknown cartographer. Subsequent editions in 1753 and 1772 incorporated many improvements, in line with the more up-to-date surveys which were made during the course of the eighteenth century, and consequently these later Morden maps are of considerable interest.

John Ogilby

One of the most colourful characters involved in cartography, Ogilby was born in Edinburgh and prospered by sheer hard work and more than a dash of good luck. A leg injury put an end to his career as a dancing master and it was then that he turned to mapmaking, though he also worked as a tutor to the family of the Lord Deputy of Ireland and later ran a theatre in Dublin till the Civil War left him temporarily destitute. He then came to England and eventually settled in Cambridge where he earned a precarious living translating Virgil and composing poetry. The Restoration meant an upturn in Ogilby's fortunes and he secured an appointment to organize the coronation revels for Charles II. In 1662 he returned to Ireland as Master of the Revels, dabbled unsuccessfully in the theatre business yet again, and later returned to London where he set up as a printer in Whitefriars and produced a number of fine books. Ogilby's latest venture was just beginning to prosper when he was wiped out by the Great Fire of 1666 which destroyed his house, presses and entire stock. Nothing daunted, he promptly secured an appointment as one of the four surveyors commissioned by the City of London to assess the fire damage. It was in the course of this work that Ogilby became interested in surveying and mapmaking, and the fruits of his labours were the magnificent town plan, published by Morgan in 1667.

In the meantime Ogilby had rebuilt his house and acquired the splendid title of King's Cosmographer and Geographic Printer. Soon after 1666 he began work on his *Britannia; or an illustration of the Kingdom of England and the Dominion of Wales*. Ogilby intended to publish this work in three volumes but only the first, containing a remarkable series of road maps, was completed and ready for publication by 1675, the year in which he died. Although considerable progress had been made in the construction of roads covering the country, no survey of them, with the distances between the principal towns, had been made before Ogilby published his great work. Most of the mapmakers over the ensuing century were greatly indebted to Ogilby. The success of this venture may be gauged by the fact that it ran to three editions in 1675 alone, and was reprinted in 1698. The maps were most unusual, in that the roads were shown in vertical strips side by side, with just sufficient physical features alongside to indicate the prominent landmarks to the traveller. The names of towns, villages, hamlets and even farms were included along the roads, with the distances between them. Rudimentary town plans were included where the main road intersected other thoroughfares. Each of the hundred maps in this series covered about 70 miles of roadway, and the whole was a survey of the principal post roads of the kingdom. In so far as the majority of these maps also coincide roughly with county boundaries they are of immense interest to the county collector. Ogilby's maps were plagiarized by later map-makers, most notably John Senex, whose rather smaller maps of 1719 were similar but without the ornamental cartouches at the top, which were an attractive feature of the Ogilby maps. Ogilby's maps were extensively copied by Owen and Bowen for *Britannia Depicta* published in 1720. The same idea was used for several road maps of the late eighteenth and early nineteenth centuries, though not nearly so attractively or successfully.

Herman Moll

This Dutch cartographer settled in London in 1690 and over the ensuing forty years he published numerous atlases and maps, not only of the British Isles but also of parts of Europe, Asia, Africa and America. His map of Scotland is of interest mainly on account of the detailed views of the principal towns which decorated its borders. In 1724 he published a set of maps of the counties of England and Wales. What they may have lacked in originality as maps they made up for in the delicate vignettes of antiquities and landmarks which decorated their borders. The following year Moll published a similar series devoted to the counties of Scotland and completed the trilogy in 1782 with a series of Irish county maps, by far the rarest of the three.

William Janszoon Blaeu

The Dutch had the reputation for producing the finest maps and much of the credit for this rested with the remarkable Blaeu family. William Blaeu began his long and illustrious career as a maker of globes and sea charts and then progressed to single continental maps and a splendid series of twenty maps of the world, on which his international reputation is firmly based. In 1630 he began publishing a series of atlases containing more detailed maps, county by county. By 1662 this stupendous work had reached eleven volumes, unsurpassed for their brilliance and beauty. Two volumes were devoted to the British Isles – volume four (England and Wales) and volume five (Scotland and Ireland). The maps of England, Ireland and Wales were based on those of Speed but stylistically were quite different, with a plethora of cherubim and rural landscapes replacing Speed's town plans. The Scottish maps were entirely new and were, in fact, the first to do adequate justice to the Scottish counties. They were the work of the Rev. Timothy Pont, who prepared a series of thirty-six maps in his spare time but died before they could be published. His widow sold them to Robert Gordon who added a few of his own and made revisions on Pont's maps. Like Pont, Gordon could not find a publisher in Britain and it was not till 1654 that they were published by Blaeu in Amsterdam. For the Scottish collector, the maps of Pont, Gordon and Blaeu are of fundamental importance since all later maps of the Scottish counties were derived from them to some extent.

Later mapmakers

Interest in maps increased significantly in the eighteenth century, in the wake of agricultural improvement, land reclamation schemes and the enclosure movement. Many landowners commissioned maps of their estates and a few of these were subsequently engraved and published, although the majority were drawn by hand and are mainly preserved in estate archives. From time to time they come to light in legal accumulations and add considerably to the interest of a county map collection. The demand for good quality, accurate, large-scale maps in the eighteenth century encouraged many publishers to enter this field. All of their maps have something to commend them, as each in its own way strove to offer the public something a little bit different. George Willdey, previously mentioned for his edition of Saxton's atlas in 1720, later produced his own maps which, though largely derivative, were ornamented with large cartouches. Thomas Kitchin worked with Jefferys and Bowen on the publication of various atlases of different sizes, and many fine county maps were included therein. The *Large English Atlas*, published in 1755, contained maps by Kitchin, Emanuel Bowen and R. W. Seale and contained some of the finest county maps ever produced. Seale's map of Middlesex, in particular, is much sought after on account of its handsome borders decorated with the arms of ninety-two City Livery Companies and the City of London. All of the maps in this atlas were exceedingly detailed and

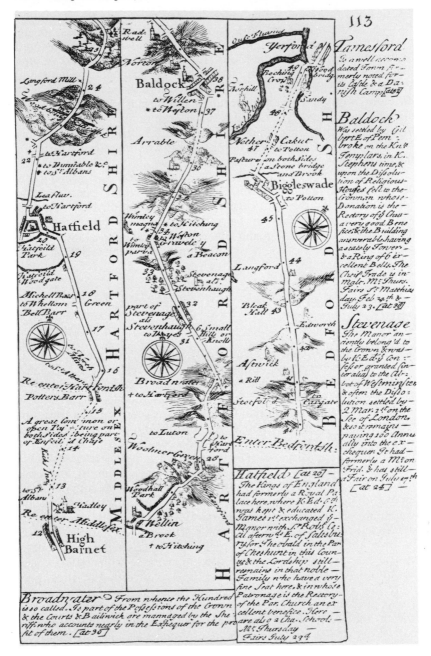

Map of High Barnet to Biggleswade by John Owen and Emanuel Bowen
1720–64 (Moreland & Bannister: *A Collector's Handbook*)

were the most accurate published up to that time. Scotland and Ireland were added to a second edition, published in 1763. Especially valuable are the details given of castles, the seats of country gentlemen, rectories, vicarages, abbeys, post stages, charity schools, mines, factories and inns. Information on market days and parliamentary representation was given for each borough and rococo cartouches contained attractive vignettes of the pastoral occupations and natural resources of each area. Wherever possible these maps were covered with minuscule engraving giving a potted history of the county and all manner of odd and unusual facts which are not to be found anywhere else. The *Royal English Atlas* (editions of 1762, 1778 and 1780) was a reduced version of the *Large Atlas* with correspondingly fewer annotations. An even smaller edition, quarto size, was published in 1765, so that the collector can find three different sizes and versions of this series. Kitchin subsequently engraved a number of English county maps for other publishers and these, too, are of considerable merit.

The brothers Christopher and John Greenwood, working at the end of the eighteenth and the early years of the nineteenth centuries, spurned the work of earlier mapmakers and undertook an entirely new survey of the country, a labour spread over seventeen years and eventually published in 1834. The forty-six folio maps were on the scale of one inch to the mile (except Yorkshire which was slightly reduced) and were the first accurate large-scale maps of the whole of England ever published. Each map bears the date of the county survey, from 1818 onwards, and is decorated with architectural landmarks. The Greenwoods also published various large-scale maps separately throughout the 1820s as their survey was in progress. James Pigot, well known for his topographical guides and directories, also published a series of county maps between 1829 and 1860 and though not so large or finely detailed as the Greenwood maps, they have attractive vignettes.

John Cary, best remembered for his *Itineraries*, a series of road maps in the Ogilby tradition, also produced numerous county maps in atlases, sets and singles. His *New and Correct English Atlas* (1787) contained forty-six quarto-sized maps and ran to several editions down to 1831. A folio atlas entitled the *English Atlas*, was published in 1809 and likewise ran to several editions till 1834. His *Travellers' Companion*, containing the famous itineraries, was published in 1790. Charles Smith rivalled Cary with his own series of folio county maps, published in 1804. William Smith published the first geological map of England and Wales in 1815 on fourteen sheets. Of much more specialist interest, these maps are now major rarities. Mostyn John Armstrong published a set of maps of the post road from London to Edinburgh but is best known for his *Scotch Atlas*, containing thirty maps of the Scottish counties (1777). Thomas

Badeslade produced a series of county maps, engraved by W. H. Toms, for *Chorographia Britannia* (1742). Thomas Moule published the last of the great series of decorated county maps in 1836 and numerous editions appeared till 1852, taking into account the rapid spread of the railway system, which gives these maps a particular interest to rail enthusiasts. Among the other publishers who produced attractive county maps in the course of the late eighteenth and early nineteenth centuries were Thomas Bakewell, John Bill, the Bowles family, John Cowley, William Darton, John Ellis, Sidney Hall, Alexander Hogg, Edward Langley, Richard Palmer, William Palmer, R. W. Seale, John Stockdale, Andrew Skinner, George Taylor, Henry Teesdale and William H. Toms. There were many others whose work may not have been in the same class but whose maps are every bit as interesting to the county collector whose aim is completeness, regardless of artistic or technical merit.

Large-scale maps

Demand for accurate large-scale maps developed during the course of the eighteenth century, a need which was recognized by the Royal Society of Arts which offered an annual prize of £100 for the finest large-scale map. The first prize was awarded to Benjamin Donn in 1765 for his map of Devon, published on twelve sheets to the scale of one inch to the mile by Thomas Jefferys. Even larger maps were published as the century progressed. In 1783 Thomas Yeakell and Thomas Gardner published their survey of Sussex on the scale of two inches to the mile. Mention has already been made of the ambitious large-scale series of county maps by Bowen and Kitchin, some of which (like Devon and Yorkshire) occupied nine sheets each. The large-scale maps were much less decorative than the small-scale maps, but much more accurate. They were, in fact, highly professional and businesslike in their compilation and engraving and are a valuable source of accurate information on topography of the eighteenth and nineteenth centuries, prior to the completion of the Ordnance Survey. One of the finest of these large-scale maps was John Rocque's 18-sheet survey of Berkshire (1761) on the scale of two inches to the mile. There were many other large-scale maps during the first half of the nineteenth century and those published by William Johnson of Edinburgh, Thomas Taylor and Thomas Martyn are particularly fine, often embellished with allegorical cartouches and vignettes of landmarks and scenery. Chapman and André published a 25-sheet map of Essex (1774) while Andrews and Dury produced a survey of Kent of similar dimensions in 1769. Many others were published from about 1750 till 1873, when the

Ordnance Survey was finally completed.

Ordnance Survey maps

The Ordnance Survey of the British Isles was instituted in 1791, taking its name from the Board of Ordnance which commissioned it. The survey was carried out by officers and men of the Royal Engineers and proceeded like a military operation – but an exceedingly leisurely one, since it took a hundred years to complete. Prior to 1873 the survey was conducted county by county, but thereafter maps were published regardless of county boundaries, and this system has continued to the present day. The first fruits of this labour began to appear in 1813 and over the ensuing sixty years the collector of county maps has an abundance of material which had the merit of being as accurate as surveying techniques and official information could make them.

The survey of Ireland commenced in 1825 and this led to a series of maps with the scale of six inches to the mile. The series for Great Britain ranged as high as 25 inches to the mile, and reduced versions on the scale of 6, $2\frac{1}{2}$, 1, $\frac{1}{2}$ and $\frac{1}{4}$ inch to the mile were also published over the years. What they lack in decorative quality, the Ordnance Survey maps make up in their accuracy and authoritative nature. They are the easiest maps of all to date specifically since the day and month as well as the year of the survey are indicated in the marginal imprint and later this information was required in order to allow users to make the necessary adjustments for annual magnetic variation. At first the maps were uncoloured, but chromolithography was used sparingly from the end of the nineteenth century to provide contrasts in roads, forests and plantations. Relief was indicated by 'sugar-loaf' hachuring in the traditional manner, but from the end of the nineteenth century contour lines were adopted and indicated in brown-red. The range of conventional symbols was gradually increased and then considerably revised in 1960 when the publication of the one-inch maps was thoroughly overhauled. The advent of metrication in the 1970s was another opportunity for major revision work. The task of the Ordnance Survey is an ongoing one, and the maps are constantly being revised and updated.

The collector concentrating on the maps pertaining to one county or area will therefore find that the Ordnance Survey maps alone add up to a formidable body of material. Variants of the Ordnance Survey maps have also been published over the past century for the use of the Post Office (showing post offices, post routes and telegraph links) and the War Department, Air Ministry and Admiralty, with overlays of information useful to the Army, Navy and RAF.

Other maps lay emphasis on railway workings and major construction projects, adding another dimension to the work of the Ordnance Survey.

Coastal maps and charts

We have already seen how some of the most decorative of the county maps were those pertaining to coastal areas, which enabled the cartographers free rein in the inclusion of sea serpents, mermaids, galleons and other ornaments of a nautical character. Since time immemorial, however, seafarers have relied on charts for safe navigation and these are among the earliest maps to have been as meticulous in their delineation as possible. This did not mean, however, that they sacrificed decorative qualities. Elaborate cartouches, armorial bearings and the obligatory dolphins and galleons were included as far as was compatible with accurate mapping of shoals, reefs, rocks and islets. The earliest sea charts were produced in Spain but are so rare as to be non-existent outside museums. The Dutch were prolific publishers of sea charts from the middle of the sixteenth century onwards. The earliest of these, and ranking among the most desirable to collectors, were published by Lucas Jansen Waghenaer, who worked as a pilot for many years and had an intimate knowledge of the coastline of Europe. He retired from the sea in 1582 and began work on a sea atlas which was published at Amsterdam in 1584. The atlas was in two volumes comprising twenty-three and twenty-two maps respectively, and a further two maps were added in 1591. The first English edition, entitled *The Mariners Mirrour*, was published by Anthony Ashley in 1588. These maps were the first to give depths in fathoms, information on tides and currents, lighthouses, buoys and beacons, reefs, rocks and offshore islands, and included elevations of the coastlines as viewed from the sea. Place names were confined to the coasts, and the inland areas were used either for the pictures of the coastal elevations or for pastoral scenery. The British coasts were covered by eight charts in both Dutch and English versions.

Blaeu's earliest work, *Licht der Zeevaert*, was a sea atlas published in 1608 and clearly based on Waghenaer. The charts in this atlas were much plainer than his predecessor's, though the cartouches and compass roses were finely engraved. Later volumes of sea charts were published by Johannes van Keulen (1680), Pieter Goos (1666), Anthonie Jacobsz (1648–1717), Henrik Donckers (1660) and Hugo à Linschoten, showing how the Dutch dominated this field. Two French cartographers worked on volumes of sea charts – Louis Rénard (1715) and Pierre Mortier (1700), but both had to go to Amsterdam to get their work published. These atlases encompassed many parts of the world other than Europe, but their chief interest to the county collector lies in those charts which showed the coasts, notably the northern and western isles of Scotland and the more prominent English coastal counties, such as Cornwall and Devon.

The first work entirely produced in Britain was *The English Pilot* published between 1671 and 1803. The publishers varied from edition to edition and some of these, such as Thornton and Mount, Mount and Page or Mount and Davidson, were prolific issuers of individual charts. John Seller, who published the first edition in 1671, also published the *Atlas Maritimus* and numerous later charts and county maps. His maps and charts were reprinted by Francis Grose between 1777 and 1787 in a series of fifty-two quarto sheets. These charts took in many other parts of the world and were by no means confined to the British Isles. The first series of charts limited to the British Isles was published in 1693 by Captain Greenville Collins whose *Great Britain's Coasting Pilot* comprised forty-eight charts. This work ran to numerous editions, the later ones being of a much poorer quality but collectable none the less. The charts of chief interest in this series are those dealing with Orkney, Shetland, the Hebrides, the Isle of Man and the Isles of Scilly. Sayer and Bennett published a *Channel Pilot* in 1777 covering the counties of the south coast. Many other sets of charts were published in the course of the nineteenth century, often based on survey work of naval officers whose names may be found on many of the charts used to this day.

Town plans

Possibly the most fascinating of all maps are those concerned with the detailed delineation of a single town or village. By confining themselves to a single town, such maps could be drawn on a much larger scale than usual and could give an incredible amount of detail. Modern town plans show streets and roads and pick out the more prominent public buildings, but the antique town plans were much more explicit, frequently naming individual householders and itemizing every shop, church, chapel, manufactury, bleachfield and toll-gate. The borders were often suitably embellished with civic arms or the emblems of the liveried companies and trade guilds, while prominent features, such as churches, town halls and other public buildings, were often engraved in separate cartouches. Among the finest of the English town plans was that published by Richard Blome of London in 1673. It was engraved by the Bohemian artist

Map of Norwich dated 1582 (Jack Mitchley)

Wenceslas Hollar and included the latter's famous panoramic view of the city. Hollar actually produced several panoramic views, both before and after the Great Fire of 1666. Prints by Hollar were also utilized in the maps published by John Bowles about 1740. Bowles had a keen appreciation of the market at that time and it is significant that his publications included a map of Elizabethan London, though the Hollar scene was quite definitely from the Restoration period.

If the Dutch excelled as naval chart-makers, the Germans were the undisputed masters of the town plan. From the late sixteenth century onwards, map-makers such as Georg Braun, Frans Hogenberg, Sebastian Munster and Johann Baptist Homann, working in Cologne, Basle and Nuremberg, produced beautiful town plans. The earliest of them were panoramic bird's-eye views and were exquisitely drawn down to the tiniest architectural detail, with the buildings shown in perspective. Braun and Hogenberg published *Civitates Orbis Terrarum* in 1572, comprising over 300 maps of towns and cities, mainly in Europe. Those of interest to the British collector were London, Oxford, Windsor, Bristol, Chester, Norwich, Canterbury, Edinburgh, Exeter, Cambridge and Nonsuch Palace at Ewell, Surrey, though why the last-named was included is a mystery. A further two plans were added to the edition of 1618, one covering the main towns of Ireland and the other the northern English cities and towns of York, Shrewsbury, Lancaster and Richmond. Not surprisingly, London figured more often in these global surveys than any other British city, and it was included in most of these atlases. Darlington and Howgego catalogued no fewer than 421 maps and plans of London between 1553 and 1852 alone. Other cities and towns were not covered to anything like the same extent, which makes the task of the local collector very much simpler. Plans of the provincial towns and cities were included in Speed's maps, but did not become common in their own right till the beginning of the eighteenth century. Pierre Mortier of Amsterdam included a number of British cities in his atlas of 1700, but the vogue for town plans did not really become established till 1720 when John Kip published a number of fine plans in his *Britannia Illustrata*. John Rocque, a French surveyor who settled in London, published his *Exact Survey* of London in 1746, consisting of sixteen sheets on a scale of 5½ inches to the mile and including London, Westminster, Southwark and the surrounding districts to a radius of ten miles. This was followed by an even more ambitious survey of central London on the scale of 25 inches to the mile, and finally a 13-inch to the mile survey on eight sheets, published in 1755. He also published large-scale plans of Bristol (1750) and Dublin (1756) but both are comparatively rare. In 1770 he published a series of plans relating to many British towns and cities.

Other fine series of town plans were produced by John Strype (1720), Richard Horwood (1799 and later editions till 1819), John Roper (1810), John Andrews (1772–1792), Thomas Moule (1836), G. Cole (1809), John Tallis (1850), James Knox (1823) and William Wood (1819 onwards). Messrs Baldwin and Craddock published a comprehensive series of town plans for the Society for the Diffusion of Useful Knowledge between 1833 and 1850. Many of these town plans incorporated armorial bearings and engravings of prominent landmarks, providing an over-all decorative effect. One should not neglect the town plans of more recent vintage. It is probably true to say that our cities, towns and villages have undergone more radical changes and expansion since 1900 than in all the centuries up to that time and this rapid transformation is vividly captured by the maps of the past eighty years. This has been the era of urbanization and industrialization, of the establishment and phenomenal growth of local government undertakings such as council housing, of the speculative builder and of the dormitory suburbs and the 'new towns'. Most of the town plans produced in the past century were not intended as mere decoration for hanging on a wall or reposing in a folio atlas. The majority were intended for the traveller's pocket and were thus designed as folding maps either sold separately within card covers, or as a pull-out supplement to a town guide. These maps vary enormously in character and quality since many of them were produced by the town council or the local jobbing printer. A few of these maps, catering primarily to tourists, have artistic pretensions, but most are quite plain. Whatever their aesthetic qualities, however, all are of more than passing interest to the local collector.

Specialist maps

Mention has already been made of the rare geological maps by William Smith (1815). Another interesting group comprise the fox-hunting maps of the English counties published by William C. Hobson in 1850. They were originally produced as an atlas containing forty-two maps, folio-sized, published by J. and C. Walker who had previously published the maps in 1837 to show the new parliamentary divisions. Hobson superimposed the names of the places where the hounds met and the areas covered by the hunts.

Other maps from the beginning of the nineteenth century onwards were intended for industrial or commercial rather than recreational purposes. The Post Office was one such organization that required accurate maps for the survey of post routes and the demarcation of the free delivery areas of letters in the period before Uniform Penny Postage. Even then free delivery was confined to a certain distance from the nearest delivery post office and it was not until 1898, following a concession granted to celebrate the Diamond Jubilee of Queen Victoria the previous year, that the Post Office made a concerted effort to provide every home in the United Kingdom with a door-to-door delivery of mail. It was necessary, therefore, for the postal surveyors and postmasters to have accurate maps showing the extent of their responsibilities, and numerous versions of these local maps were published for the Post Office down till 1907. The best of these maps were produced between 1820 and 1850 and a number of artists and engravers, such as B. R. Davis, T. Ellis, J. Gardner, Henry Martin and J. Henshull, were employed in their production. In the early states of these maps the boundaries of the free delivery areas were delineated and often coloured by hand. As the boundaries were widened amendments were made to the maps, sometimes as a result of re-engraving but more often by manuscript additions, using different coloured inks, keyed to an explanation at the foot of the map, with the date of the amendment. Postal maps covering a rather wider area were also produced when a new postal route was being proposed, or a post office was to be relocated. Sometimes, like the estate surveys of the eighteenth century, these maps were hand-drawn sketches, tinted in watercolours, but quite a few of them were engraved and printed. Different colours of ink were used to denote the various modes of postal communication – by foot messenger, by mounted messenger, by mailcart, mailcoach or railway train and, in an age when the distance a letter was conveyed affected the rate of postage, the mileages were shown as accurately as possible. In fact, not enough credit is given to the postal surveyors, with their waywisers, for making accurate surveys of the distances between towns and post offices, and the measurement of the post roads in the early nineteenth century.

Special maps were commissioned by the turnpike trusts established in the late eighteenth and nineteenth centuries for the maintenance of the highways. Diagrammatic maps were prepared by the engineers who surveyed the routes taken by the canals and later the railways. Railway maps are a large and diverse category, which range from the semi-diagrammatical kind indicating the signalling systems over a given route, to the multicoloured maps of junctions and joint lines, the different colours denoting the various companies whose rolling stock and locomotives operated over the lines. These attractive little maps – often no more than octavo size – continued until 1922 when the regrouping of that year rendered them superfluous. The railway companies also produced maps of their routes as a form of advertisement and these appeared on cards framed and glazed in the railway compartments. These maps, aimed at the rail traveller, were often more decorative, with tiny vignettes of tunnels, stations, signal boxes and locomotives.

Topographical prints

Many of the maps mentioned in this chapter were published as part of a county or national history or topographical survey. The earliest volumes, such as Camden's *Britannia*, would fetch an astronomical sum today and, dealing with the country as a whole, are outside the scope of this book anyway. But there are many county surveys, topographical or antiquarian guides, and directories which incorporated not only maps and town plans but also engravings of scenery, landmarks and other places of interest. The earliest of these works, devoted to a single county, was Sir William Dugdale's history of Warwickshire, published in 1656, containing maps of the individual hundreds and many fine topographical engravings. A much improved edition was published in 1730, with additional maps by Henry Beighton. This work was re-issued in 1756 and subsequently until 1817. This established the fashion for county histories, many of which appeared in the course of the eighteenth century and were reprinted or revized during the nineteenth century. One of the finest in this genre was P. Morant's *History and Antiquities of the County of Essex*, published in 1768 and including thirty-three engraved plates featuring historic sites and monuments. Many of the histories published in the eighteenth century laid emphasis on natural history, implied in their titles, but this was often liberally interpreted to include archaeology and antiquities and sites of more recent vintage, all of which were the subject of the engraved plates. Cynics have observed wryly that the amount of space given to individual buildings depended on the size of the owners' subscriptions to the publication of the work, which only seems reasonable in the circumstances. Textually, many of these tomes were on the ponderous side and in the nineteenth century many of them were broken up for the sake of their plates which were then mounted and framed for individual display. The originals were uncoloured but quite a Victorian industry developed in the hand-tinting of these plates. At the same time the original copper plates were often reworked and used to take pulls of the engravings quite independently of the original publications and many of these are still available at a fairly modest price. Indeed, it seems odd that many late eighteenth and early nineteenth century topographical prints are now cheaper than some picture postcards of the twentieth century.

These topographical engravings ranged in size from folio all the way down to demi-octavo and even smaller. The smallest examples, in fact, were often the same as the vignettes that graced the commercial stationery, banknotes, cheques and notepaper of the period. Conversely publishers of pictorial notepaper sometimes reprinted the vignettes used for notepaper in bound volumes. The vignettes, instead of being printed at the top of the sheets, were placed centrally so that they could be mounted and framed. I have a volume containing fifty engravings of Welsh scenery published by Newman & Company of Watling Street, London. The date of publication is not known but individual engravings in the volume bear dates from 1855 till 1870. It should be noted that the later publishers of picture postcards also reproduced the photographs from their cards in book form. At one extreme are the 'photo-folios' published by Beecham which, in effect, encompass their entire range from Land's End to John o' Groats, but of greater interest to the local collector are the slim volumes known as illustrated guides or picture albums which dealt with individual towns, districts or counties. The pictures were reproduced on art paper instead of card, sometimes with a page or two of supporting text by way of an introduction and usually handsomely encased in a gilt or pictorial binding of the type so fashionable at the turn of the century. These small albums published by the postcard companies were the forerunner of the albums of colour photographs which originated in America in the 1930s and are now so popular in Britain. Colour superseded black and white pictures in these pictorial paperbacks about 1950 and they are now one of the mainstays of the tourist industry. The best of these are the Pitkin Pictorials which were first published in the 1930s and which continue to this day, but there were and are many others, often more local in scope, which certainly merit the attention of the local collector.

Numismatics

People receiving mail from Sutton in Surrey during 1979 may have been puzzled or intrigued by the slogan postmarks which proclaimed '2000 Years of Coinage' in that area. A closer examination of the slogan revealed two reproductions of coins – a gold stater of King Commius of the Atrebates and the one-pound coin of the Isle of Man. Commius reigned about 35 to 20 BC over an area approximating to the modern counties of Berkshire, Hampshire, Sussex and Surrey so it is reasonable to suppose that whatever ancient British settlement existed on the site of the present borough of Sutton would have used these coins. Commius is not so well known as Cunobelin (the Cymbeline of Shakespeare) but he was the first of the ancient British rulers to have his name on his coins. For this reason the gold staters showing a triple-tailed horse can be attributed to a particular area and period. At the other end of the time scale, separated by two millennia, the Isle of Man coinage has a connection with Sutton in that, since 1973, the Manx coins have been struck by the Pobjoy Mint of Sutton, now the largest private mint in Europe. The idea of sponsoring the slogan postmarks to put Sutton on the numismatic map came when it was realized that the Royal Mint had moved its operations to Llantrisant in south Wales and thus ended almost 2000 years of coining tradition in London. London alone could boast a mint in existence in the Celtic period, which continued to function under Roman occupation and then emerged in the early seventh century as an Anglo-Saxon mint. From then on London has had an unbroken record of coin production which only ended in the transfer of the Royal Mint from its historic location of Tower Hill. Even London cannot claim total continuity, since minting was only revived in AD 293 during the rebellion of Carausius who established the breakaway British Empire. After the rebellion was suppressed an official Roman mint continued until it was closed down by Constantine in AD 325. Almost three centuries elapsed during the Dark Ages and the disintegration of Roman

Britain, before coining was revived by the Anglo-Saxon settlers. The tiny gold thrymsas dating from about AD 630 are extremely rare. The earlier examples had the inscription LONDVNIV on the reverse but later versions had a blundered inscription due to the illiteracy of the moneyer. The name of the city did not become a regular feature of English coinage till the tenth century and even after that time many coins were issued without a town name. They can be identified by the name of the moneyer which usually appears on the reverse.

Celtic coins

The earliest coins used in Britain were imitations of gold staters used on the Continent and were brought to eastern England by the Belgic tribes that migrated across the Channel in the second century BC. The areas in which these crude imitations were struck and circulated may be determined by the pattern of coin hoards and other archaeological evidence, and these uninscribed coins are generally classified as North or South Thames, Sussex, Weald or Kent groups. By the middle of the first century BC the quality of the design of these coins was improving and recognizable elements enable numismatists to assign many of them to specific tribes, such as the Dobunni, the Iceni, the Durotriges and the Coritani who inhabited the southeastern districts of Britain. Commius was the first to have his name on his coins and from the closing years of the pre-Christian era come many coins of the Celtic dynasties. The Atrebates and Regni of the Thames basin issued coins in the name of Commius and his successor, Tincommius. In the reign of Epillus a few gold and silver coins even included the name of the mint – Calleva (now Silchester). The Cantii, who gave their name to modern Kent, struck coins in the name of Dubnovellaunus about 15–1 BC and in the names of Vosenios (c.AD 5) and Eppillus (AD 10–25). Coins were issued by the Durotriges in west Hampshire, Dorset, Somerset and south Wiltshire and by the Trinovantes in Essex, but the best known and most prolific issues were those of the Catuvellauni who inhabited Hertfordshire and Bedfordshire. Not only do their coins bear the names of rulers such as Tasciovanus, Andoco and Cunobelin, but they often include the name of the mint at Verulamium (modern St Albans). Thus both Silchester and St Albans preceded London in having their names on coins.

Farther north coins were struck by the Dobunni in Gloucestershire, Herefordshire, Monmouthshire, Oxfordshire, Somerset, north Wiltshire and Worcestershire, by the Iceni in Cambridgeshire, Norfolk and Suffolk, and by the Coritani in Lincolnshire, Yorkshire and the east Midlands. Although all of these coins have recognizable inscriptions with the names of kings and sub-kings, none of them actually gives the place of minting. They are sufficiently closely identified to certain localities that they can be included by county collectors in any survey of their own area, though only collectors in Silchester and St Albans can claim any coins of their towns with certainty.

Roman coins

From the middle of the first century AD till the middle of the fifth century, Britannia was a province of the Roman empire. In common with other western provinces of the empire, Britain did not strike local coinage and only the issues of the imperial mint at Rome circulated. Coins were an important medium of propaganda in the Roman Empire and many of them refer to Britain. Under Antoninus Pius, for example, the Roman army advanced into what is now central Scotland and erected a wall across the Forth and Clyde isthmus. This event is recalled by a gold aureus of this reign showing Victory seated on a globe and bearing the caption BRITAN. A bronze as of the same period shows a rather dejected-looking Britannia on the reverse – the ancestor of all the Britannia coins of the seventeenth to the twentieth centuries. It is thought that these coins were struck at a temporary travelling mint in Britain. Coins of Commodus (177–192), Caracalla (198–217) and Geta (209–212) frequently refer in their inscriptions to victory over rebel tribes in Britain. In AD 287 Carausius, commander of the Roman Channel fleet, seized power in Britain and northern Gaul and opened a mint at London where silver denarii and bronze antoniniani were struck. Carausius opened a second mint at either Camulodunum (Colchester) or Clausentum and struck a wide range of coins, mainly antoniniani, with attractive allegorical subjects. In 293 Carausius was murdered by Allectus who worked for the unification of the breakaway province with Rome. Under Diocletian an imperial mint was established at London in 297 and this continued till it was closed down by Constantine in 325. Particularly prized are the large quasi-commemorative pieces of the early fourth century which depict the Roman fortress of Londinium, forerunner of the Tower of London.

Early Anglo-Saxon coins

The withdrawal of Roman troops from Britain about AD 410 was followed by a gradual deterioration of Romano-British central government which led to a rapid decline in the money supply. Incursions of Teutonic peoples, first as mercenaries, then as peaceful settlers, rather than systematic invaders, accelerated the breakdown of the old Roman system and led to further encroachments of migratory tribes from northwestern Europe. The petty kingdoms which the Germanic tribes established renewed commercial contact with Europe by the end of the sixth century, when the first attempts were made to convert the Angles to Christianity. At the same time trade with the Merovingian Franks across the Channel brought a new style of coinage to southern Britain, based on the tiny gold tremissis, worth a third of a Roman solidus. The Anglo-Saxons called them thrymsas and one of the earliest of these is a unique coin bearing the name and portrait of Bishop Leudard, chaplain to Queen Bertha of Kent. Later thrymsas even included the name of the mint, both Canterbury and London being known. Most coins did not name the mint but gave the moneyer instead, which is sufficient to assign them accurately to Kent, London, York, Mercia, South Wessex, East Anglia and Northumbria. A great deal of research remains to be done on these coins, however, and there are still many whose location has not been fully identified. The gold content of the coins was debased in the course of the seventh century, and by 675 it had given way entirely to silver sceats or sceattas. The majority of these sceats have little or no inscription but the designs were distinctive and many of them have been assigned to particular localities largely on the strength of archaeological evidence. London alone was sufficiently civilized to have its name on its coins, appearing as LONDUN, LONDVNIV or LVNDONIA, though the lettering was sometimes blundered and barely recognizable. During the eighth century the kings of Northumbria struck sceattas with their name on the obverse and fantastic animals on the reverse. From the end of the eighth century these coins also bore the moneyer's name on the reverse. A parallel series of sceattas was struck at an ecclesiastical mint in York, in the name of successive archbishops from Ecgberht (732) to Wulfhere (854–900). Most of these sceats are not too difficult to find and they pass through the salerooms regularly, mainly at a price which most collectors can afford. A few coins, such as the gold solidus of Archbishop Wigmund (837–54), are unique or extremely rare, but it should not be too difficult to put together a representative collection of the early sceattas pertaining to your own area.

Middle Anglo-Saxon coins

Pepin, King of the Franks, adopted a new silver coinage in 755, based on the denier, which was derived from the Roman denarius or penny. A few deniers were minted in Kent by Heaberht (*c.*765) and Ecgberht (*c.*780) but the first pennies minted in abundance were those struck under the authority of King Offa of Mercia about 775–80. These thin silver coins established a pattern which was to continue, with modifications, till the early sixteenth century. A crude portrait of the ruler appeared on the obverse, surrounded by his name and title, while the reverse showed a cross and the name of the moneyer. Up to about 975 the place of minting was not normally included, but with the much clearer inscriptions of king's and moneyer's names the Anglo-Saxon coins of the late eighth to tenth centuries are much easier to identify.

The coins of Kent were struck at royal mints in Canterbury and Rochester, the latter being extremely rare, and also by an ecclesiastical mint operated by the Archbishop of Canterbury. Many of the latter coins were inscribed DOROVERNIA CIVITAS (City of Canterbury), sometimes abbreviated to DRVR CITS. Coins in the name of Offa, who became overlord of southern Britain, were also struck at Canterbury and Rochester as well as London and an unnamed location in East Anglia, the moneyer's name alone appearing on the reverse. Some coins were also issued in the name of the Bishop of London.

Wulfred (Group II) silver penny of Canterbury *c.*810 (The Trustees of the British Museum)

From about 885 to 915 the Vikings issued coins in the names of the English kings for circulation in the Danelaw, the area of East Anglia which they had occupied. These Viking coins include pennies issued in the name of St Martin of Lincoln and crude copies of the pennies of Alfred the Great with the LONDONIA inscription. Similar copies of Alfred's coins were minted in Danish Northumbria in the same period. One of the most prolific series consisted of the Viking coinage at York, identified by EBRAICE CIVITAS or an abbreviated form on the reverse. A few coins are known also to have been struck in the name of Anlaf Guthfrithsson at Derby about 939–41. The kings of Wessex struck coins at Winchester, Canterbury, London and Rochester as their power ebbed and flowed. Under Alfred the Great (871–99) pennies were also struck at Gloucester, Exeter, Bath and Chester, and as his successors extended their sway to the whole of England, coins were struck at York and Lincoln and possibly some towns in the northwest, though none has been positively identified.

Late Anglo-Saxon, Norman and Plantagenet coins

In 973 Eadgar was crowned king of all England at Chester and subsequently introduced a new coinage. The royal portrait on the obverse now became much more prominent, while the name of the mint now appeared regularly on the reverse. Since most fortified towns of burghal status were permitted a mint, as well as certain ecclesiastical authorities and even some royal manors, the scope for the local collector increases enormously from the beginning of the eleventh century. By 1066 no fewer than seventy mints were active in England and Wales, though the total number of mints known to have operated at some time or another prior to 1279 was at least double. The place-names on the reverse of these silver pennies shed an interesting light on the orthography of the period and show the extent to which names have changed over the past thousand years. BRICSTO is quite recognizable as Bristol while OXNAFOR or OXENEF are obviously Oxford; but DORO (Canterbury), PICC (Droitwich) and SANTEA (Bury St Edmunds) are not so readily identifiable, although the local collector will probably have a good working knowledge of the classical and medieval names of the towns in his area. Even now, scholars are uncertain about the locations of some of these names: AESTHE (Hastings), BRYGIN and NIPAN (Shaftesbury?), DERNE or DYR (somewhere in East Anglia), DEVITVN (David's town, St David's?) ORSNAFORDA (Horsforth), WEARDBYRIG (Warborough) and EANBYRIG (unknown). These mints operated under normal conditions; but during the war between Stephen and Matilda and the subsequent period of anarchy (1138–53) coins were struck by many of the barons in their own name. These irregular coins were struck in many parts of the country, and are generally grouped by numismatists according to area – south-east, southern, south-western, north-eastern, Scottish border areas (including issues by David I of Scotland as Earl of Huntingdon and his son Prince Henry as Earl of Northumberland), and the prolific Yorkshire group.

Henry II restored law and order and introduced a reformed coinage in 1158. In line with the strong centralizing policy of this king, the number of mints was substantially reduced. Some thirty mints were utilized for the recoinage itself but after this task was completed Henry closed all but a dozen of them: London, Exeter, Lincoln, Northampton, Norwich, Oxford, Wilton, Winchester, Worcester and York. Under Richard I coin production was resumed at Canterbury, Carlisle, Durham, Lichfield and Shrewsbury. Bury St Edmunds, Chichester, Ipswich, Kings Lynn, Rhuddlan and Rochester struck coins in the reign of King John, mainly in connection with the recoinage of 1205. Under Henry III coin production was largely concentrated at London and Canterbury, though the Abbot of Bury St Edmunds continued to issue his own coins. In 1247 the Long Cross coinage was introduced, and this led to the revival of some of the provincial mints but they closed again by 1250 and only the royal mints of London and Canterbury, and the ecclesiastical mints of Durham and Bury St Edmunds remained open.

Later English provincial coins

In 1279 Edward I embarked on a major recoinage, which introduced new denominations – the groat or fourpence, the halfpenny and farthing. The moneyers' names were now abandoned, except for a few issues from Bury St Edmunds and although some provincial mints were reopened for the recoinage minting was later restricted to London, Canterbury, Durham and Bury. The provincial mints were again used for a subsidiary recoinage in 1299–1302, Berwick, Bristol, Chester, Exeter, Kingston upon Hull, Lincoln, Newcastle upon Tyne and York being involved in this operation. This pattern continued periodically till Tudor times but by the reign of Henry VIII only the royal mints in London and Canterbury, the archiepiscopal mints in Canterbury and York, and the episcopal mint in Durham were in permanent operation. The chaotic state of the coinage in the reign of Henry VIII, when it was drastically debased, followed by various attempts to restore it to its original quality in the reigns of his successors, led to a revival of production at subsidi-

Henry VII half groat of York inscribed CIVITAS EBORACI (City of York) *c*.1502–09 (The Trustees of the British Museum)

ary mints. In addition to the Royal Mint at the Tower of London, subsidiary mints in the London area operated at Southwark and Durham House in the Strand, while coins were also struck at various times in the provincial mint at Bristol. The ecclesiastical mints were closed by Henry VIII but production under royal control continued in Canterbury, Durham and York till the mid-sixteenth century.

Civil War coinage

Relations between Charles I and his Parliament deteriorated throughout his reign but even before the final breach in 1642, there was a slight revival of provincial coinage. To exploit the deposits of silver mined in North Wales a branch mint was opened at Aberystwyth in 1638, its coins identified by the mint-mark of the Prince of Wales's feathers. This mint was in Royalist hands at the beginning of the Civil War but its plant and machinery were soon transferred to the Royalist stronghold at Shrewsbury. Aberystwyth and Shrewsbury coins can be distinguished by the open book mint-mark which was applied additionally to the coins of the former, while the plumes on the Shrewsbury coins lacked the fillet or band of the Aberystwyth type. Late in 1642 the Royalist mint moved to Oxford and again the Prince of Wales's plumes were used, but with subtle variations and other changes in the general designs. At Oxford Thomas Rawlins engraved the dies for the splendid crown of 1644 showing the king on horseback over a panoramic view of the city, but this is a major rarity which few local collectors could ever aspire to. Royalist mints also functioned at Bristol (1643–45), Chester (1644), Truro (1642–43), Exeter (1643–46), Weymouth (1643–44) and Worcester (1646). Coins with two interlocked Cs have been tentatively ascribed to Coventry or Corfe Castle, while later versions of the Weymouth coins with SA mint-mark have been assigned to Sandsfoot Castle or Salisbury. Thomas Bushell, who had been concerned with the Aberystwyth mint, struck coins for the Royalist cause in the West Country in 1645–46, though scholars are divided as to whether they were minted at Lundy, Appledore, Barnstaple or Bideford or somewhere else in Devon. A mint at Furnace near Aberystwyth also flourished briefly in 1648–49, striking silver coins with a crown mint-mark.

Charles I Newark besieged half-crown 1646 (The Trustees of the British Museum)

Several towns and cities were besieged by the Parliamentary forces at various times during the war and produced obsidional currency, usually silver plate commandeered by the garrison, cut roughly into pieces approximating to the coin denominations and marked in some way to indicate their value. Newark was besieged several times in 1645–46 and lozenge-shaped coins bearing the crown and royal monogram with OBS/NEWARK and the date on the reverse were struck. Lozenge-shaped, octagonal or circular pieces valued at one or two shillings were minted at Pontefract between June 1648 and March 1649. After the execution of Charles I in January 1649 Pontefract struck coins in the name of his youthful successor. The most prolific of the siege coins were the roughly rectangular pieces struck at Scarborough between July 1644 and July 1645. Two types are known, showing a castle with a gateway to the left or a castle with two turrets, and the range of denominations is incredible, from the groat to five shillings and eightpence, in odd amounts which reflected the exact weight of the piece of silver. Most of these Scarborough pieces are extremely rare. Carlisle was besieged in 1644–45 and issued shilling and three-shilling pieces in a circular format but these, too, are very scarce.

Later provincial coinage

Coin production was finally centralized at the Tower of London under the Commonwealth and this practice continued after the Restoration. As before, however, drastic overhaul of the coinage was sometimes too great for the Tower mint to cope with. Branch mints were reopened in 1696 to replace the badly worn and clipped silver coins which were still in circulation, despite the introduction of milled coinage in 1662. Bristol, Chester, Exeter, Norwich and York were involved in this operation and coins may be recognized by an initial letter below the king's bust on the obverse. Thereafter all coins for use in the United Kingdom were produced by the Royal Mint at Tower Hill with a few notable exceptions. The Royal Mint perennially suffered production problems, exacerbated in the eighteenth century by a dearth of silver which meant that few coins were struck in this metal. In particular the smaller denominations were forced out of existence by inflation, their place taken by tokens discussed later in this chapter. Base-metal farthings and halfpence had been struck by royal patent since 1613 and by the Royal Mint since 1672, but only sporadically in the reign of George III from 1770 till 1775. There was then a gap of twenty-two years before copper coinage, including pennies and twopences, was sanctioned. Production was contracted out to a private company, the Soho Mint operated in Birmingham by Matthew Boulton and James Watt. The cumbersome 'Cartwheel' twopence and penny of 1797, weighing two and one ounces respectively, were followed by halfpence and farthings in 1799 and then a much smaller and neater series in 1806–07. Though circulated nationally they are of particular interest to Birmingham collectors.

Matthew Boulton founded his Soho Manufactory in 1770 and teamed up with the Scottish inventor James Watt in 1775 to produce steam engines for industry. Boulton and Watt were born entrepreneurs who turned their inventive minds to everything and anything mechanical or metallurgical and established Birmingham as the leading producer of metalware of all kinds. When the infant United States was struggling to achieve a national identity it was Boulton and Watt who helped establish the Philadelphia Mint and produced coins and tokens for the various states before the Federal issues of 1792–93. Much of their business was concerned with the minting of tokens for circulation in Britain but they were also involved in the production of blanks and coining strip for other countries. In 1850 the Soho Mint was purchased by Ralph Heaton who continued to supply tokens, his first order being from Messrs Annand Smith of Australia. Their first foreign order came from Chile in 1851 and from then onwards the famous H mint-mark of Heaton's was to be found on coinage in many parts of the world, notably in Latin America, China, Egypt and many colonies and protectorates of the British Empire. They also minted copper pence, halfpence and farthings as subcontractors for the Royal Mint from 1853 onwards, whenever the Royal Mint was unable to cope with the demand. Most of these coins bear no identifying mint-mark. In 1874–76, however, the Royal Mint presses were out of commission for prolonged periods and the bulk of the bronze coinage of Britain dated 1874 and 1875 and all of that dated 1876 was struck by Heaton's and can be recognized by the H mint-mark below the date. This was repeated in 1881–82, 1912 and 1918–19 when the H mint-mark again appeared below or alongside the date. In 1918–19 the demand for bronze pennies was so great that part of the contract was farmed out to a rival firm, the Kings Norton Mint, Birmingham, now a part of Imperial Metal Industries, and pennies of those dates may be found with the mintmark KN to the left of the date.

Heaton's were by no means the only private mint in existence in England. William Wood of Bristol struck token coins in Bath metal for circulation in England, and Ireland and is best remembered for his 'Rosa Americana' coins and Wood's Halfpence which circulated in colonial America. James Watt & Company, a derivative of the original Soho Mint, was established in the mid-nineteenth century and won a major contract to supply the bronze coins for Britain in 1860, and shared with Heaton's the contract for Romanian coinage in 1867–68. In 1920–21 Acroyd & Best of Morley, near Leeds produced coins for British East Africa, using an A mint-mark. In 1920 J. R. Gaunt & Sons of Birmingham, better known as makers of badges and buttons, shared with Heaton's in the production of coins for British West Africa. Both Watt's and Gaunt's were absorbed by Heaton's or its successor, the present Birmingham Mint Group. Heaton's passed out of family control in 1935 and was renamed The Mint, Birmingham Ltd, and restyled The Birmingham Mint in 1974. Along with Imperial Metal Industries, it is the major contractor to the Royal Mint for coining equipment and coin blanks and still produces coins for the Royal Mint. Coins minted by this mint independently of the Royal Mint, however, continue to bear the famous H mint-mark.

Many other firms were engaged in the manufacture of tokens, medals, masonic and civic regalia, badges and buttons and had the die-sinking equipment necessary for coin production but only one of these, other than the brief flirtation with coinage by Acroyd's and Gaunt's, developed into coin-minters on a large scale. The Pobjoy Mint was formed in the 1960s out of the firm of Ernest Pobjoy Ltd which had been manufacturing jewellery since 1894. Though medals and tokens accounted for the bulk of production the Pobjoy Mint diversified into coinage in 1973 when it won a contract to supply gold coins to the Isle of Man. Since then it has also produced the ordinary circulating coinage of the island and commemorative silver crowns, and produced coins for a number of foreign countries as far afield as Bolivia, Tonga, Senegal and Macau. The company moved from Streatham in south London to Sutton, Surrey in 1960 – hence the boast of the borough of Sutton to have been associated with coinage over a period of 2000 years!

Scottish coins

Scotland lagged behind other parts of the British Isles in producing its own coins which were not minted till 1136 when the Scots captured Carlisle and gained possession of an established mint and nearby silver mines. Subsequently mints were opened at Edinburgh, Berwick and Roxburgh and silver pennies, similar to the English style, were struck in the name of King David I. His son, Prince Henry, Earl of Northumberland and Huntingdon, issued pennies from his mints at Bamborough, Carlisle and Corbridge, including some in the name of King Stephen who was his feudal overlord in respect of his English estates. In 1157 Northumberland and Cumbria were surrendered to the English and henceforth Scottish coins were minted at Berwick till it was seized by Edward I in 1296. During the reign of William the Lion (1165–1214) minting extended to Perth and 'Dun', an abbreviation which may have been Dunfermline. Berwick and Roxburgh continued to be the main mints during the reigns of the three Alexanders, but other mints were opened at Glasgow and Stirling early in the reign of Alexander III (1249–86) and others followed shortly thereafter. In all, some eighteen mints were in operation during this long and prosperous reign. Three of these are of doubtful location – 'Dun' already mentioned, 'Fres' (possibly Dumfries) and 'Wilanerter' (which may have been a variant of Perth, which previously had coins with the curious form 'Eter'). From 1280, however, the mint names were omitted but a system of mullets and stars in the interstices of the cross on the reverse served to identify the mint; e.g. Perth (26 points), Roxburgh (25), Berwick (24), Aberdeen (23) and Edinburgh (20). This system must be treated with caution, since it has not been fully proven, and the identity of the mints which produced the relatively scarce coins with 28, 27, 22 and 21 points has not been established. The coins of this reign were well struck and abundant, and not expensive even now.

Under John Baliol (1292–96) pennies were restricted to Berwick and St Andrews. Few coins are known from the turbulent reign of Robert the Bruce and, though unnamed, they probably coincided with the recapture of Berwick in 1320. Under the Stuart kings pennies were minted at Aberdeen, Berwick (till 1333), Edinburgh, Dundee, Perth, Dumbarton, Inverness, Linlithgow, Stirling and Roxburgh, reaching the peak of provincial production in the mid-fifteenth century. After that, production was restricted to a few mints but one of these was Berwick, again in Scottish hands for a few years. In the reign of James III (1460–88) the range of coins was increased and included gold, billon (a base alloy of copper with some silver), copper and brass. There was considerable production of pence and farthings in base metal from ecclesiastical mints – certainly Bishop Kennedy of St Andrews was a prolific issuer. From 1488 onwards, however, minting was confined to Edinburgh, apart for an issue of base metal bawbees (sixpence Scots or an English halfpenny) from Stirling in the reign of Mary Queen of Scots. The Edinburgh mint continued to strike distinctive Scottish coins till the of Queen Anne. The Union of Scotland and England in 1707 resulted in the production of English coin types at Edinburgh in 1707–09, distinguished by the mint-mark E below the queen's bust. The Edinburgh mint closed in 1709 and no coins have been struck north of the Border since that time.

Irish coins

Although the coinage of Ireland dates back almost 150 years before the Scottish series it has a sparse and sporadic history. The earliest coins were silver pennies minted by the Viking rulers of Dublin about 995. Sihtric III produced coins closely modelled on the Crux and Long Cross pennies of Aethelred II of England. The Hiberno-Norse coins continued till about 1150, the last series consisting of bracteates – very thin coins with the design showing through from the obverse to the reverse. Anglo-Irish coins began shortly after Henry II visited Ireland in 1171 and was proclaimed Lord of Ireland. He subsequently bestowed this title on his 10 year-old son John and coins in his name were minted in Dublin, Carrickfergus, Kilkenny, Limerick and Waterford. Sporadic issues of coins were made by later kings, and also by John de Courcy (at Carrickfergus and Down-patrick in Ulster). The most prolific of the Anglo-Irish coins were produced in the name of Edward IV (1461–83) and included groats and copper or brass farthings as well as silver pennies. Coins were struck at Cork, Drogheda, Galway, Trim and Wexford in addition to the earlier mints, but from 1483 onwards minting was restricted to Dublin and Waterford. Groats and half groats were struck at Dublin in 1487 in the name of Lambert Simnel who took the title of Edward VI. In the reign of Henry VIII coins were struck only at Dublin and from 1553 onwards they were minted at London and Bristol and then shipped to Dublin. Distinctive coins featuring the Irish harp on the reverse continued till the reign of George IV, but were of English manufacture.

During the Great Rebellion, as the Civil War of 1642–49 is known in Ireland, coins of a very crude appearance were struck in a number of towns besieged by Parliamentary forces. They were preceded by copper halfpence and farthings issued in June 1642 at Kilkenny following the meeting of the Confederated Catholics. In 1642–46 pieces of gold and silver, stamped with a certified weight, were issued by Lord Inchiquin, Vice-President of Munster and ranged from the gold double pistole to the silver threepence. In 1643 silver coins, from the crown to the half groat, were struck by the Marquis of Ormond and crowns and half-crowns with a distinctive cross potent obverse were issued in 1643 by the Confederated Catholics. A small amount of obsidional currency, in copper, brass, pewter and silver, was issued at Bandon, Kinsale, Cork and Youghal during the Parliamentary campaign of 1645–47 in Munster. The so-called Blacksmith's Money, consisting of very crude half-crowns, was struck at Kilkenny in 1649.

During the Williamite Wars of 1689–91, when James II attempted to regain his throne by a campaign in Ireland, mints were established at Dublin and Limerick for the production of 'gunmoney', thus named since it was struck in brass and base metal from obsolete cannon and church bells. Apart from tokens, mentioned later in this chapter, Ireland did not strike coins of its own again until 1928 when the 'Barnyard' series of the Irish Free State was introduced. Since then coins have been struck at the Irish Mint in Dublin but none has been struck in any of the provincial towns.

The Crown Dependencies

Although there is some controversy over whether a Hiberno-Norse mint existed in the Isle of Man in the late tenth century, or whether the coins found in hoards on the island were, in fact, minted at Dublin, a few isolated examples of coins from medieval times have been recorded, both gold and copper coins having been struck in 1324–29 during the Scottish occupation. In the seventeenth century Irish base metal tokens circulated on the island but were officially superseded by local tokens, known as Murrey's pence, which, being declared a legal tender by Tynwald (the Manx parliament) may be regarded as the first Manx coins of modern times. They were produced in Birmingham in 1668 and became legal tender in 1679. Thirty years later James, tenth Earl of Derby, issued copper pennies and halfpence in his capacity as Lord of Man. These coins were cast, possibly somewhere in England though there is a strong local tradition maintaining that they were minted at Castle Rushen on the island. William Wood of Bristol struck various pattern coins for the island in 1721–25 and 1732, but no further coins appeared till 1733 when coins in Bath metal were struck by Amos Topping and Samuel Dyall at Castle Rushen with the Derby arms and Manx triskeles on obverse and reverse. Coins with the crowned monogram of James, second Duke of Atholl and Lord of Man, were struck, probably in England, in 1758. After the Duke of Atholl sold his rights to the Crown in 1765 regal coins, bearing the profile of George III were struck at the Royal Mint (1786) and the Soho Mint (1798 and 1813). The last Manx coins were struck at the Royal Mint with the portrait of Queen Victoria in 1839 and consisted of copper pence, halfpence and farthings. They were withdrawn as a result of the Copper Riots when Tynwald attempted to bring the Manx shilling (14 Manx pence) into line with the mainland system of 12 pence. The islanders thought they were being cheated out of twopence in the shilling and this led to considerable outbreaks of violence which were only resolved by abolishing the distinctive coinage. The island had a surprisingly large and varied output of tokens in copper and silver in the nineteenth century, as well as tokens in brass, card and plastic at the internment camps during both world wars, but Manx coinage was not resumed till 1965. Since then a prolific series of coins, both circulating and commemorative, in platinum, gold, silver and various base metals, has been produced. It should be noted that the Isle of Man has led the way in the issue of a circulating pound coin (1978), a £5 coin (1981) and the first twenty-pence coin in the British Isles (April 1982).

Apart from various trade tokens of the eighteenth and early nineteenth centuries no distinctive coins were issued in the Channel Islands till 1830, though collectors of this area may like to include the ancient Armorican coins which pre-dated the Roman occupation at the beginning of the Christian era and circulated in Normandy and the offshore islands. Guernsey led the way, with an issue of copper coins in denominations of one, two and four doubles (8 doubles = 1 penny sterling). Eight-double coins followed in 1834. From 1885 till 1949 these coins bore the H mint-mark of the Heaton mint in Birmingham. A threepenny piece was added in 1956 and a rectangular ten-shilling, commemorating William the Conqueror, was issued in 1966. Jersey's coinage, introduced in 1841, was based on the shilling sterling, with denominations expressed as fractions of the shilling: 1/52, 1/48, 1/24, 1/13 (1841–71), 1/12 (1877–1966), 1/6 and 1/4 being issued at various times up to 1966. In addition silver tokens tariffed at eighteen pence and three shillings were issued in 1813, and a cupro-nickel crown was issued in 1966. Both Guernsey and Jersey, in common with the Isle of Man, have issued decimal coinage since 1971, including commemorative sets. These decimal coins are generally in the same sizes, weights and alloys as the United Kingdom series, but have attractive pictorial designs on the reverse, reflecting the scenery, fauna, flora and traditions of the respective islands.

Mention has already been made of the bronze puffin and half-puffin coins authorized by Martin Coles Harman. Though illegal, these bronze coins with the profile of Mr Harman on the obverse and a puffin on the reverse are much sought after. Proof sets containing four coins were issued by the National Trust in 1965 but had no legal validity and can only be regarded as curiosities, as are some spoof coins of Brecquou in the Channel Islands, struck about 1970.

Tradesmen's tokens

The diarist John Evelyn, writing in 1697, described tokens 'which every taverne and tippling house . . . presum'd to stamp and utter for immediate exchange . . . payable through the neighbourhood

. . . though seldom reaching further than the next street or two'. He was referring to the plethora of base metal pieces which filled the gap left by successive governments who were either unable or unwilling to issue low-denomination coins. During the Civil War and subsequently the Commonwealth the value of money fell and there was need of a base metal subsidiary coinage to replace the silver penny and meet the requirements for halfpence and farthings. It was not until 1672 that halfpence and farthings were issued by the Royal Mint. During a period of twenty-six years it was left to tradesmen and innkeepers to issue their own tokens. Between 15,000 and 20,000 different types are believed to have been produced in that period. Token halfpence and farthings were also issued by towns and villages, by parish and ecclesiastical authorities and manufacturers. They were officially suppressed in August 1672 but several years passed before they died out altogether. They were struck or cast in lead, brass, copper or pewter in a wide variety of shapes and sizes and ranged from simple designs giving the date and the initials of the issuer to elaborate types with pictorial elements and lengthy inscriptions. They were extensively used in England and Wales, less common in Ireland and the offshore islands but hardly used at all in Scotland where the Edinburgh mint produced an abundant supply of base metal low-denomination coinage. The tokens, issued only by William Dick of Braid (*c*.1648) and George Coombs of Dunbar (1668), are extremely rare.

In the eighteenth century silver coinage virtually died out but the Government were reluctant to strike base metal coins. Even half-pence and farthings ceased to be struck after 1775 and no copper coins were issued in Britain till 1797. In the interim there was an immense shortage of coins which was not filled till 1787 when the Parys Mine Company of Anglesey began minting halfpennies and pennies from locally mined copper. The Anglesey Druids, as these tokens were called after their obverse design, were immediately popular all over the country and soon imitated by distinctive tokens everywhere. The number of different tokens produced in the late eighteenth century is astronomical and almost every town and village had its own series. Unlike the seventeenth century tokens, these were often well struck and highly artistic in their designs. Many of them were latterly struck as a form of advertisement and were even produced specifically for sale to collectors. Consequently this is an area where a considerable amount of material exists at a relatively modest price even to this day. These tokens were issued in every part of the British Isles, including Scotland which also had a penchant for locally countermarked Spanish and American dollars.

The Cartwheel coinage of 1797 and subsequent copper coins of 1798–1807 did not satisfy the demand for subsidary coinage and from 1808 till 1816, when the coinage of Britain was completely

A selection of tradesmen's tokens *from left to right*

Top: John Allen of Braintree, seventeenth century, inscription reads
            BRANTRE IN ESSEX A IG; William Martin of Braintree,
            probably seventeenth century, inscription reads BRAYNTRY IN
            ESSEX WM; Peeter Pearce of Braintree, probably seventeenth
            century, inscription reads IN BRAINTREE PP

Middle: Woodbridge Almshouses, 'PUBLISHED BY R. LODER 1796'
            on rim; Penny token, 1797, 'I promise to pay on demand the
            Bearer one Penny' on rim; Dunmow token, 1793, inscription on
            reverse MAY DUNMOW PROSPER

Bottom: 1813 penny token of British Copper Company Smelting Works
            at Landore; 1794 token, 'Payable at W. Goldsmiths Braintree
            Essex' on rim; Borough of Maldon token 'Payable at W. Drapers
            Watchmaker Maldon Essex' on rim (Ivan R. Buck Collection)

reformed, tokens were again in use. The early nineteenth-century
tokens, in copper, tin, white metal, pewter or lead, are less common
that their eighteenth-century counterparts and consisted mainly of

advertisement farthings. Even after the Great Recoinage of 1816 tokens continued to be struck for a variety of reasons. They were issued in the 1820s and 1830s by public bodies, institutions and workhouses and could be exchanged for meals, lodgings or goods. Benevolent societies and trade unions struck tokens, often with a philanthropic or political motif. Factories and mines issued tokens which could be exchanged by their workers at the factory shop or canteen. These were abolished by the Truck Acts of the late 1830s since the barter system which they represented was widely abused. At an even later date, however, tokens and checks were issued by co-operative societies, grocers and other shopkeepers as a form of discount to their customers. From the mid-nineteenth century onward date the gaming tokens used in the hotels and public houses of the Isle of Man, right down to the cupro-nickel crown-sized £1 token of 1979. Many of the railway companies of the late nineteenth and early twentieth centuries issued canteen tokens to their employees, while numerous local authorities down to the present day have issued transportation tokens for use on trams, buses and suburban trains by their staff on official duties. All of these tokens add up to a formidable branch of numismatics, and there would be few counties or districts which could not boast some representation.

Communion tokens

John Calvin is credited with the invention of the communion token, a small piece of metal which served as a ticket of admission to the sacrament of communion. This idea was embraced by the Calvinist and Presbyterian churches in the British Isles, but predominantly in Scotland where they are known to have been used by 1560. Examples from the sixteenth and seventeenth centuries are rare but thereafter they were used by every parish church, and also by the various breakaway sects or Free Churches. They gradually died out in the early years of this century, being superseded by communion cards, although a few churches have issued them from time to time, either as commemorative pieces or as souvenirs. They were produced in lead, often struck or cast locally from matrices held by the church elders. The later and more sophisticated examples were struck in pewter, brass, bronze or white metal and bore pictorial motifs, such as the burning bush (emblem of Presbyterianism), the communion plate or even views of the church itself. The early tokens bear the initials of the parish but by 1800 the full name was generally given. As they were issued mainly in connection with the annual communion services, the vast majority of tokens are dated, which adds greatly to their interest and range. Though mainly of Scottish

A selection of Scottish communion tokens
Top: Parish of Leadhills, 1867; Wanlockhead Church, 1859; New
            Ardrossan, 1851
Bottom: Arbroath, 1814; Parish of Lesmahagow, 1806; Irongray, 1821
            (James Mackay)

interest they may be found in parts of Ireland, Wales and England
where Presbyterian churches were established.

Commemorative medals

Medals celebrating historic events, personalities and anniversaries
originated in Italy in the middle of the fifteenth century and spread
rapidly throughout western Europe. The earliest British medals
were mainly concerned with events of national or international
importance. Many of them celebrated coronations, jubilees, royal
weddings and births, while others were quasi-political with a strong
propaganda element advocating a particular viewpoint in national
or international politics. Medals of more limited interest developed
slowly from the 1760s onwards. A few medals of this period paid
tribute to famous people, such as the Marquis of Granby (1761) or
the Bishop of Winchester (1761), and might qualify for inclusion in
a county collection on the grounds of their connection with
Cambridgeshire and Hampshire respectively, but the earliest medal
associated with a particular place was that struck in 1762 to mark
the foundation of the Catch Club in London. The following year the

Commemorative medals
Top: The opening of the New Wesleyan Schools, Cheadle in 1872; the
            consecration of St Nicholas Church, Hetton-le-Hole, 1901; the
            opening of Madeley National School in 1844
Bottom: The visit of Queen Victoria to Warwick in 1858; the opening of
            Southport Salt Water Baths in 1871; the International Exhibition
            of Industry, Science and Art in Edinburgh, 1886 (Christopher
            Eimer)

first medal with a truly local character commemorated the foundation of the North Bridge in Edinburgh. The manufacturer of this silver medal is unknown, but the obverse bore a very lengthy Latin text referring to the laying of the foundation stone by George Drummond, Lord Provost of Edinburgh, while the reverse showed a view of the bridge. This is a very rare item, a specimen being in the National Museum of Antiquities in Edinburgh. Almost as rare is the bronze medal of 1765 in memory of William Stukeley and depicting a view of Stonehenge on the reverse. Several medals were issued in various metals in 1766 to celebrate the restoration of Alnwick Castle and from then onward medals of local interest steadily proliferated, though this did not become a torrent until the 1780s. From that period come the enormous range of medals commemorating the foundation or inauguration of public buildings – churches, schools, town halls, stock exchanges, hospitals, libraries and market halls. Bridges, viaducts, canals and harbours were favourite subjects which have long had immense appeal to transport enthusiasts, but this was as nothing to the spate of medals issued from the late 1820s with the theme of railways. The railway lines, cuttings and bridges, the stations and the locomotives themselves were the subject of seemingly endless issues of medals in bronze, pewter, potin, white metal, brass or silver. The railway engineers and locomotive builders were similarly honoured but such medals only qualify for inclusion in this survey if they are linked to local lines.

Probably the most fertile area of local medals concerned churches. The zenith of church-building in the British Isles was from 1800 till 1900 and as this century coincided with the peak of interest in the commemorative medal the scope is considerable. In addition several medallists published long sets of medals with a particular theme and these included the series of English cathedrals begun by J. Davis in 1835 with a medal showing St Paul's and continuing at intervals into the 1840s. The Wesleyan chapels and the free churches also issued medals with considerable enthusiasm. The temperance movement, founded in 1829, was responsible for numerous medals of local interest. Medals commemorating local demonstrations of people 'signing the Pledge' against alcoholic drink were issued at Lisburn, Guernsey, Birmingham and London (1837), Cork, Glasgow, Portarlington and Rathfarn (1838), St Pauls and Kilkenny (1839) and Arklow, Anaghlone, Cork, Gorey and St Andrews (1840). About the same time Isaac Parkes produced an extensive series of temperance medals for no fewer than thirty-eight different temperance societies in Ireland alone, mainly in connection with the campaign organized by Father Mathew.

Personal medals also increased in number and diversity in the course of the nineteenth century. It became fashionable for medals to honour the marriage or death of the local squire or landowner, the coming of age of his eldest son, the birth of an heir male and so on. Visits of royalty and other famous people to a locality were automatically the subject of medals. At the same time national events, such as the coronations of 1831, 1838, 1902 and 1911 and the jubilees of 1809, 1897 and 1935, were celebrated at a local level by numerous medals. By the end of the nineteenth century medals of this type were issued by many civic corporations, parochial boards and even individuals for distribution at their fetes and garden parties associated with these events. Increasingly also businesses commissioned medals for distribution to their employees, and similar issues were made by school boards to the pupils in their areas.

Commemorative medals went out of fashion during the First World War, and relatively few were struck for local events from the 1920s. Interest revived in the early 1960s and led to something of a boom, mainly in medals struck in gold for investment purposes. After this bubble was pricked by anti-gold legislation in 1966 collectors switched their interests to silver and other metals. In 1982 an Art Medal Society was formed in London with a view to promoting interest in medals as an art form. In the intervening years a steady trickle of medals has appeared at a county or borough level for such events as the Silver Jubilee (1977) and the wedding of the Prince of Wales (1981).

Prize medals

Gold, silver and bronze medals sculpted by R. Yeo were presented by the Earl of Aylesbury between 1761 and 1765 as prizes for competition at Winchester College and prize medals were instituted by the Royal Academy in 1768, and the Medical Society of London in 1773. These were the earliest in what eventually became one of the most prolific of all classes of medal. By the beginning of the nineteenth century every college and university, every learned society and institution, had established prize medals. By the 1850s this practice had extended all the way down the educational system to the level of the parish schools. Often such medals were named after the benefactor whose profile might grace the obverse. Other subjects might be the coat of arms of the school, the county or town, or the donor of the medals. In a few cases a picture of the school or college buildings graced the obverse. As a rule the reverse had a space within a laurel wreath for the recipient's name and the details of the award. School medals may be found from every county in the British Isles. Those struck in pewter, white metal or bronze, having no intrinsic value, have probably survived in larger quantities than the gold and silver medals, many of which were melted down for their scrap value. This is a category of medal which is only now beginning to attract serious interest, and consequently examples are comparatively inexpensive. Another interesting group comprises school attendance medals. The medals themselves were often inscribed 'For Perfect Attendance' and were awarded to pupils who had attended school without any absence over a specified period. They were often intended for wear and fitted with a suspension bar and pin. Continued perfect attendance was recognized by the award of an additional bar, or bars, inscribed 'One Year', 'Two Years' and so on. Since every school board at the turn of the century issued medals of this kind, they provide a fertile subject for the local collector.

Prize medals at a more adult level consist mainly of those awarded by horticultural and agricultural societies, either for competitive entries at the county or district shows, or for long service to local industry and agriculture.

Medals of organizations and institutions

As long ago as 1766 the London Brotherhood of Freemasons issued a bronze medals, sculpted by R. Kirk, and thus set an example to masonic lodges all over the country. Many of these medals celebrated the foundation or anniversaries of the individual lodges, while others were struck for award to their members. Consequently this is a vast subject in itself, but one which impinges on every part of the country at the level of individual towns and even villages. Other bodies, such as the temperance societies previously mentioned, the Rechabites and the Independent Order of Good Templars, the Red Cross, the Boy Scouts, Girl Guides and Rotary, have had medals struck for issue at a local level.

Notaphily and scripophily

These two pseudo-scientific words were coined in the 1970s by Stanley Gibbons and *The Times* respectively to cover the study and collecting of paper money and security documents, such as stock and share certificates. The need for such words reflected the dramatic upsurge of interest in these subjects as collectables during that period. Banknotes had long been regarded as a sideline of coin-collecting but lack of comprehensive catalogues had militated against widespread acceptance. This is now a subject which has been well researched and documented and there are numerous catalogues dealing with banknotes at both national and local level. The study of stock and share certificates is of more recent origin, and the literature is not yet so extensive. Even more recently attention has been focused on cheques, bills of exchange, sight notes and promissory notes and though interest in this area is growing rapidly it has not yet acquired the accolade of a pseudo-scientific name, despite attempts by some Americans to foist the obscure term syngraphics on the collecting world.

Banknotes

Paper money was known to the Chinese during the T'ang period (AD 650–800) and continued until the end of the Ming dynasty in 1644. At a somewhat later date paper money was invented independently by Johann Palmstruch, a Dutchman residing in the Latvian city of Riga, then under Swedish government, and first issued by the Stockholm Bank in 1661. These credit notes replaced the cumbersome copper currency then in use. In Britain banking was in the hands of the wealthy court jewellers and goldsmiths and paper money of a sort consisted of the receipts given for valuables deposited by merchants and the aristocracy for deposit in their vaults.

These receipts could be used as securities to get a loan and, like the later promissory notes, tended to circulate quite widely as a form of currency. Banknotes in the strict sense, however, began in 1695 when the Bank of England, founded by William Paterson the previous year, issued notes in denominations from £10 to £100. William Paterson founded the Bank of Scotland the same year and its first notes, from £5 to £100, were issued shortly afterwards. Banking developed along quite different lines in England and Scotland, reflecting the legislation which governed the activities of the banks. The Bank of England had a monopoly of note issuing within a radius of 65 miles of Charing Cross and prior to the Bank Act of 1833 Bank of England notes were legal tender only for amounts above £5. In effect this meant that gold coin had to be used within the 65-mile radius, but beyond that limit numerous local banks issued their own notes mainly in denominations of one to five guineas (and later pounds).

The Bank of England enjoyed considerable government backing and privileges and influenced the course of legislation in England which restricted the growth of banks outside London. The number of partners in a banking concern was limited to six, and this effectively precluded the development of large banks (as in Scotland) with branches all over the country. Instead a great number of small banks operated on a fairly localized basis, but this makes their issues of banknotes all the more interesting and relevant to the local collector. The English banks were divided into joint stock banks (whose shares might be held by the public) and private banks, with the latter predominating. By the beginning of the nineteenth century there were more than 900 country banks in England and Wales, and about 500 of them are known to have issued their own notes. These banks received a severe setback in 1826 when they were forbidden to issue notes under £5. Their notes had only limited validity unlike those of the Scottish banks which, because of their widespread branch system, were readily acceptable all over Scotland. To be sure, many of the smaller banks existed on the shakiest of foundations and the economic upheavals of the period after the Napoleonic Wars took a heavy toll. The failure of Sir Peter Cole and Company in 1825 triggered off the collapse of sixty-three private banks. By 1837 the number of independent banks in England and Wales had been reduced to 351, most of which operated from a single office. In Scotland at the same time, by contrast, there were only twenty-four banks but among them they had 274 branches.

Joint stock banks were not permitted in England till 1833, in a belated effort to stabilize the situation but bank failures continued at an alarming rate, due in no small measure to the reckless habit of over-issuing notes. This was subject to strict control under the Bank Charter Act of 1844 which stipulated that no person other than a banker issuing his own notes by 6 May 1844 should be permitted to do so after that date, that any banker ceasing to issue through bankruptcy would not be allowed to resume, the issue of notes to be limited to the average circulation during twelve weeks preceding 27 April 1844, and on amalgamation the authorized issues could be combined providing the total number of partners of the new bank did not exceed six. Separate legislation for Scotland the following year permitted note issuing in excess up to the limit of the security afforded by the total amount of gold in the bank's possession – an important concession denied to the English banks. The results of the 1844 Act were the sharp decrease in the number of English provincial banks issuing their own notes since they tended to amalgamate and form larger banking groups which were thus debarred from issuing. The number dwindled until 1921 when the last of the English provincial banks, Fox, Fowler & Company of Wellington, Somerset (now part of the Lloyds group) ceased issuing its own notes.

Private banknotes continued to appear in the Isle of Man until 1961 when the Manx government took over the privilege. Since then notes have been issued by the Isle of Man Bank under the authority of the Manx Treasury. In the Channel Islands banknotes were issued by the private banks from 1797, while the States of Guernsey issued its first government notes in 1826. Of particular interest are the notes, ranging from sixpence to £5, issued by Guernsey and Jersey

Five-pound note issued by Fox, Fowler & Company in 1921 (Lloyds Bank Limited)

during the German occupation of the Second World War. Attractive pictorial banknotes are produced to this day by the state banks in both bailiwicks.

The Bank of Scotland enjoyed a monopoly of note issuing until 1727 when the rival Royal Bank of Scotland was established. Rivalry between these banks was intense and each tried to embarrass or cripple the other by hoarding their rival's notes and then presenting them for payment all at one time. This led the Bank of Scotland to introduce the option clause in 1730 making payment on demand or in the option of the directors six months after presentation with the addition of interest. The British Linen Company entered the banking arena in 1746 to promote the linen trade but from 1750 notes were issued as part of the company's normal banking activities. The Scottish banks grew steadily in the latter half of the eighteenth century and reached their peak in the first decades of the nineteenth century. About ninety different banks were in existence at one time or another, issuing their own notes. Many of these little banks were short-lived, casualties of the economic depression after the Napoleonic Wars. Others crashed spectacularly at other times and in other circumstances, the most notable being the failure of the Ayr bank of Douglas Heron & Company in 1772, the Western Bank (1857) and the City of Glasgow Bank (1878). This led to the incorporation of all but the three great chartered banks under the Companies Act of 1879 and the adoption of limited liability. By the beginning of this century there were only ten banks of issue in Scotland. The Caledonian and the Town and County ceased soon afterwards but the eight remaining banks continued to issue their own notes until the 1960s. At the present time note issuing is confined to the Bank of Scotland, the Royal Bank and the Clydesdale Bank. The pattern of note issuing by the small banks of the eighteenth and nineteenth centuries was not as widespread as in England and Wales but still sufficient for the county collector to find representative examples from his or her own locality.

Banking was a relatively late development in Ireland, where the Bank of Ireland was chartered in 1783. Prior to that, however, banking was in the hands of merchants, such as George Touche whose finance house was founded in Dublin in 1725 and was absorbed by the Munster Bank in 1878. Banking tended to develop along provincial or national lines, as in Scotland, with branches in many parts of the island, rather than small localized banks as in England. The scope for the county collector is therefore much less. Between 1927 and 1942 notes in standardized designs were issued by the Irish Free State's Currency Commission for use by the eight shareholding banks, only the names of the banks and the signatures of their treasurers differing. A separate series by the Currency Commission itself, portraying Lady Lavery as an Irish colleen, was issued from 1928 till 1942. Thereafter similar designs were issued by the Central Bank. The notes of the private banks continued after 1928 only in Northern Ireland, including distinctive designs by some of the consolidated banks using the Currency Commission designs in the Irish Free State. Of the six banks which issue notes in the province to this day, however, only those of the Belfast Banking Company can be regarded as having a local character, and even this is misleading, since the Company has branches all over the province.

Cheques

Not all of the small provincial banks are known to have issued bank-notes, but all of them would have issued cheques as a fundamental part of their activities. It follows, therefore, that cheques are a far more widespread record of banking than banknotes. Furthermore, they are relatively more plentiful and still much cheaper than bank-notes. Banknotes, representing real monetary value, were usually redeemed by their holders. Even if the issuing bank had ceased to exist its notes were usually honoured by the bank which had taken over its business. Very few banknotes survived in private hands as a result. Cheques, on the other hand, are financial instruments which, having performed their duty, cease to have any monetary value. Since it was (and often still is) bank practice to return used cheques to the drawer large accumulations of old cheques have been preserved in family and estate papers and in the attics and cellars of country solicitors and have subsequently percolated through to collectors, via the scrap-paper merchants.

The earliest cheques were entirely written by hand and examples are known from the seventeenth century. By the 1790s, however, some element of formal printing was emerging, though inscriptions tended to be in a standard copperplate style, simulating handwriting. From about 1810 onward printing became more prominent and varied, with a wide range of different type faces which gave cheques a more ornamental appearance. By the 1830s this was being combined with various forms of security underprint, often in a contrasting colour, which gives cheques greater visual appeal. In the 1840s small pictorial vignettes became fashionable, at first confined to the left-hand vertical margin, often straddling the perforations that separated the cheque from its counterfoil, but later occupying a more prominent position across the upper portion of the cheque. The zenith of pictorial cheques was reached in the second half of the nineteenth century though many fine examples will be found before and after that period. After 1900, however, cheques tended to become more functional in appearance, reflecting the amalga-

Provincial banks cheques. Note the vignette of York Minster on the York City and County Banking Company Limited cheque (David Shaw)

mation of banks and the need to standardize designs. In recent years there has been a return to the earlier pictorialism and some banks now offer multicoloured cheques in thematic series.

Apart from the standard designs used by ordinary customers, the banks offered a service to their more important clients. Businesses and institutions could have special cheques, in which their name was much more prominent than that of the bank, and the vignette was often in the form of an advertisement for the company or organization concerned. These special cheques were thus a parallel development to the pictorial letter and bill headings popular at the same time. Indeed, pictorial special cheques have continued to the present day. Even though the banks may be national in character these days, the special cheques they provide have an attractive local flavour which should commend them to the town or county collector.

Other financial instruments analogous to cheques which should be considered include bills of exchange, the entirely handwritten forerunners of cheques. Unlike cheques, they were not drawn on a bank but on a person or firm. Thus there was always a much stronger individual, personal element which meant that printed bills of exchange, of the period 1850–90, are often highly pictorial and decorative. They were superseded by the firms' special cheques previously mentioned. During the shortage of silver in circulation, a chronic problem for much of the eighteenth and early nineteenth centuries, many firms issued vouchers of a stated value in payment of wages. These vouchers carried a statement to 'persons in trade' requesting them to take them as money and present them in due course for cash at the firm's premises, or some designated bank. Bankers' orders, the written instructions by clients to the bank to make a payment or series of payments, were subject to stamp duty and, in the nineteenth century, were written out on cheque forms specially designed to show the amount and the periodicity of payments. Bank drafts, drawn by one bank on another, or inscribed 'Pay to Ourselves or Bearer', were widely used in the era of the small private banks, so they, too, are eminently collectable. Even the cheques of the bigger, nationwide banks should be considered, since the majority of them refer to the branch on which they were drawn and this automatically gives them a local character. Furthermore, interest is now growing in the firms of security printers who produced these cheques. The imprint usually appears on the left hand side, parallel to the counterfoil ornament. As some banks used several firms to print their cheques, this adds another dimension to the subject.

Stocks, bonds and share certificates

Joint stock companies had their origins in Tudor times when chartered companies were formed for exploration and trade overseas. The Muscovy Company, founded in 1553, was the first of these organizations of merchant adventurers, shortly followed by the Guinea Company the same year. The East India Company, founded in 1599, was the largest and longest-lived of these great trading companies. At first investors put money into individual ventures, often confined to a single trading voyage, but this practice was extended and finally, in 1657, investments were made on a permanent basis, with the proviso that shareholders could transfer their interests to third parties. This principle triggered off a spate of company flotations in the period following the restoration of the monarchy in 1660. The Bank of England was one such venture, formed as a joint-stock company incorporated by royal charter until 1946 when it was nationalized. The joint-stock principle was now extended to all forms of internal trade and industry. The early and highly spectacular success of the South Sea Company (founded in 1710) encouraged a wave of speculation in which numerous companies were formed and share issues floated for all manner of projects. The bubble burst in August 1720 and though the South Sea Company managed to weather the storm many of the more ephemeral companies were discredited. The impressive share certificates and

Share certificates
Top: A Wharfdale Railway Company £15 share certificate; the cow in the vignette was the famous 'Craven Heifer' born 1807, which grew to eleven feet four inches long, weighed 312 stone, died 1812
Bottom: A £25 share certificate of The Whitby and Robin Hood's Bay Steampacket Company Limited issued in 1867 (Herzog Hollender Phillips & Co, 9 Old Bond Street, London W1)

prospectuses of the period are a graphic reminder of an extraordinary episode in British financial history.

The joint stock companies played a pre-eminent role in the development of communications that presaged the Industrial Revolution. In the second half of the eighteenth century hundreds of companies were launched to develop canals and other inland waterways. The canal mania of the period was to be echoed by the railway boom of the 1840s, and both crashed just as spectacularly as the earlier South Sea Bubble. The companies are all but forgotten, their memory perpetuated solely by the attractively printed and engraved share certificates which, worthless at the time, were preserved by optimistic shareholders and have lain undisturbed in legal accumulations for over a century. In the second half of the nineteenth century there was a significant growth of local authority projects and the development of public utilities at civic, municipal and county level. These trends are faithfully reflected in the share certificates of the period. Aesthetically the certificates of the nineteenth and twentieth centuries are the most attractive, with their handsome engravings of scenery, factories, railways, shipping and public buildings appropriate to the undertaking. The most desirable are the share certificates and dividend warrants of the various railway companies, but now greater attention is being focused on the local authority bonds and shares, many of which are exceedingly handsome. This is a field which has been relatively neglected until now. Often the local authority certificates are ornamented with the very same scenic engravings as are to be found in the topographical prints of the period, often at a fraction of the price. Now that the commercial angle in these certificates is more fully appreciated the market is hardening. Much of the interest in scripophily when it was taken up enthusiastically by the major London dealers and sale-rooms lay in the colourful and exotic Chinese and Russian bonds whose value soared correspondingly. When this particular bubble burst in 1981 the resulting slump affected all categories to some extent, but significantly it is the less spectacular British bonds and share certificates which have held their own and actually increased steadily in value.

Militaria

The organization of the British Army is virtually unique among the great armed forces of the world. The regimental system, developed gradually over a period of two centuries, was, from the earliest, organized along territorial lines. While some countries, such as the United States, use geographical criteria in the organization of militia, national guards and local defence forces, this is deliberately ignored for the regular, permanent forces as part of the centralizing, unifying policies of the national government. In Britain, on the other hand, local patriotism has long been recognized as a powerful morale-booster and the *esprit de corps* which it engenders has been deliberately fostered. This applies mainly to the infantry but territorial units of engineers, artillery, signals and other support formations have strong local ties, while the cavalry, and latterly armoured units, were traditionally organized along the lines of the old yeomanry in which local affinities were most keenly developed. Despite severe retrenchment in the armed forces, and the amalgamations of regiments or the disbandment of others, the old county and regional loyalties survive and in many respects are felt more keenly than ever. Regimental traditions and past glories play a prominent part in building the morale and discipline of a regiment. The highly developed professionalism of the modern army goes hand in hand with the reputation which the regiment and its predecessors has built up. Regimental history forms a vital part of every recruit's basic training and regimental tradition figures prominently in the parades and ceremonial which are the more colourful highlights of modern soldiering. Even in these days of standardization certain regiments maintain idiosyncrasies, such as the Glosters with their two cap badges, fore and aft – an allusion to a desperate engagement in the Napoleonic Wars when the regiment fought back-to-back to repel the French.

Since time immemorial the military forces of the British Isles were organized on a local basis. In Anglo-Saxon times the king had his hus-carles or personal bodyguard of elite cavalry, but the rank and file were drawn from the peasantry, called to arms in moments of national crisis. Under the feudal system introduced by the Normans, military service was a condition of vassalage which permeated right down from the greatest of the nobility to the lowest ranks of freemen – the origins of the yeomanry which were originally foot soldiers armed with the longbow. Long after feudalism had decayed and disappeared the mustering of soldiers for temporary service, both in civil wars and overseas campaigns, was conducted on a local basis. It was the duty of the lord-lieutenant of the county, assisted by his deputy-lieutenants and the justices of the peace, to call out able-bodied men of the county or parish for service. The idea of a permanent, standing army was anathema to the English who were ready enough to spring to arms when the occasion demanded.

In Scotland a similar system operated, but was strengthened (and complicated) by the tribal divisions of the country, known as the clan system. The clans (from Gaelic *clanna* = children) owed their loyalty to their chiefs through ties of kinship, real or imagined, and the bond of a common surname. The clannishness for which the Scots and Irish were famous was a unique form of solidarity derived from common blood, stronger even that the territorial ties found in English regiments. The Scots had a warlike reputation which tended to be channelled into more constructive uses by exporting them as mercenaries. Scottish regiments, including the famous *Garde d'Ecosse*, served in the regular French army, and others were raised for service under Gustavus Adolphus of Sweden in the Thirty Years War. Sir Donald Mackay of Farr raised a force numbering several thousands from among his clansmen and they served with great distinction all over northern Europe in the seventeenth century, remembered to this day in the Mackay regiment of the Royal Nether- lands Army. The regimental system in Britain, in fact, originated out of an independent company raised in 1625 by John Hepburn for regular service. This became the Royal Scots 'First of Foot and Right of the Line', nicknamed Pontius Pilate's Bodyguards because of their antiquity. It was from the small Berwickshire village of Coldstream that General Monck, later Duke of Albemarle and Commander-in-Chief, raised the first of the guards regiments, and the only one to bear a local name to this day. The Coldstream Guards were recruited as a bodyguard for Charles II at the time of his Restoration in 1660. Long after that date, however, the standing army was kept to the minimum and it was the attempts by James II to overawe the citizens of London with a large force camped at Hounslow that helped precipitate the revolution of 1688 and the downfall of the Jacobite cause.

The army of William of Orange was commanded by Sir Hugh

Mackay of Scourie, a veteran of service in the Continental armies and the backbone of the Williamite forces consisted of picked Scottish mercenaries. During the campaigns of 1690–1 against the Jacobites regiments were raised by members of the nobility from the men on their estates. One of these was the 26th Foot, raised by the Earl of Angus from his Lanarkshire estates and known from its inception as the Cameronian Regiment, from the Covenanter, Richard Cameron, executed during the period of religious persecution in the 1680s. The Cameronians, later known as the Scottish Rifles, retain their links with Lanarkshire, though both regiment and county have been swallowed up by the Lowland Brigade and Strathclyde region respectively. Other Scottish regiments have clan names rather than county names. The Gordon Highlanders, originally raised as the 92nd Regiment, were personally recruited by the Duchess of Gordon who gave each recruit a kiss as well as the king's shilling. The Seaforth Highlanders were raised by Mackenzie of Seaforth from among his clansmen, while the Queen's Own Cameron Highlanders have a similar origin.

The bulk of the regiments in the British Army today trace their origins to the volunteer and fencible regiments raised for temporary service during the French Revolutionary and Napoleonic Wars. As this period of hostilities spanned a whole generation (1792–1815), what started as a temporary measure eventually became a permanent feature. The vast colonial empire acquired during and after this period required troops for garrison duty and thus developed a professional regular army recruited mainly from specific counties and districts. At the same time the idea of temporary reserve forces was not lost entirely. It lay dormant for some years but the fears of a French invasion in 1859 led to a revival of the volunteer movement. The regiments of volunteer militia were specifically for the defence of their own localities but in times of national crises they could be sent overseas following the necessary enabling legislation by parliament. The volunteers were not disbanded after the invasion scare subsided but continued, more social than military, organized along the prevailing lines of social and economic classes. The militia (infantry) and yeomanry (cavalry) served with distinction in the Boer War (1899–1902) and many new formations were raised in that period. In 1908 the system was thoroughly overhauled and replaced by the Territorial Army. Though officers and men were largely part-time volunteers, a leavening of professional officers and NCOs ensured that standards of training and efficiency were of the highest level. The territorial battalions formed a valuable adjunct to the small regular forces – 'the Old Contemptibles' – in the British Expeditionary Force sent to France in 1914. The recruitment of men for service in Flanders escalated sharply. The county regiments, consisting of 1st and 2nd battalions before 1914, were rapidly expanded. The Highland Light Infantry, mostly recruited in the Glasgow area, held the record of thirty battalions serving in the First World War. Many of the temporary wartime battalions echoed the old Scottish clan sentiments, in the form of the 'pals battalions' consisting of men from the same towns, streets and factories whose bonds of friendship were an additional dimension. On one day alone (13 September 1914) 1100 employees of Glasgow Corporation Tramways Department enlisted *en masse*, to form the 15th HLI Tramways Battalion. The 16th battalion was entirely recruited from former members of the Boys Brigade, a youth movement founded in Glasgow in 1883. The four companies of the 17th battalion were recruited from students of the Royal Technical College (A Coy.), former pupils of the city's schools (B Coy.), and employees of city business houses (C and D Coys). London, Manchester, Birmingham, Sheffield and other large cities recruited on a similar basis.

Prior to 1881 the regiments of the regular army were distinguished by a number, although most of them had strong county or city links and were often known by county names. In 1881 the regiments were reorganized and the numbers dropped in favour of names, largely of county origin. There were some amalgamations at the time and hitherto independent regiments became the second battalions. In some cases regiments merged in this way adopted joint county names, such as the Argyll and Sutherland Highlanders, the Bedfordshire and Hertfordshire Regiment and the Oxfordshire and Buckinghamshire Light Infantry. During the phenomenal expansion of the battalions of line regiments during the First World War some of these battalions adopted county or city names. After the war many of them reverted to their territorial role and were reactivated at the beginning of the Second World War. The contraction in the armed forces led to the amalgamation of many regiments in 1960 and subsequent years, but, here again, vestiges of the old county regiments remained at territorial level.

The collector looking for material pertaining to his county regiment will find that, in addition to the badges and insignia of the period 1881–1960, there is an abundance of material relating to the earlier militia regiments many of which were absorbed into the 1881 system as 3rd and sometimes 4th battalions. In addition the line regiments also absorbed the local volunteer regiments, as volunteer battalions, and as many as seven or eight battalions might exist in this manner at the turn of the century. In addition to the infantry formations, there were the other 'teeth arms' often recruited locally. The yeomanry regiments formed from 1793 onwards formed the basis of cavalry in the Boer War and armoured units in the Second World War. The Royal Artillery units of the modern Territorial Army and Volunteer Reserve include many which were originally raised either as yeomanry or as Royal Garrison Artillery Volunteers on a local basis.

Similarly units of the Royal Engineers can trace their origin back to formations such as the Scottish Engineer Volunteers. The major line regiments and support arms all have regimental museums, located in towns and cities which were originally their headquarters or the centre of their recruitment area. These museums include the militaria associated not only with the regiment itself but with all the territorial, volunteer, militia, fencible, national guard and other units associated with it. A complete list of regimental museums will be found in *A Guide to Military Museums* by T. Wise (Hemel Hempstead, 1971). At the present time there are some 109 regimental museums in England, twelve in Scotland, four in Wales and four in Northern Ireland, not to mention material of regimental interest in most county and borough museums. A visit to your local regimental museum will give a good idea of the scope of the military collectables.

Badges

Perhaps the most colourful and plentiful of militaria, badges formed a part of the uniform of British regiments from the middle of the eighteenth century. Prior to 1751 regiments were identified by the name of their commanding officer but regimental numbers were then introduced. The earliest badges consisted of large numerals embroidered on the tall mitre caps and other headgear. Gradually, however, pictorial elements, often derived from the personal arms of the colonel or the locality where the regiment was recruited, were incorporated. The badges embroidered in metal wire were superseded by metal badges about 1790. The regimental numbers were stamped out of sheet brass or copper, sometimes also incorporating a name. These relatively simple badges continued till about 1810, but by 1800 more elaborate badges or helmet plates, incorporating armorial designs and mottoes, were coming into use. Officers helmet plates were often extravagantly decorated with cast silver or gilt ornament, whereas the badges of the rank and file were usually cast or struck in brass. When the stovepipe shako was introduced in 1815 the size of the badge was increased accordingly. The period from 1815 to 1830 witnessed some of the largest and most elaborate badges, in brass for the enlisted men and usually in silver, parcel gilt, for the officers.

The bell-topped shako was adopted in 1830 and this required an entirely new type of badge, with the regimental emblem superimposed on a Brunswick star. Though smaller than the preceding type this star-pattern badge was still quite large and ornate. The lower-crowned shako adopted during the Crimean War required a much smaller badge but the Brunswick star background was retained. The

A selection of cap badges, shoulder titles and buttons

Top: Sherwood Foresters bakelite cap badge, issued and worn only in the Second World War (The Sherwood Foresters Regimental Museum); First World War North East Lancashire Volunteers cap badge (K. J. Smale); Essex Regiment cap badge from Second World War (K. J. Smale)

Middle: Shoulder title of the Durham Light Infantry (left) and Suffolk Regiment (right) (K. J. Smale)

Bottom: Essex Regiment button from Second World War (K. J. Smale); button of 1st Derbyshire Militia dating from 1855–81 (The Sherwood Foresters Regimental Museum)

blue cloth helmet adopted in 1879 required a much larger badge so there was a return to the large star-pattern type. Since many new regiments had been formed since 1855 the range of badges of this type was considerable. These badges were short-lived since the Cardwell reforms of 1881 drastically reorganized the regiments and placed greater emphasis on the county connections. The numbers were dropped in favour of county names and this meant a major change in the design of the badges. The badges used on helmets and other headgear were invariably surmounted by a royal crown. Prior to 1901 this was an imperial crown with a flattened top and slightly curved arches. After the death of Queen Victoria, however, a new pattern, known as the 'king's crown' was adopted. This was, in fact, the single-arched Tudor crown which continued in use until 1953 when badges reverted to the imperial crown.

The adoption of the Broderick service-dress cap about 1910 led to a need for much smaller badges with a metal clip. Even smaller versions were adopted for use with forage caps and berets (first used briefly during the First World War and revived in the Second World War). The cap badges of 1910–53 are probably the most prolific of all, since they spanned a period that saw numerous changes in the regiments, combined with countless variations in design and even materials. Officers' badges continued to be made of silver or silver-gilt, but those worn by the other ranks ranged from brass and white metal to bronze and even plastic materials. The badges of county regiments with the imperial crown adopted in 1953 are often more elusive than the earlier examples, since many of these regiments were phased out within a decade.

Apart from the cap badges, there were numerous other badges. The largest and most impressive of these were the plaid belt badges worn by Highland regiments, the regimental insignia being mounted on a large brass plate. Modified and miniaturized versions of the cap badge include those worn on sporrans, collars, epaulettes. There were also smaller versions of the cap badges for wear with the Glengarry bonnet (worn by many English as well as Scottish regiments from 1874 till the First World War) and for mounting on the puggaree of tropical helmets. Rather similar to the plaid belt plates in general appearance were the brass plates which adorned a soldier's bed space in barracks. These were made of sheet brass, usually rectangular or octagonal in shape, and bore the regimental insignia and the name of the unit. The most desirable (and expensive) of all items decorated with the regimental insignia were the gorgets worn by officers and warrant officers of the British Army from the beginning of the eighteenth century. Made of gilt copper, they were often decorated with regimental insignia in silver but they gradually died out by 1830. The waistbelt buckles of the eighteenth and early nineteenth centuries were also decorated with the regimental insignia. Like the Highland regiments the infantry regiments, including volunteers and militia formations, had elaborate shoulderbelt plates but these were abolished in 1855. They were intended to hold the crossbelts, worn over the shoulders, in place where they intersected on the soldier's chest, and for this reason are sometimes known misleadingly as breastplates. These shoulderbelt plates came into use about 1780 and before they disappeared in 1855 underwent numerous changes. The earlier ones were roughly rectangular but in the 1790s they were successively chamfered or rounded so that an elongated oval shape became fashionable. This continued till about 1820 when a rectangular pattern was reintroduced to provide more ample space for the recitation of the regimental battle honours acquired during the recent Napoleonic Wars. The best of the shoulder-belt plates date from this period, down to 1855 when they were abolished.

Buttons

The earliest buttons on military tunics seem to have been confined to the uniform worn by officers. These were of thin gilt or silver metal, the rims turned over a bone or wooden base, and the two sections soldered together. Buttons worn by the rank and file were originally of plain brass, but from 1767 onwards the regimental numbers were stamped on them. This system continued till 1871 for the other ranks and 1881 for the officers. In 1830 officers in regular line regiments changed from silver to gilt buttons and thereafter only volunteer and militia regiments wore silver buttons. The coatee worn by other ranks had small buttons made of pewter or brass, often semi-circular in section and usually fairly plain in design. The change to the tunic adopted during the Napoleonic Wars was matched by the introduction of much larger, rimmed buttons which permitted greater ornamentation. General Service buttons, bearing the royal coat of arms, replaced regimental buttons for the other ranks in 1871 but ten years later new regimental patterns were introduced for officers and NCOs, at the time of the change to county names. These buttons from 1881 onwards were much more pictorial in design and were immensely popular with collectors from their inception. This induced the manufacturers about 1900 to re-issue them for the collector market. These re-issues can be distinguished from the originals by the words 'Special Made' which replaced the makers' names on the backs, but they are quite collectable none the less. Brass buttons for wear by private soldiers were reintroduced in 1920 and have continued down to the present day, reflecting changes in the county regiments. Black or brown plastic replaced brass buttons during the Second World War while the king's crown was superseded by the queen's or imperial crown in 1953 though not all regiments featured a crown on the insignia shown on their buttons. One can collect matching sets of buttons, the largest being worn on greatcoats, with smaller buttons on tunics and the smallest buttons on the chinstraps of headgear.

Medals and decorations

The collector of British militaria is singularly fortunate in that, from the early nineteenth century onwards, the majority of campaign medals have borne the number, rank and name of the recipient, together with his regiment, formation, squadron or ship. These details were impressed on the rims of campaign medals according to a prescribed pattern. Confirmation of these awards may be obtained from the muster rolls maintained by county record offices and regimental museums, giving details of the men present at various actions and campaigns. Apart from isolated examples, such as the medal awarded by Parliament to its forces serving at the battle of Dunbar in 1651, the system of awarding campaign medals only developed at the end of the eighteenth century and was then confined mainly to military units in the army of the East India Company. The first medal awarded generally to all ranks of the British Army was that struck after the battle of Waterloo in 1815. General service medals, with campaign bars for individual battles, were not awarded to the veterans of the French Revolutionary and Napoleonic Wars till 1848, long after many of the participants in these campaigns were dead. From then on, however, medals were awarded at the time of the campaign and this system continues to the present time. The only medals issued unnamed were the stars and medals awarded for service during the Second World War, but since they often appear in groups with other, named medals the problem of authenticity and identification is not too great.

As well as campaign medals, there have been awards for long service and good conduct, proficiency in the volunteers, yeomanry and territorial units, and some (though not all) gallantry awards. Fortunately, from the army viewpoint, the commonest of the bravery awards, the Military Medal, was invariably issued with the recipient's details impressed on the rim. The practice of naming medals is virtually unique to the British and immediately gives them a personal quality lacking in other countries. It is possible to research the recipient's life and military career once his number and rank and formation name are known. The regimental name is most important to the collector wishing to specialize in the medals awarded to soldiers in the county regiment. This may seem a fairly straightforward task, but the further one delves into military history the more one comes across instances of small detachments from a regiment seconded for service elsewhere. This is particularly true of the campaigns and expeditions in Africa during the nineteenth century. Whereas most regiments could put up an excellent showing of medals awarded to their men in the Boer War (1899–1902) few would be able to produce examples of the Africa General Service Medal with the bars for Lango (1901) or Nandi (1905–06), or the

Tibet Medal (1903–04). Full details of the distribution of each campaign medal and its bars may be found in *British Battles and Medals* by L. L. Gordon (London, 1979).

Apart from the 'official' medals, there was a vast array of unofficial awards, especially in the period between 1800 and 1914. Before the institution of the Victoria Cross in 1856 individual acts of heroism were often recognized by the award of a medal given on the initiative of the regimental commander. Some of these medals were individually fashioned from silver plates by the regimental blacksmith, their designs engraved by hand. Later each regiment might have a distinctive medal awarded for acts of gallantry or in recognition of special services. Such medals were usually struck by one of the great Birmingham or London firms of medallists, but the details of the award, and the name of the recipient, might be hand engraved on the reverse. Ribbons in the regimental colours or tartans were fitted to these medals and early photographs indicate that soldiers habitually wore these medals, often on the right breast whereas offical awards were worn on the left. This practice died out at the turn of the century, but survived longest in the militia and volunteer units.

Miscellaneous militaria

Shoulder titles made of metal (brass for the other ranks and gilt-metal for officers) were worn on the scarlet tunics of the British Army till the early years of this century, and on the service dress khaki uniforms from then onwards. When battledress was introduced shortly before the Second World War these metal badges, giving the regiment's name or initials, were superseded by cloth strips embroidered with the name. Cloth shoulder titles had a relatively short life, being discontinued in the 1960s when battledress was phased out.

Helmets and headgear from the mid-eighteenth century till the eve of the First World War bore the regimental badge. Nowadays the badges are usually collected separately and the collecting of complete helmets with their badges in position would be costly and impractical. Nevertheless, the inclusion of a few Albert helmets, shakoes, busbies, bearskins and cavalry tschapkas or lance-caps considerably enhances any collection of militaria. From the local collector's viewpoint, even the black japanned tin boxes in which these helmets and other head-dress were stored are of interest since they were usually decorated with the regimental insignia. Bandoliers, ammunition pouches, and sabretaches of brightly polished leather bearing the regimental crest in brass or silver are scarce and correspondingly expensive, but of immense interest. Larger items, such as lance-pennants, guidons, regimental colours and drums decorated with the regimental insignia and battle-honours are seldom encountered outside museum collections.

Among the assorted ephemera associated with the county regiment are the beautiful embroidered silk postcards which were a great favourite with the troops during the First World War. Many of these were picked out in the regimental colours and emblems, and embellished with patriotic sentiments. Even the more conventional postcards and photographs, from the carefully posed regimental group, to the informal snapshots of troops on manoeuvres, territorials and volunteers attending their annual summer camp, or studio photographs of small groups of soldiers add considerably to the interest of a collection of badges, buttons and medals. Army paybooks, travel warrants, commissioning certificates, citations for gallantry awards or testimonials for long service and good conduct, are among the more common types of ephemera. Recently a friend of mine, while clearing out the accumulated papers in a country solicitor's attics, unearthed several bound volumes of the early nineteenth century which turned out to be the offical diaries of the county regiment. Records of this kind are best deposited for safe keeping in the regimental museum for the lasting benefit of all students of military or local history.

Glass

Glass-making in Britain dates from the late sixteenth century when French and Italian glassworkers settled in the London area and began practising their skills in the manufacture of plate glass for windows and blown glass for bottles and vessels. In 1623 Sir Robert Mansell obtained a monopoly of glass-making and at the same time the government introduced a prohibition on the sale of wine in bottles. The heavy tax on glass meant that bottles were expensive and they tended to be carefully preserved. The more affluent classes of society, who drank table wines, had to buy their wines in casks from which they were decanted into bottles for convenient handling at the table. These bottles were distinguished by a circular seal impressed on their sides bearing the name or initials of the owner and the date of manufacture. By the end of the seventeenth century glass-making had long ceased to be a monopoly and John Houghton, writing in 1696, identified no fewer than 42 glassworks in England and Wales, spread evenly all over the country, producing about three million bottles a year. Unfortunately glass was a commodity that was frequently subject to legislation and taxation. The prohibition on wine bottles for the retail trade lasted till 1860, while heavy taxes were levied from time to time to raise large sums in times of war and national crises. Taxation almost killed the indigenous glass industry at the beginning of the nineteenth century. The glass tax was not abolished till 1845 and its repeal had the immediate effect of stimulating the industry. Machinery for moulding bottles greatly accelerated expansion and by the end of the nineteenth century glass bottles were being produced in over 250 glasshouses all over the British Isles. Even though most of the smaller glasshouses have long since disappeared their products have survived in vast quantities, due to the Victorian policy on refuse disposal. Prior to 1910, when municipal destructors and incinerators were installed, rubbish was disposed of by dumping it in disused gravel pits, marshy gound, ravines, old coal-workings and along the coasts and estuarial waters.

Down in the dumps

Rubbish lay undisturbed for a century or more until the late 1960s when the hobby of dump-digging was born. This rather jejune sport has since been developed and refined into a reputable branch of industrial archaeology, allied to the study of old civic records and the systematic excavation of the former burghal or municipal refuse sites. River banks, especially in estuaries, have since proved to be a fertile source of all kinds of urban detritus – coins, buttons, badges, pottery and non-ferrous metalware as well as glass, but glass is the subject most closely associated with this activity, partly because it was the commonest material dumped and partly because it is comparatively free from the ravages of time, weather and salts in the soil. Before the middle of the nineteenth century bottle manufacture was carried on at a local level and the pattern of distribution of bottled goods other than wines tended to be fairly localized. For these reasons, therefore, the excavation of former dumps is a useful indication of manufacture and distribution of bottles in any given area. Occasionally bottles from farther afield will be unearthed but, for the most part, they tend to belong to clearly defined and limited areas.

Sealed bottles

Although a bottle bearing a seal dated 1562 is reported to have been found at Chester in 1939 its present whereabouts are not known and this surprisingly early date cannot be verified. The earliest bottle seal now extant is dated a century later and bears the name and coat of arms of John Jefferson and the date 1652. Bottles bearing actual seals still intact are known from roughly the same period. Two bottles with the initials RW are thought to have belonged to Ralph Wormeley who died in 1651. These seals, roughly an inch in diameter, were impressed on the sides of the bottles at the time of manufacture and the detail on them was raised in relief by means of iron or brass matrices, not unlike the seals used with sealing wax on letters. By the beginning of the eighteenth century such seals were commonplace. The most desirable examples incorporate a date, although an approximate idea of the date can be deduced from the shape and colouring of the bottle. Those with the initials of the owner are obviously not as desirable as those with the name in full, while those that also incorporate the owner's crest are the most sought after of all. After the ban on wine bottles was rescinded in 1860 the need for personalized bottles rapidly disappeared, although sealed bottles may be found with dates down to about 1875. Where

Sealed bottle, moulded not blown. The date 1771 is thought to refer to the founding of W. Leman's business in Chard, Somerset (Harvey's Wine Museum, Bristol)

they can clearly be assigned to a particular family they automatically qualify for inclusion in a local collection. Sealed bottles were also used by inns and taverns and those bearing the names of the public houses and appropriate symbolism are the most interesting and attractive of all. A little-known aspect of these sealed bottles is that Thomas Bewick the engraver, best remembered for his topographical prints and engravings for endpieces in books, engraved the dies used for these seals and worked in partnership with Ralph Beilby in Newcastle. Ralph's brother William was the author of the famous Beilby enamelled glassware discussed later in this chapter. Sealed glassware has its modern, if rather attenuated, counterpart in the ornament found on some spirit bottles. In recent years there have been desultory attempts to revive sealed bottles and drinking glasses as a commemorative medium, but I have not encountered any examples at a local level.

Left: Seal of T. Lawrence, 1819. Perhaps the painter Sir Thomas Lawr-
ence (1769–1830) much patronized by King George III and King
George IV (Harvey's Wine Museum, Bristol)
Right: Seal showing the coat of arms of the Chadwick family which can be
traced back to William the Conqueror (Harvey's Wine Museum,
Bristol)

Mineral water bottles

Experiments were conducted by Joseph Priestley (1772) and Jacob
Schweppe (1790) in search of a satisfactory method of sealing bottles
containing soda water and other aerated mineral waters. Previously
gaseous liquids were sold in earthenware bottles fitted with a tight
cork secured with wires, but the cork often shrank, permitting the
gases to escape and ruining the mineral water. In 1809, however,
William Hamilton of Dublin patented a bottle with a deliberately
rounded or pointed end. This prevented it being stood upright and

this meant that the cork would be permanently soaked in liquid and therefore kept from shrinking. This simple device was most effective, and Hamilton 'torpedo' bottles were widely used till the 1870s. The fact that they could not be stood upright, however, was a problem for shopkeepers, so other methods of keeping a gastight fit were sought. John Henry Johnson (1864) patented a stopper using an indiarubber ball held against the mouth of the bottle by the pressure of the gas, while Adams and Barrett (1868) invented an internal wooden stopper, but the problem was not solved till 1872 when Hiram Codd patented his distinctive bottle with its glass marble stopper held tightly against an indiarubber washer in an annular groove. Countless thousands of these Codds must have been broken by small boys trying to get at the marbles, but an abundant supply of Codds survived such vandalism and were consigned to the dumps between 1875 and 1930, eventually to be retrieved by the dump-diggers and transformed into collectables of considerable interest. Codd had numerous imitators: Sutcliffe & Fewing, Brefitt, Cherry, Edwards, Deeks, Edmonds, Lamont, Macvay, Nuttall, Rose, Sykes, Tapp and Trotman are among those whose bottles incorporated some distinctive feature in the sealing device. But the only rival to Codd who came close to him in sheer inventiveness and the variety of devices used, was Dan Rylands of Barnsley, remembered by collectors for his Premier, Bulb and Valve patent stoppers. These devices invariably affected the shape of the bottles, and this adds considerably to their fascination.

Codds are the generic name, regardless of manufacturer, given to these marble-stoppered bottles so popular at the turn of the century. They were usually made of aquaglass, with its distinctive greenish tint, but they may also be found occasionally in dark green, amber, brown or deep cobalt blue glass. What makes these bottles so important to the local collector, however, was the fact that the name and address of the retailer using them was impressed into the glass at the time of production. The name and address of the bottle manufacturer was also sometimes given, but generally in a subordinate position, either near the foot of the reverse side, or on the slightly raised foot rim underneath. Techniques of glass-moulding improved from 1908 onwards when American machinery for this purpose was imported into Britain, and it is from this date that the most attractive bottles were made. A great deal of pictorialism could be injected into the design of a bottle, and its sides covered with a veritable bas-relief in glass. Since the manufacture of mineral waters was virtually a cottage industry, requiring only a good supply of artesian well-water (whose qualities could be praised by the local medical doctor), sugar, colouring and the necessary aerating and bottling equipment, most towns could boast several rival establishments who appreciated the value of presenting their wares in as

Glass mineral water bottles *from left to right*
Above: Chapman's Patent internal rubber stoppered bottle, used by
              Gulliver, Aylesbury *c*.1877; Sutcliffe's Patent bottle *c*.1880, used
              by C. Wooding & Sons, Wellingborough; internal bullet-
              stoppered bottle *c*.1890, used by Praeds, Wellingborough
Page 185:   Internal bullet-stoppered Hamilton-type bottle *c*. 1875 made by
              Nuttal & Co, St Helens, used by W. Preston & Co of Liverpool
              and Southport; rare Codd-Hamilton hybrid bottle with no cross
              pinch across the shoulder, used by Wallis, Derby *c*.1871 (repro-
              duced courtesy of *Finders Keepers/New Collecting Lines* maga-
              zines)

attractive a manner as possible. Codds may be found with local landmarks embossed or moulded on their sides. Another favourite
subject consisted of local worthies, ranging from the heroes of folk-
lore such as Robin Hood, to celebrities of more recent vintage, such
as Shakespeare, Robert Burns and the naval heroes of the Napoleonic and later wars. In many cases a motif from the firm's trade-

mark would be amplified into a full-blown pictorial device, subject to subtle alterations and modifications with the passage of time, so that the collector may find an astonishing range of design variants as well as sizes in the bottles used by a single company.

Other bottles

From about 1880 other improvements in sealing bottles included the swing stopper and the internal screw stopper. In 1905 the crown cork was invented and this greatly simplified the design of the lip and mouth of both mineral and beer bottles. As the design of bottles became more streamlined, the tendency to decorate their sides with embossed lettering and moulded ornament receded. Beer bottles traditionally were less decorative than mineral bottles but quite a few may be found with a pictorial trademark as well as the name and address of the brewery. The brewing of ales and beers was also conducted at virtually parochial level and the variety of bottles from

Medicine bottles and cream jar from the Leicestershire area, dating from the late nineteenth to early twentieth century (Leicestershire Museums, Art Galleries and Record Service)

the era of real ale is truly enormous. Before the advent of the giant breweries and the spread of 'tied houses' most public houses brewed their own beer or at least insisted on having their own brand name, reflected in the inscriptions found on the bottles.

Chemists made up patent medicines and poisons and accordingly their names and addresses were often embossed on the sides of the bottles. Poison bottles in particular tended to have highly distinctive shapes, to make them stand out from bottles containing harmless liquids. Sometimes the pseudo-scientific names beloved by the patent medicine manufacturers were embossed on the bottles. The most desirable are the safe-shaped bottles used by Warners Safe Cure, and the bottles for hop bitters which traditionally took the shape of a log cabin. These 'novelty' bottles may also be found with the name and address of the neighbourhood chemist embossed on them, an additional factor of interest to the local collector. Flat, pocket-sized flasks were made in a wide variety of shapes and either embossed, moulded or etched with the name of a public house and sometimes also its landlord. These public house spirit flasks, for whisky, gin, rum and brandy, were very popular in the period 1880–1914. At the same time the distillers developed brand names for whisky and packaging was an important factor in their promotion. Unusual shapes, such as the VAT 69 sealed bottle and the famous Haig 'dimple', survive to this day, but at the turn of the century they were far more numerous. The distiller's name, address and brand name were embossed on the glass, but the more desirable examples also included a trademark or even a moulded picture. Many of the railway companies had licensed restaurants on their stations, and also sold wines, beers and spirits in their dining cars, and thus bottles and spirit flasks may be found with their names and coats of arms embossed on their sides.

Commemorative glassware

During the eighteenth century Newcastle was the centre of an industry producing some of the most elegant drinking glasses ever manufactured in England or elsewhere. Because of the light, clear metal used, these glasses were the ideal medium for delicate wheel-engraving and this accounts for the fact that they are so often found with their sides lavishly decorated. This ornament might be purely symbolic (grapes and vine leaves) or bear the armorial crest of the owner. Other glasses had a more deliberately commemorative character, with dates and inscriptions relating to specific events and individuals, trades and institutions. But while the glasses were made in Newcastle almost all of the fine engraving was done across the North Sea in Holland, and consequently the majority of Newcastle engraved glassware has subjects of Dutch, rather than British, interest. Clearly this was a two-way traffic, since quite a few glasses of undoubted Dutch engraving, possess English motifs, but the Dutch motifs predominate. Among those with an undoubted English subject are the large so-called marriage goblets, bearing engravings of two different coats of arms side by side. These goblets were extremely popular as wedding presents among the landowning classes all over the British Isles and the crests represented on them are known from

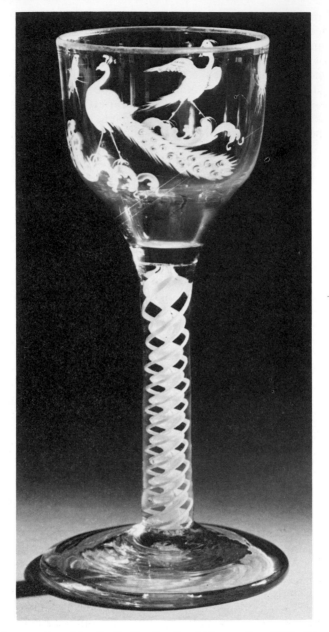

Wine glass produced by the Beilby family of Newcastle *c*.1770, 16 cm high, decorated with white and pale blue enamel, with a double series twist stem (Pilkington Glass Museum)

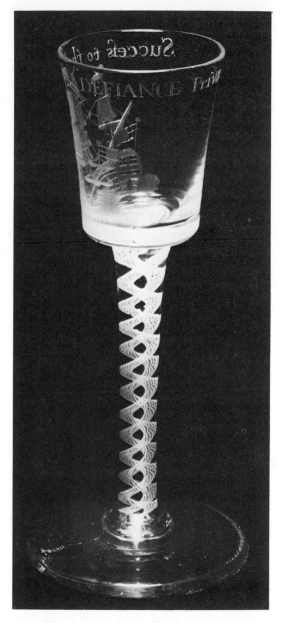

Bristol Privateer wine glass of 1760, 15.5 cm high. The bucket bowl is engraved with a sailing ship in full sail, the rim is inscribed 'Success to the Defiance Privateer'. The stem has a multi-ply double series opaque twist (Harvey's Wine Museum, Bristol)

every part. The indigenous glass-engraving industry, though not as refined or sophisticated as the Dutch, had a considerable output of goblets, bowls and drinking glasses. The decoration and inscriptions on this glassware might seem crude by comparison with the Dutch, but it possesses a certain vigour and naive charm. Heavy-footed rummers or firing glasses were a particular favourite of the masonic lodges, but there were numerous political, debating or drinking clubs in the late eighteenth and early nineteenth centuries who favoured engraved glassware of this type. Trade and professional guilds, civic corporations and similar bodies also made extensive use of engraved glasses, all of which merit inclusion in a local collection.

Commemorative engraving on rummers was quite commonplace but the vast majority of examples seen these days celebrate the opening of Sunderland Bridge in 1796. One suspects that many of these Sunderland Bridge glasses were engraved long after the event, but it is amazing how diverse is the range of glasses which may be found with this very striking motif. Much more elusive, and doubly desirable, are the engraved rummers with slogans alluding to long-forgotten election campaigns, bearing the names of the candidates and the date. Others were more personal in their nature and some of the obscure inscriptions found on them refer to in-jokes of a purely domestic nature. A rummer inscribed 'Success to Nent Force Level' probably has immense significance to some local collector somewhere, if one only knew what or where Nent Force Level was. Others are cryptic, in their use of initial or oddly abbreviated names, which doubtless give the collector endless entertainment in their deciphering.

Glasses were also enamelled or painted. Enamel colours, being fired at a high temperature close to the melting point of the glass, are generally much brighter and more permanent than painted glass, where the painting was only lightly fired, if at all, and tends to rub off rather easily. By far the most important glass enamellers in England were the Beilby family of Newcastle. Most of their handiwork is found on opaque twist wine glasses and goblets but they sometimes enamelled decanters, bowls and vases. Their subjects were pastoral scenes, but included landmarks, famous ruins, sporting subjects and armorial devices, all of which may be attributed to particular areas. Like the engraved glassware, painted glasses were a favourite medium for all kinds of commemoration, from national and international events down to weddings, christenings, birthdays, coming of age, deaths and other family matters. Many of these glasses have an electioneering or nautical flavour, wishing success to a particular ship, and were obviously an attractive memento of the eighteenth and early nineteenth centuries. Like everything else, there have been some creditable attempts to revive decorative glassware in recent years, and all of the traditional tech-

niques – wheel-engraving, acid-etching, enamelling and painting –
may be found on modern commemorative glassware, though little
of this, as yet, has a purely local flavour.

Pictorial paperweights

Glass paperweights were fashionable in Bohemia, Silesia and France
in the mid-nineteenth century and today the exquisite *millefiori*
weights from the great French glasshouses at Baccarat, Clichy and
St Louis are highly prized and correspondingly expensive. At the
other end of the value scale, however, are the shallow-domed glass
weights with a pictorial motif affixed to the base. These pictorial
paperweights were immensely popular with tourists in Victorian
times. In their heyday they would have been sold at watering places,
spas, seaside towns and holiday resorts for a matter of a few pence.
Today they fetch as many pounds but are still modestly priced and
relatively unconsidered. Most of them are quite small, with an
average diameter of two inches (5 cm). The pictures were usually
chromolithographed on paper which was glued to the base and
backed with a disc of leather for added protection. At the turn of
the century there was a vogue for monochrome pictures, consisting
of actual sepia-toned photographs, a spin-off from the contemporary
postcard industry. Less common are the larger rectangular weights
with a flat top bevelled at the edges. Like so many other souvenirs
of Victorian and Edwardian holidays, they died out during the First
World War. A few latter-day weights have been seen, using multicolour photographs of landmarks and scenery, but they are much
more elusive than the turn-of-the-century types. They possess a
distinctly naive, artless quality, their original kitsch overtones having
mellowed with the passage of time. Nothing is known about their
manufacturers, since they were issued unsigned and unmarked, but
they were very widely distributed and have been recorded with
scenery and landmarks from every part of the British Isles, so it
seems that their manufacture was not confined to any one area.
Stylistically, however, the chromolithographed weights probably
emanated from Bavaria and Saxony, like the postcards on which
they were closely modelled.

Ceramics

The craft of pottery is one of the oldest known to mankind and crudely fashioned clay pots, sun-dried or baked in a kiln, were probably made in every locality since time immemorial. From the local collector's viewpoint, however, pottery only becomes interesting at a period when it was customary to apply a mark to it identifying the pottery. For all practical purposes, therefore, identifiable local pottery begins in the seventeenth century when distinctive styles of earthenware and stoneware and an increasingly varied range of glazes emerged, and production came to be concentrated in certain areas, such as Burslem in Staffordshire or Wrotham in Kent, famous for their lead-glazed earthenware and yellowish-green slipware respectively. Among the distinctive styles of decoration dating from this early period are the so-called 'Cistercian' wares associated with the abbeys of Yorkshire and the so-called 'Metropolitan' slipware found on sites in and around London but now known to have been manufactured at Harlow in Essex. Many of the mugs, tygs, posset pots, chamber pots, chargers and rack-plates of the seventeenth century were lavishly decorated with trailed slip and moulded clay ornament and personalized with names, dates and pious sayings, evidence of their having been produced as presents on family occasions such as births, betrothals and marriages. From the late seventeenth century onward it became increasingly customary for the potter to apply his mark to the base or underside of the piece, a tradition which continues to this day and enables identification of ceramics to be fairly straightforward. At the present day the manufacture of commercial pottery is carried on mainly in Staffordshire but during the eighteenth, nineteenth and early twentieth centuries production was very widely diffused, as far afield as East Kent and the Outer Hebrides. Interest in these local commercial wares is strong and they have been exhaustively studied and their products well documented. There are few counties or regions of the British Isles where commercial pottery, mainly domestic tablewares, was not produced at some time or another, thus providing a basis of plentiful material for the collector. Since these potteries produced the full range of wares – domestic, sanitary and industrial – one can form an interesting collection devoted to the output of a single local pottery, covering all aspects and periods of production.

Certain areas specialized in distinctive types of pottery. Tin-enamelled Delftware or faience was made at Aldgate and Southwark in the London area from the 1620s, at Lambeth (from 1630), Brislington near Bristol (c.1650), at Liverpool from the late seventeenth century, and at Wincanton, Somerset, Delftfield, Glasgow, Dublin and Limerick during the eighteenth century. Salt-glazed stoneware was first produced in England by John Dwight at Fulham in 1672 and subsequently by the Elers brothers of Bradwell, Josiah Wedgwood at Burslem and James Morley of Nottingham, before it spread to every part of the country, though now mainly associated with the Royal Doulton company. Wedgwood pioneered the distinctive black basaltes and jasper wares which continue to this day. White stoneware was a speciality of Castleford, near Leeds, while polychrome wares, such as tortoiseshell, agate and marbled earthenware, were specialities of John and Thomas Astbury and Thomas Whieldon of Staffordshire. Creamware, or cream-coloured earthenware, was pioneered by Wedgwood but later associated mainly with Leeds, Liverpool and Swansea. Underglaze coloured earthenware, also known as Prattware after its inventor, Felix Pratt, was produced in many of the Staffordshire and Yorkshire potteries. Pearlware, also pioneered by Wedgwood, later became a Spode favourite, though the most desirable pieces emanated from the Leeds pottery. Apart from the enormous range of different kinds of pottery, porcelain, both soft-paste and hard-paste, has been produced in the British Isles since the mid-eighteenth century. At first confined to a few areas, such as Chelsea and Bow (London) and Derby, it spread to every part of the country, as far afield as Lowestoft and Worcester and Belleek in Northern Ireland.

Studio pottery and porcelain

Reaction against the stereotyped quality of the pottery and porcelain produced by the commercial potteries in the second half of the nineteenth century led to the cult of studio pottery, produced by individual artists and craftsmen in small workshops using traditional methods of handcraft. The renaissance of pottery as a craft rather than a mechanized industry began in England as a result of the efforts of the Art Unions, the increasing importance of art schools and colleges, and the attention paid by exponents of the fine arts

The Mason Vase produced at the Della Robbia Pottery, Birkenhead in 1898. Designed and decorated by Cassandia Annie Walker, it commemorates the visit of H.R.H. Princess Louise to the pottery (Williamson Art Gallery and Museum, Birkenhead)

(painting and sculpture) to the applied arts, of which pottery was that most capable of practical expression. Valiant attempts were made by some of the commercial potteries, notably Minton and Doulton, to encourage artists and art students to produce designs capable of interpretation by mechanical processes but, by and large, the major potteries produced what the general public wanted – decorative and useful wares in traditional and neo-classical patterns.

Artist pottery, inspired by the teachings of John Ruskin and William Morris, was produced haphazardly in the late nineteenth century, much of it of startling simplicity or of bold originality compensating for crudeness in technique and finish. By 1900, however, several studio potteries enjoyed a precarious existence, producing tiles and majolica, like the De Morgan enterprise at Merton Abbey and Sand's End, and the Della Robbia Pottery in Birkenhead, or grotesquerie in the art nouveau idiom, like the distinctive vases and figures produced by the Martin Brothers of Fulham. Nevertheless, studio pottery continued to be an esoteric subject into the late 1920s. A few teachers and designers, such as Gordon Forsyth and H. W. Maxwell, produced excellent handmade pottery and encouraged their students to do likewise, but their chief aim was to raise the artistic standards of the commercial potteries. The Ashtead potteries were established in the Twenties to give employment to disabled ex-servicemen and produced a considerable amount of figures and table wares remarkable for their good design and tasteful blend of beauty and usefulness. A sense of idealism also imbued the early efforts of the Poole Pottery, which John and Truda Adams, Phoebe and Harold Stabler, J. Radley-Young and Erna Manners formed out of an old-established tile-making company, Messrs Carter of Poole. Much of the domestic and ornamental pottery produced before the Second World War was handmade for a small but discerning public. This pottery continues to this day, producing all kinds of decorative wares of a very high artistic standard.

The most original work, however, was that produced by the individual craftsmen, such as W. Staite Murray and Bernard Leach, both of whom were strongly influenced by Chinese and Japanese artist potters. They, in turn, exerted a considerable influence on the other studio potters of the inter-war period, particularly the craftsmen of the Poole Pottery and such artists as Stella Crofts, Gwendolen Parnell, Harry Parnell, Charles Vyse and Dora Lunn. Leach encouraged the studio potters of the Twenties and Thirties to revive old techniques such as throwing and slipware. His example stimulated the gradual development of interest in studio pottery which came to maturity in the 1950s. Since then many artist-potters have set up small studios all over Britain. It has been estimated that more than 300 studio potteries were in operation in the early 1970s alone, producing slipware, stoneware, slabware, coiled pots and figures. Much of the more recent work has a sculptural quality which verges on the fine arts. Conversely, many of the commercial potteries now deliberately try to simulate the qualities of studio pottery in their domestic wares. Many of the studio potteries of the past three decades have been ephemeral, the problems facing all small companies in these difficult times being often exacerbated by a lack of business sense or a surfeit of artistic temperament. Many of these potteries were launched on a wave of optimism and original ideas by young men and women fresh out of art college, but were under-capitalized and went out of existence after a relatively short period. Their wares, often interesting and unusual, were confined to a few outlets in craft shops and tourist centres, and the collector concentrating on the studio pottery of his own area may find many of these wares extremely elusive. This is a subject which requires the collector to be constantly on the look-out for new talent in local art exhibitions, as well as continually scouring the countryside craft shops.

Commemorative pottery and porcelain

Mention has already been made of the seventeenth and early eighteenth century earthenwares which had trailed slip decoration commemorating family events. This tradition continued on two levels down to the late nineteenth century, but the more localized domestic tradition gradually died out as the manufacture of pottery came to be concentrated on certain areas. Wares with inscriptions and pictorial motifs celebrating events of national and even international importance have, however, continued to flourish to the present day, as witness the spate of mugs and plates which greeted the silver jubilee in 1977, the royal wedding in 1981 and even the turbulent events in the South Atlantic in 1982.

Between these extremes, of purely family commemoration, and the celebration of national events, there is a vast range of pottery commemorating events and personalities at county, town or parish level. In some cases a personality of national significance might be the subject of commemorative pottery with a purely local angle. Thus although Robert Burns has been widely honoured in pottery from every part of the country my interest is confined to the mugs and rack-plates which pertain to the events in the closing years of his life, when he resided in Dumfries. Numerous examples of commemorative pottery were produced from 1796 onwards, the year of his death, and bear his portrait or depict his mausoleum, or the house in which he died, and subsequent pottery with a Dumfries inscription celebrated the centenaries of his birth (1859) and death (1896). From the time of Gladstone and Disraeli onward the cult of the political personality has ensured that visits by politicians to all but the remotest parts of the country would be celebrated by a rack-plate or mug suitably inscribed. Where the visit coincided with the inauguration of a church, town hall, bridge, railway or some other public building or utility, the local interest was considerably

Criminal commemorative pottery
Above: Staffordshire figure *c*.1850, 9½ inches high, of Dick Turpin, eight-
            eenth-century highwayman, thug and killer, associated with
            Essex, Cambridgeshire, London and York (Red Dragon Picture
            Co)
Page 199: William Corder, 8 inches high, and Maria Marten, 6 inches high,
            Staffordshire figures *c*.1828 depicting the criminal and his victim,
            murdered in the Red Barn, Polstead, Suffolk in 1827 (The Royal
            Pavilion, Art Gallery and Museums, Brighton)

strengthened. Nothing seems to have been too trivial, however, for
this form of commemoration. As late as 1917 plates were still being
produced to celebrate visits of David Lloyd George to munitions
factories up and down the land. This localized medium, however,
died out rather abruptly after 1918 and has seen little attempt at a
revival.

Folk heroes of the Napoleonic Wars, such as Jack Crawford (who
nailed his ship's colours to the mast at the Battle of Camperdown,
1797) or Dolly Pentreath, (who tricked the French invaders of

Pembrokeshire into surrender in 1798) were the subject of pictorial rack-plates long after the time of their exploits. Famous preachers, like John and Charles Wesley, social workers and philanthropists like Hannah Moore and William Wilberforce, were immortalized in figures and busts which circulated nationwide, but they were also portrayed on plates, bowls and mugs with inscriptions of more local interest. Parliamentary elections were assiduously commemorated in the eighteenth century, rack-plates bearing the names of candidates, dates and political slogans being a speciality of the Bristol delftware factory in the 1750s and 1760s. Though most of these electioneering plates relate to events in Gloucestershire, Devon, Dorset and Wiltshire, there have been isolated instances, in glazed earthenware, from other areas right down to the present time. The best-known and certainly the most prolific group of commemorative pottery and porcelain consists of plates, mugs, tankards, vases and bowls decorated with transfer-printed motifs highlighting events and celebrities associated with the expansion of the railway system. The subjects ranged from pictures of the early locomotives and rolling

Edward VII Coronation mug, 1902, distributed in Harlow, Essex (Jack Mitchley)

stock, to views of stations, viaducts, railway bridges, tunnels and cuttings. Rack-plates in particular were a popular medium for the opening of new stations in Victorian times or the inauguration of new lines, or anniversaries of George Stephenson and other famous locomotive engineers. Since much of this pottery bore inscriptions relating to specific railway lines or events in company history, they are of immense interest to the local collector.

Royal events have been celebrated in ceramics since the sixteenth century and to this day it is traditional to present schoolchildren with mugs commemorating coronations and jubilees. Although many of these souvenirs have been produced by the giant potteries for distribution on a national level the royal events from the Golden Jubilee of Queen Victoria (1887) to the Coronation of King George VI (1937) were often celebrated by mugs and beakers which, if not actually manufactured locally, were often inscribed for distribution in a specific area and often decorated with the coat of arms of the local landowner or benefactor or the town or corporation making the issue. A few boroughs and county councils even commissioned mugs which were entirely distinctive to them in their pictorial motifs. Other royal events, notably the investiture of the Prince of Wales, precipitated a rash of commemorative wares which, produced worldwide, would be relevant to any collection of material associated with Caernarvon.

Although commemorative rack-plates were out of fashion from 1918 onwards they enjoyed a considerable revival in the 1960s, as collector interest in the older plates was rekindled, and this has led to a vast output of material from the leading companies, such as Wedgwood, Spode, Minton, Doulton, Worcester and Rosenthal. It is customary nowadays for local authorities to commission plates to celebrate important local anniversaries. Among the more noteworthy examples in recent years have been plates celebrating the 350th anniversary of the departure of the *Mayflower* from Sutton Harbour, Plymouth (1970), the centenary of Girton College (1969), the eighth centenary of the martyrdom of St Thomas à Becket (1971), the 1900th anniversary of York (1971), various landmarks associated with European Architectural Heritage Year (1975), anniversaries of Westminster, Selby and Iona abbeys (1966–72), the millennium of Tynwald, the Isle of Man's parliament (1979), the centenary of the Royal Albert Hall (1971), the 150th anniversary of the Stockton-Darlington Railway (1975) and of the Liverpool-Manchester Railway (1980).

Two mugs commissioned by Brighton Borough Council to commemorate (left) the Jubilee of Queen Victoria in 1887 and (right) the marriage of the Duke of York and Princess May in 1893 (Spode Limited Museum Collection)

Crested china

William Henry Goss founded the Falcon Pottery at Stoke-on-Trent in the late 1850s and for about a quarter of a century concentrated on porcelain tablewares and Parian figures. In the early 1880s, however, his son, Adolphus William Henry Goss, became a director of the company and it was he, a heraldry enthusiast, who pioneered miniature porcelain souvenir hollow-wares bearing the crests of towns and counties all over the British Isles. He obtained permission from the cities and boroughs in 1887 and produced his first souvenirs the following year. A wide range of items was produced, covering almost every conceivable ceramic shape and style, from Graeco Roman times to the present day. The tiny bowls, vases, lamps and vessels were made of plain white porcelain decorated in bright polychrome enamels with the crests of the towns and cities. From the outset Goss only retailed these objects in the town whose crest was depicted, and immediately these souvenirs became immensely popular with the public looking for a cheap memento of their visit. Goss china enjoyed a tremendous following at the turn of the century. During the First World War a patriotic note was struck and, at the same time, the range of collectables greatly extended, by the production of miniature porcelain versions of guns, tanks, ships, aircraft, shells, soldiers, dispatch riders and even war memorials, all suitably embellished with local crests. After the war Goss searched farther afield for material for his crested novelties and in the Twenties and Thirties all manner of novelty shapes and folk objects, often

Two examples of Goss crested china produced between 1900 and 1910. Roman ewers from (left) Felixstowe and (right) Henley-on-Thames (Goss and Crested China Ltd)

derived from other cultures and civilizations, were marketed with these local crests. After the firm was taken over by the Cauldon Pottery group in 1936 production of these popular souvenirs continued, though the quality in the latter years was not so good. Production ceased abruptly in 1940 when the Goss factory was destroyed. Inevitably Goss had their imitators and similar examples of crested china may be found with the names and marks of Arcadian, Civic, Crescent, Florentine, Carlton, Grafton, Queens, Regency, Shelley and Swan among others. Though generally inferior to Goss, these wares are eminently collectable on account of their local heraldic devices. Pre-1914 Goss china bore a serial number, corresponding to the registered design numbers listed at the Patent Office, and these help in the dating of specimens. Goss and other forms of crested china now have a large following, with regional collectors' clubs and a steadily increasing volume of specialist literature. Since every part of the country was covered, there are numerous examples of these souvenirs to be found with the crests of every place which had even the slightest pretension to an armorial device.

A selection of toothpaste potlids from 1885–1915 (Robert Opie Collection)

Prattware and other transfer-printed potlids

The collector's term for this transfer-printed underglaze ware is derived from the firm of F. & R. Pratt of Fenton, Staffordshire who, if not actually the first in the field, were certainly the largest and most prolific producers of these wares. Mayer & Company of Burslem and the Cauldon Pottery Company were also manufacturers of potlids in this genre, but Prattware is in a class of its own, due mainly to the superb engravings by Jesse Austin whose name appears on many of them. Earthenware pots were used in the packaging of various consumer goods, especially bear's grease pomade, fish pastes, potted meats, shrimps, tooth paste, cold creams, shaving creams, healing unguents and even confectionery. Prior to 1846 the lids of these pots bore a printed paper label or an underglaze transfer print in black or brown, but henceforward techniques for colour printing were developed. The earliest of the polychrome pictorial potlids were intended for bear's grease pomade, the hair dressing then fashionable, and tended to feature humanoid bears in various whimsical situations. This idea was soon copied by the retailers of shrimp paste and they chose scenery in and around Pegwell Bay near Ramsgate in Kent. This was later extended to other subjects in east Kent, such as the new jetty and pier or the harbour at Margate, Royal Harbour and the fashionable terraced houses of Nelson Crescent in Ramsgate, and the castles at Walmer and Sandown. Several different views of Pegwell Bay are also known transfer-printed on the sides of the jars themselves. These shrimp paste lids and jars were used by the retailers, S. Banger or Tatnell & Son but apart from one lid showing the Belle Vue tavern with a Tatnell cart in the foreground, these paste manufacturers did not obtrude themselves on to the lids.

The idea was soon followed by other manufacturers of fish pastes and potted meats. Many of the subjects were patriotic in character, with scenes in India and the Crimea. Others depicted general scenery and landscapes from all over the world, but those with a local flavour are of specific interest. The British landmarks reproduced in potlids include the Alexandra Palace, St Paul's Cathedral, the Royal Exchange, Windsor Castle, Shakespeare's birthplace, Ann Hathaway's cottage, Holy Trinity Church, Stratford-upon-Avon, Conway Castle, Buckingham Palace, Drayton Manor, Sandringham, Osborne House, the Houses of Parliament, the Tower of London, Westminster Abbey, the Albert Memorial, Charing Cross, Blackfriars Bridge, the Thames Embankment, the Chapel Royal at the Savoy, Trafalgar Square, Holborn Viaduct, St Thomas's Hospital and Strathfieldsay, the residence of the Duke of Wellington. Others had a dual role, depicting landmarks and commemorating events. The visit of the Prince and Princess of Wales to London Bridge in 1863 was celebrated by potlids, while a lengthy series hailed the Great Exhibition of 1851 and depicted the interior and exterior of the Crystal Palace, and the opening and closing ceremonies. This inspired later potlids for similar events at home and abroad, including the Dublin Industrial Exhibition (1853) and the International Exhibition in London (1862). Some of these transfer prints were later used in less utilitarian forms and may be found decorating plates, vases, jugs, bowls, candlesticks, porringers and tureens of the 1870s.

The potlids used for tooth paste, shaving cream and other cosmetic products continued the earlier monochrome tradition and were generally far less decorative. What they lacked in that respect, however, they made up in their use of names and addresses of the

Examples of late nineteenth-century and early twentieth-century stoneware cream pots, ginger beer and water bottles (Reproduced courtesy of *Finders Keepers/New Collecting Lines* magazines)

manufacturers, dentists and chemists, and thus provide a more diverse range of local interest. While the pictorial potlids of which Jesse Austin was the leading exponent died out in the 1890s, the more utilitarian monochrome lids continued into the present century, and though they have largely been superseded by other methods of packaging a few survive to this day.

Stoneware bottles and jars

The leading potteries put up a very stiff rivalry to the glass manufacturers in the nineteenth and early twentieth centuries and many products were bottled in earthenware or stoneware provided by such firms as Doulton & Watt, the Denby Pottery and James Stiff, Stephen Green & Company. These potteries produced a wide range of whisky flasks, gin bottles, blacking pots, ink bottles, meat, clotted cream, jam, preserve and fish-paste jars, hot-water bottles and bottles for vinegar or ginger beer. As the glass manufacturers made their wares more attractive with lavish embossing and moulding, so the potteries enlivened their vessels with incised ornament and underglaze transfer-printing. The most attractive pictorial bottles and jars date from 1880 till 1920, but I can remember quite vividly the brown earthenware jars in which jam was sold as late as the Second World War. Even now these pottery jars are used for the packaging of foodstuffs, from exotic cheeses and fish-pastes to jam and preserves, aimed at the high-class market. Sometimes these traditional forms of packaging are used for commemorative purposes. The jars of drambuie-flavoured marmalade sold in 1981 as souvenirs of the royal wedding depict St Paul's Cathedral but would also appeal to collectors in Strathclyde, since they emanated from Newton Mearns in that region.

Metalware

At first glance it would not seem that there was much scope at the town, county or parish level to interest the local collector in metalware, and yet this is a field offering a great deal to those fortunate enough to be concentrating on certain areas. Obviously collectors in Birmingham and Sheffield are better placed than most since these cities have for centuries been the centres of manufacturing industries in all aspects of metalcraft, 'from a needle to an anchor'. Apart from the military aspects discussed in Chapter 10, there is immense scope for the local collector in the livery buttons worn in former times by servants. These buttons, decorated with the arms of the employer, may be found in every part of the country. In the nineteenth century buttons with pictorial motifs including famous landmarks were fashionable.

Silver and pewter

Assay marks, guaranteeing the fineness of the metal, are known to have been applied to silver articles in London as long ago as 1300, when the leopard's head device was introduced. The silversmiths of London adopted individual maker's marks in 1363 and a date letter, changed annually, in 1463. Scotland followed suit in the late fifteenth century. The Edinburgh assay office used a mark consisting of three small towers, derived from the city's coat of arms, and this was struck on all articles assayed from 1485, although marks applied by the manufacturer and the deacon of the guild of hammermen were obligatory from 1457. Silversmiths were active in Dublin from the thirteenth century but no formalized assay marks were used there till 1605 when the city council decreed that articles should bear lion, harp and castle marks in addition to the maker's mark. The figure of Hibernia was added in 1731. Elsewhere in the British Isles distinctive marks were introduced gradually as provincial assay offices were established. The Chester used a triple wheatsheaf mark from 1686, Exeter had a triple-towered castle from 1701 till 1883, while Newcastle had a mark of three towers intermittently from 1702 till 1884. York, as the second oldest city in England and an important archiepiscopal centre, had a complex system of assay marks from 1411 onwards. Originally a mark of a demidiated leopard and fleur-de-lis was used, but a half-rose was substituted for the latter in 1632–98 and thereafter a cross charged with five lions passant (the city's arms) was used until the assay office was closed in 1857. Assay offices were established at Birmingham and Sheffield in 1773 using an anchor and a crown respectively. Glasgow's silversmiths used a sequence of date letters from the sixteenth century till 1705 when the present mark, derived from the civic arms and showing a tree, salmon and bell, was introduced. Additionally Edinburgh silver bears a thistle mark while Glasgow has a lion rampant, while the English assay offices had marks showing a lion passant and a crowned leopard's or lion's head.

Although only ten cities have, or had, assay offices, hallmarks which were tantamount to assay marks were widely used before they were abolished by Act of Parliament in 1836. In Scotland alone, for example, distinctive town marks have been recorded from Aberdeen (ABD, three castles or three crosses), Arbroath (portcullis), Canongate (stag with or without a cross between its antlers), Dundee (lily-pot or the town name), Elgin (ELN or name in full, or a mother and child), Greenock (anchor or thistle), Inverness (INS, or a dromedary), Montrose (rose), Perth (lamb, double-headed eagle or single-headed eagle), Peterhead (PHD), St Andrew's (saltire cross), Tain (town name or figure of St Duthac flanked by letters SD) and Wick (town name). A similar pattern of town marks may be found on silver from England, Wales and Ireland. Furthermore, the use of emblems or initials to denote the silversmith, when taken in conjunction with a town mark or assay office mark, enables the collector to identify a piece of silverware accurately and assign it to a particular town. Interest in provincial silver is increasing and many collectors now specialize in articles manufactured in their own localities. Apart from the various marks which distinguish silver, considerable interest attaches to inscriptions and armorial devices engraved on silver, much of which was produced for presentation purposes. Prize cups are an obvious category, but all kinds of silver, from snuffboxes to cake-baskets and candelabra, may be found with commemorative inscriptions.

Although snuffboxes are probably the commonest type of small silverware found with presentation or personalized inscriptions, dental cases, lancet cases, stamp boxes, pounce boxes, patch boxes and vinaigrettes may also be found thus embellished. Most of this decoration was applied in a form of shallow engraving, views of Brighthelmstone and other watering places being particularly fashionable but by the mid-eighteenth century cast and repoussé ornament was also very popular. Many of the snuffboxes and vinaigrettes dating from about 1780 to 1840 were elaborately die-stamped with ornament and pictorial scenes and landscapes were very fashionable. These boxes were the product of the Birmingham and Sheffield diesinkers who catered to prevailing public taste by providing their customers with such subjects as Birmingham Town Hall, Hampton Court, Windsor Castle, York Minster, Ann Hathaway's cottage, Abbotsford, Holyroodhouse, Edinburgh Castle, St Paul's Cathedral, St George's Hall, Liverpool, the Houses of Parliament, Southampton Bar Gate, the Tower of London and Tower Bridge. Similar techniques, allied with bright-cutting and acid-etching, were later used for larger objects, such as card-cases and cigarette cases, many of which perpetuated the pictorial theme down to the early years of this century. Even quite small objects, such as penknives, could be decorated with embossed or engraved vignettes along their sides. This was a favourite device commemorating the public fairs and exhibitions of the Victorian period, from the Great Exhibition of 1851 to the international exhibitions in Glasgow (1888), Cork (1902), Dublin (1907) and Edinburgh (1911).

Pewter, an alloy of tin and lead, was extensively used as a cheap substitute for silver and, when new, had a bright silvery sheen which could be maintained by constant scouring and burnishing. Pewterers went to great lengths to give their wares the appearance of precious metal, even to the extent of stamping articles with marks in imitation of silver hallmarks. Pewter touchmarks were carefully regulated by the guilds of hammermen and pewterers but other marks were included, such as a quality mark and a maker's mark. Since the manufacture of pewter was far more widespread than silver the range of marks is enormous, though mainly in the period from 1600 to about 1750 when pewter was largely ousted by Sheffield plate and later by electroplating. Pewter marks were often extremely elaborate and, in the late eighteenth century even included patriotic or political slogans. Sheffield plate, the close fusing of thin plates of silver to a copper base, was, as the name suggests, practised mainly in Sheffield and had its own elaborate system of pseudo hallmarks, but far more widely diffused was the manufacture of Britannia metal (an alloy of tin and antimony) which enjoyed a certain vogue in the mid-nineteenth century. Little interest has been shown so far in electroplate, pioneered by Elkington's in the 1840s. Articles may be found with the initials E.P.N.S. (electroplated nickel silver) or, more rarely, E.P.B.M. (electroplated Britannia metal) and the pseudo hallmarks of the manufacturer. As this material is still largely neglected it can often be picked up for very little.

Boundary marks and fire insurance marks

Small shield-shaped, oval, circular or oblong plaques, cast in iron or lead, were used to mark the boundaries of parishes, wards and other administrative units of local government, and were affixed to the walls of churches, public buildings and even private houses on street corners. The vast majority of extant examples date from the early eighteenth century and continued down till about 1900. In most cases they bear a date, indicating when they were erected or boundaries were fixed. In their simplest form they consist of shields bearing the initials of the district but some of the more elaborate nineteenth century examples have a pictorial motif derived from the local coat of arms or equestrian figures in bas-relief. These marks tend to come on the market as a result of inner city redevelopment and the demolition of old buildings. Fire insurance marks are similar to, but generally more elaborate than, boundary marks. These plaques bear the emblems of the insurance companies which organized their own fire brigades in the eighteenth and nineteenth centuries and were affixed to the walls of buildings by these companies to ensure that their brigades only dealt with fires on the premises of their clients. The Royal Exchange Company instituted this practice in 1722 and other companies soon followed suit. They ceased to have any validity from about 1865 when municipal fire services were organized, though they survived in provincial towns to the end of the nineteenth century in some cases. These marks were cast or embossed in iron, lead, copper, brass or stamped out of sheet iron and painted or enamelled or left in a natural state.

Fire insurance marks of (left) Leeds Fire Office, 1777–82 and (right) Bristol Crown Fire Office, 1718 (The Chartered Insurance Institute)

Enamelled metal signs

As branded goods developed in the mid-nineteenth century signs made of sheet iron with enamelled decoration proliferated and reached their peak at the turn of the century when every available space was littered with them. Although intended mainly to advertise goods known nationally they were often combined with the name and address of the local grocer, tobacconist or stationer. The larger signs are rather cumbersome, but there were many smaller signs, ranging from window pieces to door furniture (the small plates affixed near the doorhandle to protect the paintwork from fingerprints).

Horse brasses

These objects, designed partly to decorate horse harness and partly to ward off evil spirits, have been recorded from medieval times. The earliest examples were cut, filed and chiselled from latten or sheet brass, but since about 1830 the vast majority of them have been cast in brass. Lightweight brasses, aimed at the late-Victorian and Edwardian tourist trade, were die-struck from thin brass sheet and lack the primitive appearance and evidence of chasing and afterwork found in the seventeenth and eighteenth century brasses. In recent years there has been a revival of brasses cast in the traditional idiom, for the tourist 'repro' market which is much more discriminating these days than its late-Victorian counterpart. The vast majority of brasses have motifs derived from medieval amulets and good-luck symbols and cannot be categorized on a local basis. Quite a few subjects, however, have a pronounced local character and these would certainly qualify for inclusion in a local collection. From the Isle of Man, for example, come brasses depicting the triskeles or three-legged emblem, the tailless Manx cat, the Tower of Refuge in Douglas Harbour and, more recently, a Tourist Trophy motor cyclist. Brasses showing landmarks from other parts of the British Isles include those depicting York Minster, St Paul's Cathedral, the Tower of London, the birthplace of Robert Burns at Alloway, Ann Hathaway's cottage, Stratford, Balmoral and Windsor Castles, and the Crystal Palace.

Portrait brasses with a local character include those showing John Peel the Cumbrian huntsman, literary figures, such as Shakespeare, Burns and Scott, politicians like Disraeli, Gladstone, Joseph Chamberlain and Lord Randolph Churchill, or sporting personalities, such as the great Victorian jockey Fred Archer. Brasses commemorating Derby winners were a great favourite at the turn of the century,

A selection of horse brasses found in the Chelmsford, Essex area and dating from the late nineteenth to early twentieth century. From left to right:

Top: Fly terret, usually worn on the crown of the horse's head where the harness went around the ears and sometimes on the harness going across the horse's shoulders; dimension brass, usually attached to the shoulder harness; a light rein passed around the brass tongue kept the horse's head upright

Middle: Brass rosette, attached to the reins just below the horse's ear by means of an iron loop; eye brass, attached to leather blinkers. Both the brass rosette and eye brass illustrated carry the owner's initials.

Bottom: Tonn brass, worn by dray horses (G. L. Bailey)

while brasses celebrating royal events, such as Victoria's jubilees and the coronations and royal weddings of more recent years, were often given a local slant in their inscriptions. Brasses were often produced as mementoes or prizes at county shows and similar local events, while many of the heraldic brasses have motifs derived from the coats of arms of the local landowners. A large but relatively neglected field consists of saddlers' brasses, the less decorative items found on saddlery and bearing the names, addresses and trademarks of the harness makers. Among the more desirable brasses are those bearing civic or regimental emblems, worn by horses employed by local authorities or the cavalry regiments, while brasses bearing the arms or initials of the railway companies (which employed large numbers of horses for the transportation of passengers and freight to and from the stations) are much sought after.

Trivets and iron stands

Metal stands for sadirons and cooking pots were wrought or cast in iron, brass or bronze and decorated with moulded, cast, stamped or pierced ornament. Trivets were very popular in an age before cooking stoves and ranges became fashionable, while iron stands were widely popular until the advent of the self-standing electric iron in fairly recent years. Both trivets and iron stands may be found with figural, heraldic or commemorative motifs but the latter are far more plentiful and provide a much wider range of subjects, especially those of local interest. Cast brass stands date from 1820 but the heyday of the really decorative types was 1880–1920 when they were regarded as an ideal medium for the commemoration of all manner of events and personalities. The more utilitarian iron stands survived till about 1940 but those from 1870 onwards, usually in cast iron, often included firms' names and advertisements.

Tins and tinware

Improved machinery for canning, introduced in 1870, greatly extended the usefulness of tinplate for packaging of all kinds of branded goods. A decade earlier, however, Benjamin George had patented a method of transfer-printing on to metal and this, coupled with the developments in the making of tins and canisters, considerably enlivened the packaging of confectionery, cakes, biscuits, tobacco and other goods in the last quarter of the nineteenth century. The advent of offset-lithography in 1880 made the decor-

A selection of tinware dating from the 1920s (Robert Opie Collection)

ation of tinware even more elaborate and colourful. Embossing was added to the range of processes in 1888 and at the turn of the century there was a craze for novelty tinware in every kind of shape and decorative treatment. Though tins became more prosaic in shape from 1920 onwards the pictorial ornament has steadily improved. Many of the tins produced over the past century are irrelevant to a local collection, other than those produced for goods of local manufacture, but the custom adopted by biscuit-makers and confectioners of embellishing their tins with scenery and landmarks, often in thematic sets, provides the local collector with an abundance of material in this medium. Tins of sweets given to children as part of the celebrations of coronations and jubilees were often decorated with the coat of arms of the local authority, in the same manner as the commemorative mugs, and therefore also qualify for inclusion in a local collection.

Treen

This generic term signifying anything made of wood is confined at the local level to a few highly distinctive categories of woodware popular throughout the nineteenth century and surviving, in some cases, till the 1930s. Snuffboxes carved or fashioned from wood were the poor man's counterpart of the elegant silver objects of vertu discussed in the previous chapter. They were a speciality of Scottish craftsmen, working in and around Laurencekirk, Kincardineshire, where the crippled woodworker, Sandy Stivens, invented the concealed integral wooden hinge. The top, base, front and back of

'Treen' sycamore wood, transfer-printed Solway snuff box, 1823. Souvenir of the Maryport to Newcastle Canal (By courtesy of Birmingham Museums and Art Gallery)

these wooden snuffboxes could be decorated with engraved scenery, portraiture and even maps. The Pinto collection, now in the Birmingham Museum, had a spendid Solway snuffbox decorated with a portrait of Robert Burns, a view of his mausoleum in Dumfries, and a map of the Solway coast, with a presentation inscription for good measure! Snuffboxes made of pieces of wood with some association with Robert Burns or William Shakespeare were decorated with pictorialism appropriate to these literary figures. Similarly boxes that purported to be made of pieces of the Boscobel Oak showed the dramatic escape of the youthful Charles II after the Battle of Worcester. In the nineteenth century enterprising craftsmen would salvage timber from the wrecks of famous ships and fashion snuffboxes decorated with pictures of these ships. This adds up to a fairly primitive form of folk-art aimed largely at the embryonic tourist market. Out of this developed two quite distinct forms of applied art which played a major part in the local souvenir trade of the nineteenth century.

Tunbridge ware

Decorative woodware was produced at Tunbridge Wells and Tonbridge in Kent from about 1660, distinguished by its surface decoration of marquetry composed of tiny pieces of wood stained, dyed or bleached in contrasting colours and shades. From this minuscule art form developed the characteristic wood mosaic about 1820. This mosaic was composed of very thin rods of wood of different types and colours glued together to make a picture when viewed in section, and then cut into thin slices which could be affixed to the surface of boxes and other useful articles in the same manner as marquetry veneers. The more intricate pictorial motifs appeared about 1827 and continued over the ensuing sixty years. Towards the end of that period there was a vogue for large boxes with a pictorial mosaic panel showing scenery and landmarks. Although Tunbridge ware was eventually sold by souvenir shops in the resorts all along the south-east coast they continued to be predominantly souvenirs of the Tunbridge Wells and Tonbridge area and consequently most of the pictorial motifs have a Kent interest. The most popular motifs were Eridge, Dover and Tonbridge Castles, the stately homes such as Knole and Penshurst Place, ruined abbeys like Battle and Muckrose and the celebrated Pantiles where many of the Tunbridge ware manufacturers had their shops. From 1887 onwards, however, Tunbridge ware was largely confined to simpler geometric patterns and the industry gradually dwindled, until it was killed off by the outbreak of the Second World War.

Tunbridge Ware jewel cabinet *c*.1860. Decorated with mosaic inlay; panel with Warwick Castle on top; panels with floral bouquets on back and doors and floral banding based on Berlin woolwork patterns. Van Dyke border round base characteristic of work done by the Wise family. Label on inside drawers 'From G. Wise, Jun. Manufacturer Tunbridge' (Tunbridge Wells Museum)

Mauchline ware

Sometimes regarded as the Scottish answer to Tunbridge ware, this type of souvenir was entirely different and, by contrast, was clearly aimed at the tourist market of the nineteenth century everywhere. It took its name from the small Ayrshire town of Mauchline where the firm of A. & A. Smith, established about 1820, were originally engaged in quarrying stone for razor hones. Their earliest essay in woodwork was the manufacture of the cases for these hones and razor strops but they very quickly expanded to the manufacture of wooden boxes and cases of all kinds to meet the growing tourist trade of the early nineteenth century. At first these boxes, made of white sycamore, were decorated by hand in pen and ink but they moved on to hand-painted tartan decoration and (about 1840) began producing boxes on which the tartan decoration was printed on paper glued on to the wood. Originally the tartan was intended as a frame to hand-drawn or painted portraits of Robert Burns, who had very close connections with Mauchline, but Bonnie Prince Charlie was soon added to the repertoire, to cash in on the rising tide of Romanticism fostered by the writings of Sir Walter Scott. The tartan boxes – snuffboxes, pillboxes, rouge pots and stamp boxes – have no local relevance, beyond the use of the many different Scottish tartans which, by 1850, were identified in gilt lettering. Since most of the Scottish clans have a territorial affinity the tartan boxes can be collected on a county or regional basis.

About the middle of the century, however, the Smiths found their true metier. The laborious hand-drawn designs were replaced about 1845 by black transfer prints taken from steel or copper engravings. The prints were fixed by varnishing the sycamore wood into a distinctive tawny colour. As the range of useful articles to which these transfer prints could be applied grew – Edward Pinto had listed over 120 different categories from photograph albums and bezique markers to wool-ball holders and work boxes – so also did the range of pictures increase. They reached their peak between 1860 and 1900 but continued till 1933 when the Mauchline boxworks was destroyed by fire. At their zenith the Smiths also had a factory and warehouse in Birmingham, then very much the centre of the British souvenir industry. The copper and later steel plates from which the Smiths took transfers were engraved in Birmingham, Sheffield and London and from the outset the range of subjects was very wide, including hotels, public buildings, monuments and identifiable scenes in all the towns and cities of England and Wales which attracted visitors. A volume of *Views for Sycamore Work*, used by Smith salesmen, lists over 450 views in the south and west of England and Wales alone, from Abergavenny asylum to Wilton church and presumably other volumes, covering the rest of the British Isles, also existed. Their range of Scottish views was even more detailed and few places, no matter how remote or obscure, were not the subject of a Smith transfer print at some time or other. The Smiths also produced an astonishing range of views of European countries, as well as Australia, India, Canada and the United States. The Smith family did for woodware what Goss did for china, providing the tourist and day-tripper with an inexpensive souvenir of their holiday outings.

Textiles

The craft of needlework was one of the necessary accomplishments of all women until the middle of the present century and part of the education in this skill consisted of working a sampler. Pieces of linen were neatly embroidered by girls and young ladies from the early seventeenth century onwards. The earlier samplers were instructional, demonstrating the range of stitches which had to be mastered, with the letters of the alphabet and the numerals in cross-stitch, and usually the name of the youthful seamstress and the date on which it was completed. Such samplers, spanning a period of three centuries, are not uncommon, but their relevance to a local collection is governed by whether one can identify the seamstress and assign her to a definite locality. Since relatively few of these instructional samplers include the name of the school or the village or town, this is no easy task. Ornamental samplers, however, came into fashion in the 1790s and became something of a craze which peaked in 1830–70, then tailed off till the time of the First World War. These samplers were often worked on prepared sheets of linen stencilled with views of famous landmarks and scenery, but the more imaginative and ambitious young ladies sometimes struck out on their own and worked a picture copied from the *Graphic* or the *Illustrated London News*. One is more likely to come across an ornamental sampler with a motif of local interest. Stencilled canvas sheets were also published by Berlin manufacturers, hence the term Berlin woolwork given to the specimens of ornamental crewelwork and worsted-work which were also popular for much of the nineteenth century. These tapestries were worked in short thrums of coloured wool, and they continue to this day. As a medium of local expression, however, woolwork tapestry is limited, since the majority of the pictures relate to a few instantly recognizable subjects, such as Tower Bridge, Windsor Castle, the Forth Bridge and the Clifton Bridge.

Handkerchiefs

Hand-embroidered pocket handkerchiefs of the finest linen were very expensive and confined to the wealthier classes, but from about 1820 printed calico or those woven on Jacquard looms became increasingly plentiful and were very much cheaper. At first simple floral motifs were favoured, but by the middle of the nineteenth century more elaborate pictorial designs were commonplace. By the 1860s this medium was widely used to commemorate events and personalities or even for political or religious propaganda in the same manner as the broadsheets and tracts of an earlier generation. Printed handkerchiefs with portraits of Queen Victoria, Disraeli, Gladstone and other celebrities, both royal and political, were immensely popular in Britain in the second half of the nineteenth century. From the 1870s till the outbreak of the First World War printed or woven handkerchiefs were produced for fairs and exhibitions, for jubilees and coronations and, most of all, as tourist souvenirs of holiday resorts. The finely engraved vignettes contained in ornamental cartouches, usually one in each corner, with a larger picture in the centre, echoed the pictorial notepaper of the same or slightly earlier period. Such trifles went into eclipse during and after the First World War but in recent years have made a comeback, with the additional benefit of full colour.

Stevengraphs

The boom in cheap woven pictorial handkerchiefs was triggered off by the removal of restrictions on the importation of foreign silk goods. The French dominated this market and within two years the indigenous industry had almost collapsed. Thousands of textile workers in and around Coventry, the centre of the English silk-weaving trade, were thrown out of work. It was then that Thomas Stevens came to the rescue. He had started up in business only in 1854 and was experimenting with various new ideas when the slump came. Not a man to give up easily, he persevered and by 1862 had succeeded in adapting the Jacquard loom to manufacture small multicoloured silk pictures. His earliest products consisted of narrow silk bookmarkers but they were an immediate success and Stevens was soon exploring other media, turning his silk pictures into greetings cards, calendars, sashes, ribands, badges and favours. Almost single-handed, Stevens generated an entirely new market and the public clamoured for his attractive pictorial silks. The major breakthrough was the distribution and sale of these silks through booksellers and stationers, a complete change from the normal drapery

Woven silk picture or stevengraph of The Lady Godiva Procession, Coventry. Design registered March 1880 (Herbert Art Gallery and Museum, Coventry)

outlets of the Coventry silk manufacturers.

In 1874 Stevens hit upon the idea of making larger and more ambitious woven silk pictures, mounting them on cardboard ready for framing and hanging on walls. The woven texture of these pictures gave them a startling three-dimensional effect and, again, Stevens had an instant success. Over the ensuing thirty-odd years countless thousands of these pictures, which he termed stevengraphs, were sold. Stevens himself died in 1888, but the business was carried on by his sons. In the early years of this century, taking note of trends in public taste, the Stevens company began manufacturing woven silk postcards. The vogue for stevengraphs declined after the First World War and comparatively few new pictures were added to the repertoire, the most notable being those celebrating the coronation of 1937. The firm went out of business, being totally destroyed during the Coventry blitz in 1940. From 1879 onwards, when Stevens personally demonstrated his skills at the York Industrial Exhibition, portable looms were installed at all the major national and international exhibitions and stevengraphs commemorating the occasion were woven on the spot for sale to visitors.

In many respects stevengraphs did for silk what the Staffordshire flat-back figures did for pottery; they furnished a medium for the portrayal of the popular heroes of the nineteenth century. Both American and European subjects were included in the range, as well as scenes drawn from classical mythology and the Bible. At a more local level, however, many of the exhibition stevengraphs merit attention. In addition to the York silks of 1879 these included stevengraphs produced in commemoration of the Edinburgh International Exhibition (1886), the Glasgow International Exhibition

(1888), the Manchester International Exhibition (1887) and the Royal Jubilee Exhibition, Newcastle (1887). Although Stevens produced special silks for international exhibitions in America, France and Germany it is surprising that he did not exploit this idea more fully in Britain. It may be significant that the exhibition silks were all manufactured in his own lifetime.

The scenic stevengraphs with identifiable views and landmarks include Balmoral, Conway, Kenilworth, Warwick and Windsor castles, the Clifton suspension bridge and the Old Tyne bridge, general views of Coventry, the original Coventry Cathedral (flanked by tiny vignettes of Coventry old and new), the Crystal Palace, the Forth Bridge, the Houses of Parliament, various silks of Lady Godiva and the Godiva procession through the streets of Coventry, the Mersey Tunnel Railway, Ye Old Crown House, Birmingham, the seafront at Blackpool, the Winter Gardens, Blackpool, William of Orange at the Battle of the Boyne, and the Tower of London. Several of his sporting silks may be assigned to definite localities. It is thought, for example, that the stevengraphs entitled 'The Last Lap' show the finish of a cycle race in Coventry, which was also the home of the British cycle industry. Similarly some of the coaching and railway stevengraphs depict specific coaches and locomotives, such as the London-York coach and the Lord Howe and Stephenson locomotives, which are relevant to a local collection. Stevens produced a vast number of portrait silks honouring royalty and heads of state, politicians, soldiers and sailors, sportsmen, religious figures and historical or mythical characters, and many of these have a local relevance. They include Peeping Tom and Lady Godiva (Coventry), Grace Darling (Northumberland), General Macdonald (Ross-shire), W. G. Grace (Gloucestershire), Robert Burns (Ayrshire) and John Bright (Yorkshire). The silk postcards published by the Stevens company from 1903 till 1915 covered much the same ground as the stevengraphs but included a few new subjects, including Ann Hathaway's Cottage, Grey Friars Green, Coventry, the Laxey Wheel, the Tower of Refuge, and the Loch Promenade in Douglas, Isle of Man, the Liverpool Landing Stage, Princes Street, Edinburgh, Shakespeare's Birthplace, St George's Hall and St George's Square, Liverpool, St Paul's Cathedral and, Tower Bridge.

Many other textile companies cashed in on the success of the stevengraphs and published their own silk pictures. Although few equalled Stevens in quality and vivid colouring they are not without merit, and those with a local character deserve serious consideration. Among the firms which also produced woven silk pictures the most notable were E. Wilson of Macclesfied, William H. Grant of Coventry, Welch & Lenton of Coventry, and J. & J. Cash of Coventry. Of these, the last-named is still active in this field, though nylon rather than silk is used nowadays. To Messrs Cash is due the credit for keeping the textile picture business going through the lean years and in more recent times they have produced a wide range of calendars, woven pictures, postcards and even first-day covers for the latest issues of stamps.

The Grant company continued in business until 1960 when it was taken over by J. & J. Cash who have nobly continued the tradition of woven pictures. Though Grant silks are not so well documented as the more famous stevengraphs they are of immense interest. The pictorial silks covered the same ground as the stevengraphs, but, continuing to be more active in this field over a longer period, their range is wider and includes All Hallows Church, Blarney Castle, the Bradford Exhibition (1904), the Cartwright Memorial, Bradford. Clovelly Harbour, Birmingham Council House, Stonehenge, the Dublin Exhibition (1907), a fine range of Edinburgh scenes, the Cork International Exhibition (1902–03), the Scottish National Exhibition, Edinburgh (1908) and the Scottish Exhibition, Glasgow (1911), the High Level Bridge, Newcastle, Holyrood Palace, Jesmond Dene, Newcastle, Killarney, Lister Park, Bradford, the City Chambers, George Square and the Art Galleries, Glasgow, Old Bishopsgate, London, Peel Castle, Isle of Man, Sackville Street and the Cascade, Stephen's Green, Dublin, Edinburgh Old Tolbooth, Glasgow University, and York Minster. More recent silks, by Grant, Cash or Brocklehurst Fabrics of Macclesfield, include the old and new cathedrals of Coventry, Sulgrave Manor, various public houses in and around Macclesfield, Prestbury, Hurdsfield House and Gawsworth Rectory. Since 1968 woven pictures used for First Day Covers have grown in popularity. The earliest of them were produced by Keith Clayton under the trade name of the Silk Art Company and featured Shakespeare's birthplace. Later Mr Clayton registered the name 'Textiles and Philately' and under this name produce silks which included Coventry Cathedral and Caernarvon Castle (celebrating the investiture of the Prince of Wales). More recently a wide range of first-day cover silks has been marketed by A. Buckingham of the Benham company for Britain, Guernsey, Jersey and the Isle of Man in more recent years.

Appendix

List of collectables arranged in county or regional order

As a guide to collectors twenty-four of the more popular categories of collectable have been analysed on a geographical basis. Certain categories, such as railwayana, trade ephemera (bills and letterheads), tickets, newspapers and periodicals, postal history and postmarks, maps and topographical prints, cheques, militaria, bottles, crested china and Mauchline ware apply to every county and region. At the other extreme, communion tokens are mainly confined to the Scottish and northern Irish counties. Pictorial potlids are of specific interest to collectors in only a handful of counties, though if the commercial monochrome toothpaste lids were included they would probably be relevant to almost every county. Similarly pictorial horse-brasses are restricted to subjects relevant to few counties, but named saddlers' brasses would considerably augment that. The list covers the counties and major cities of England and Wales, the counties of Northern Ireland, the regions of Scotland, and the Crown Dependencies of Guernsey, Jersey and the Isle of Man.

The following categories are coded numerically:

1   Railwayana
2   Trade ephemera (trade cards, bills, letterheads)
3   Tickets
4   Cigarette cards
5   Newspapers and periodicals
6   Picture postcards
7   Local postage stamps
8   Postal history material and postmarks
9   Maps and topographical prints
10 Coins (Roman, medieval, Civil War and/or more modern periods)
11 Tradesmen's tokens and checks
12 Communion tokens

13 Commemorative and prize medals
14 Provincial banknotes
15 Cheques
16 Stock and share certificates
17 Militaria (regimental badges, buttons and insignia)
18 Glass bottles, stoneware ginger beer bottles
19 Goss and other crested china
20 Pictorial potlids
21 Crested caddy and teaspoons
22 Horse brasses
23 Mauchline transfer-printed woodware
24 Stevengraphs and other woven silk pictures

ENGLAND

Avon	1	2	3	4	5	6	7	8	9	10	11	—
	13	14	15	16	17	18	19	—	21	22	23	24
Bedfordshire	1	2	3	4	5	6	—	8	9	10	11	—
	13	14	15	16	17	18	19	—	21	—	23	—
Berkshire	1	2	3	4	5	6	7	8	9	10	11	—
	13	14	15	16	17	18	19	20	21	22	23	24
Birmingham	1	2	3	4	5	6	7	8	9	10	11	12
	13	14	15	16	17	18	19	—	21	22	23	24
Buckinghamshire	1	2	3	—	5	6	7	8	9	10	11	—
	13	14	15	16	17	18	19	—	21	22	23	—
Cambridgeshire	1	2	3	—	5	6	7	8	9	10	11	—
	13	14	15	16	17	18	19	—	21	—	23	—
Cheshire	1	2	3	4	5	6	—	8	9	10	11	—
	13	14	15	16	17	18	19	—	21	—	23	—
Cleveland	1	2	3	4	5	6	—	8	9	10	11	—
	13	14	15	16	17	18	19	—	21	—	23	—
Cornwall	1	2	3	—	5	6	7	8	9	10	11	—
	13	14	15	16	17	18	19	—	21	22	23	—
Cumbria	1	2	3	4	5	6	7	8	9	10	11	12
	13	14	15	16	17	18	19	—	21	22	23	—
Derbyshire	1	2	3	4	5	6	7	8	9	10	11	—
	13	14	15	16	17	18	19	—	21	—	23	—
Devon	1	2	3	4	5	6	7	8	9	10	11	—
	13	14	15	16	17	18	19	—	21	—	23	24
Dorset	1	2	3	—	5	6	—	8	9	10	11	—
	13	14	15	16	17	18	19	—	21	—	23	—
Durham	1	2	3	—	5	6	7	8	9	10	11	—
	13	14	15	16	17	18	19	—	21	—	23	—
Essex	1	2	3	—	5	6	7	8	9	10	11	—
	13	14	15	16	17	18	19	—	21	—	23	—
Gloucestershire	1	2	3	4	5	6	—	8	9	10	11	—
	13	14	15	16	17	18	19	—	21	—	23	24

Hampshire	1	2	3	4	5	6	7	8	9	10	11	—
	13	14	15	16	17	18	19	—	21	—	23	—
Hereford & Worcester	1	2	3	4	5	6	—	8	9	10	11	—
	13	14	15	16	17	18	19	—	21	—	23	—
Hertfordshire	1	2	3	—	5	6	—	8	9	10	11	—
	13	14	15	16	17	18	19	—	21	—	23	—
Humberside	1	2	3	4	5	6	7	8	9	10	11	—
	13	14	15	16	17	18	19	—	21	—	23	—
Isle of Wight	1	2	3	—	5	6	7	8	9	10	11	—
	13	14	15	16	17	18	19	—	21	—	23	—
Kent	1	2	3	—	5	6	7	8	9	10	11	—
	13	14	15	16	17	18	19	20	21	—	23	24
Lancashire	1	2	3	4	5	6	7	8	9	10	11	12
	13	14	15	16	17	18	19	20	21	—	23	—
Leicestershire	1	2	3	—	5	6	—	8	9	10	11	—
	13	14	15	16	17	18	19	—	21	—	23	—
Lincolnshire	1	2	3	4	5	6	7	8	9	10	11	—
	13	14	15	16	17	18	19	—	21	22	23	—
Liverpool	1	2	3	4	5	6	7	8	9	—	11	12
	13	14	15	16	17	18	19	20	21	22	23	24
London	1	2	3	4	5	6	7	8	9	10	11	12
	13	14	15	16	17	18	19	20	21	22	23	24
Manchester	1	2	3	4	5	6	7	8	9	—	11	12
	13	14	15	16	17	18	19	—	21	—	23	24
Norfolk	1	2	3	4	5	6	7	8	9	10	11	—
	13	14	15	16	17	18	19	20	21	—	23	—
Northants	1	2	3	4	5	6	7	8	9	10	11	—
	13	14	15	16	17	18	19	—	21	—	23	—
Northumberland	1	2	3	4	5	6	—	8	9	10	11	12
	13	14	15	16	17	18	19	—	21	—	23	—
Nottinghamshire	1	2	3	4	5	6	—	8	9	10	11	—
	13	14	15	16	17	18	19	—	21	—	23	—
Oxfordshire	1	2	3	—	5	6	7	8	9	10	11	—
	13	14	15	16	17	18	19	—	21	—	23	—
Salop	1	2	3	4	5	6	7	8	9	10	11	—
	13	14	15	16	17	18	19	—	21	—	23	—
Somerset	1	2	3	4	5	6	—	8	9	10	11	—
	13	14	15	16	17	18	19	—	21	—	23	—
Suffolk	1	2	3	4	5	6	7	8	9	10	11	—
	13	14	15	16	17	18	19	—	21	—	23	—
Surrey	1	2	3	4	5	6	7	8	9	10	11	—
	13	14	15	16	17	18	19	—	21	—	23	—
Sussex (E & W)	1	2	3	4	5	6	7	8	9	10	11	—
	13	14	15	16	17	18	19	—	21	—	23	24
Tyne & Wear	1	2	3	4	5	6	—	8	9	10	11	12
	13	14	15	16	17	18	19	—	21	—	23	24

	1	2	3	4	5	6	7	8	9	10	11	12
West Midlands	1	2	3	4	5	6	7	8	9	10	11	—
	13	14	15	16	17	18	19	20	21	22	23	24
Wiltshire	1	2	3	4	5	6	7	8	9	10	11	—
	13	14	15	16	17	18	19	—	21	—	23	24
Yorkshire	1	2	3	4	5	6	7	8	9	10	11	12
	13	14	15	16	17	18	19	—	21	22	23	24

WALES

	1	2	3	4	5	6	7	8	9	10	11	12
Clwyd	1	2	3	—	5	6	7	8	9	10	11	—
	13	14	15	16	17	18	19	—	21	—	23	—
Dyfed	1	2	3	—	5	6	7	8	9	10	11	—
	13	14	15	16	17	18	19	—	21	—	23	24
Glamorgan	1	2	3	4	5	6	7	8	9	10	11	—
	13	14	15	16	17	18	19	—	21	—	23	—
Gwent	1	2	3	4	5	6	7	8	9	10	11	—
	13	14	15	16	17	18	19	—	21	—	23	—
Gwynedd	1	2	3	4	5	6	7	8	9	10	11	—
	13	14	15	16	17	18	19	—	21	—	23	24
Powys	1	2	3	—	5	6	7	8	9	10	11	—
	13	14	15	16	17	18	19	—	21	—	23	—

SCOTLAND

	1	2	3	4	5	6	7	8	9	10	11	12
Borders	1	2	3	—	5	6	—	8	9	10	11	12
	13	14	15	16	17	18	19	—	21	22	23	—
Central	1	2	3	—	5	6	7	8	9	10	11	12
	13	14	15	16	17	18	19	—	21	—	23	—
Dumfries &	1	2	3	—	5	6	7	8	9	—	11	12
Galloway	13	14	15	16	17	18	19	—	21	—	23	—
Fife	1	2	3	—	5	6	—	8	9	10	11	12
	13	—	15	16	17	18	19	—	21	—	23	—
Grampian	1	2	3	4	5	6	7	8	9	10	11	12
	13	14	15	16	17	18	19	—	21	22	23	—
Highland	1	2	3	—	5	6	7	8	9	—	11	12
	13	14	15	16	17	18	19	—	21	—	23	—
Islands	1	2	3	—	5	6	7	8	9	—	—	12
	—	14	15	—	17	—	19	—	21	—	23	24
Lothian	1	2	3	4	5	6	7	8	9	10	11	12
	13	14	15	16	17	18	19	—	21	—	23	24
Orkney	1	2	3	—	5	6	7	8	9	—	—	12
	13	—	15	16	17	18	19	—	21	—	23	—
Shetland	1	2	3	—	5	6	—	8	9	—	—	12
	13	—	15	16	17	18	19	—	21	—	23	—
Strathclyde	1	2	3	4	5	6	7	8	9	10	11	12
	13	14	15	16	17	18	19	—	21	22	23	24
Tayside	1	2	3	4	5	6	7	8	9	10	11	12
	13	14	15	16	17	18	19	—	21	—	23	—

NORTHERN IRELAND

Antrim	1	2	3	—	5	6	7	8	9	10	11	12
	13	14	15	16	17	18	19	—	21	—	23	24
Armagh	1	2	3	—	5	6	—	8	9	—	11	12
	13	14	15	16	17	18	19	—	21	—	23	—
Belfast	1	2	3	4	5	6	7	8	9	—	11	12
	13	14	15	16	17	18	19	—	21	—	23	—
Down	1	2	3	—	5	6	7	8	9	10	11	12
	13	14	15	16	17	18	19	—	21	—	23	—
Fermanagh	1	2	3	—	5	6	—	8	9	—	11	12
	13	14	15	16	17	18	19	—	21	—	23	—
Londonderry	1	2	3	—	5	6	7	8	9	—	11	12
	13	14	15	16	17	18	19	—	21	—	23	—
Tyrone	1	2	3	—	5	6	7	8	9	—	11	12
	13	14	15	16	17	18	19	—	21	—	23	—

CROWN DEPENDENCIES

Guernsey	1	2	3	—	5	6	7	8	9	10	11	—
	13	14	15	16	17	18	19	—	21	—	23	24
Jersey	1	2	3	—	5	6	7	8	9	10	11	—
	13	14	15	16	17	18	19	—	21	—	23	24
Isle of Man	1	2	3	4	5	6	7	8	9	10	11	12
	13	14	15	16	17	18	19	—	21	22	23	24

Suggested reading

Industrial Archaeology

Butt, John, *The Industrial Archaeology of Scotland*. Newton Abbot, 1967
Donnachie, Ian L., *Industrial Archaeology of Galloway*. Newton Abbot, 1971
Hume, John R., *Industrial Archaeology in Scotland*. London, 1976

Ephemera

Gladwish, Victor E. R., *The Third Book of Proven British and British-imported Matchbox Label Brands*. Huntingdon, 1978
Hill, C. W., *Collecting Cigarette and Trade Cards*. Southampton, 1979
Lewis, John, *Collecting Printed Ephemera*. London, 1979
Luker, J. H. *The Matchbox Label Collector's Catalogue*. London, 1978
Mitchell, David C., *Entered at Stationers' Hall*. London, 1978
Mullen, Chris, *Cigarette Pack Art*, London, 1979
Osborne, Keith W., *The International Book of Beer Labels, Mats and Coasters*. London, 1979; *The Beer-drinker's Guide to Labology*. Farnborough, 1980
Rickards, Maurice, *This is Ephemera; Collecting Printed Throwaways*. Newton Abbot, 1978
Robinson, W. Heath, *The Subtle Art of Advertising*. London, 1979

Deltiology

Byatt, Anthony, *Picture Postcards and Their Publishers*. Malvern, 1978
Duval, William and **Monahan, Valerie**, *Collecting Postcards in Colour, 1894–1914*. Poole, 1978
Gascoigne, Bamber, *Images of Richmond to 1900*. Richmond, 1980
Hewlett, Maurice, R., *Picton's Priced Catalogue and Handbook of Pictorial Postcards*. Chippenham, 1981
Holt, Toni and **Valmai**, *Stanley Gibbons Postcard Catalogue*. London, 1981
Monahan, Valerie, *Collecting Postcards in Colour, 1914–1930*. Poole, 1980
Sidey, Tessa, *Valentines of Dundee*. Dundee, 1979
Staff, Frank, *The Picture Postcard and its Origins*. London, 1979
Welsch, Roger L., *Tell-tale Postcards: A Pictorial History*. London, 1978

Philately

Backman, A., *The Channel Island of Jethou Priced Catalogue.* 1981
Barefoot, S. *Guernsey and Jersey Revenues.* 1979
Bourdi, M., *Catalogue des Timbres de Grève* (1971 Postal Strike stamps), Paris
Dagnall, H., *Perfins of Great Britain* (3 vols). 1978
Ecclestone, *Railway Letter Stamps of Great Britain and Ireland, 1891–1941.* n.d.
Gibbons, Stanley, *Channel Islands Specialised Catalogue; Collect Channel Islands Stamps.* London, various editions, published every two years, *Collect Isle of Man Stamps.* London, 1981
Hunter, Stanley, *The Scottish Stamp Catalogue.* Glasgow 1963; *The Scottish Stamp News* (monthly, with catalogue supplements)
Jackson, H. L., *The Railway & Airway Letter Stamps of the British Isles, 1891–1941.* Batley, 1979
Jones, Lionel D., *United Kingdom Savings Stamps, Labels and Coupons.* London, 1979
Lister, Raymond, *College Stamps of Oxford and Cambridge.* London
Lowe, Robson, *Encyclopaedia of British Empire Postage Stamps*, vol. I. London, 1952
Mackay, James A., *The Parcel Post of the British Isles.* Dumfries, 1982
Newport, O. W., *The People's League Delivery Service.* London, 1963; *Stamps and Postal History of the Channel Islands.* London, 1972
O'Neill, C. P,, *Newspapers Stamps of Ireland.* Enniskillen, 1978
Patton, Dr Donald, *Farthing Delivery – a Fight for Cheaper Postage.* London, 1964
Potter, David, *Great Britain Railway Letter Stamps, 1957–80.* London, 1980
Rosen, Gerald, *Catalogue of British Local Stamps.* London, 1979
Whitney, Dr T. J., *Yn Post Manninagh.* Thundersley, 1976; *Isle of Man Catalogue of Stamps and Postal History.* Hadleigh, 1979; *Isle of Man Stamps and Postal History.* Chippenham, 1981
Woodward-Clarke, R. L., *Registration Labels of Great Britain and Ireland*, 2 vols. Sutton Coldfield, 1979–81

Postal history

Auckland, A. Bruce, *Edinburgh Penny Posts.* Edinburgh, 1972; *Mileage Marks of Scotland.* Edinburgh, 1965; *Postal Markings of Scotland to 1808* Edinburgh, 1978; *Penny Posts of Scotland.* Edinburgh, 1982
Austin, Brian, *English Provincial Posts.* Chichester, 1978
Beith, Richard, *Scottish Airmails.* Glasgow, 1981; *Yorkshire Airmails.* 1983
Boyes, Dennis, *The Postal History of Bradford to 1884.* Sheffield, 1979
Britnor, L. E., *The Postal History of Reigate, Redhill and District.* Redhill, 1979
Buckley, Eric, *Wakefield Postal History.* Sheffield, n.d.
Bullamore, Colin, *The History of Whitby's Post.* Whitby, 1979
Calvert, Charles, *The History of the Manchester Post Office, 1625–1900.* Manchester, 1965
Cowell, J. B., *The Bangor Penny Post.* Beaumaris, 1978; *The Postal History of Beaumaris.* Beaumaris, 1981

Feldman, David and **Kane, William**, *Postal History of Ireland to 1840*. Dublin, 1975

Gade, F. W., *The Postal History of Lundy*. Bideford, n.d.

Homer-Wooff, G. H. R., *The Postal History of Bracknell*. 1981; *Wokingham*. 1981; *Newbury*. 1982; and **Jones, Peter**, *The Postal History of Reading*. Wokingham, 1982

Jarand, G. M., *Isle of Man Slogan and Special Postmarks*. Nottingham, 1976

Jones, R. G., *The Postal History of Caernarfon*. Colwyn Bay, 1979

Kemp, N. P,, *The Postal Service of the Isle of Man*. Onchan, 1982

Lewis, Eric, *Sheffield's Posts in Peakland and the Hope Valley*. Sheffield, 1979

London Postal History Group, *London's Postal History*. (In progress since 1974)

Mackay, James A., (all published at Dumfries); *Circular Name Stamps of Scotland*: 1978; *Skeleton Postmarks of Scotland*. 1978; *Scottish Postmarks Since 1693*. 1978; *The Floating Post Offices of the Clyde*. 1979; the *Islands Postal History Series* – 12 vols on the Scottish islands and the Isle of Wight. 1979–81; *English and Welsh Postmarks Since 1840*. 1980; Irish Postmarks since 1840. 1982; *Registered Mail of the British Isles*. 1983

Mann, John C., *Meter Stamp Catalogue of the United Kingdom and Eire*. London, 1972

Massy, A. J. P. *Isle of Man Postmarks*. Douglas, 1969

Mayo, A. J. *Lancashire and Cheshire Local Receiving Offices*. Manchester, 1979

Morgan, Sybil and **Scott-Archer, Michael**, *The Postal History of Cardiff*. Cardiff, 1974

Oxley, Geoffrey M., *English Provincial Local Posts, 1765–1840*. Bridport, 1973

Oxley, H. M. and **Williams, D. R.**, *A Postal History of Durham City*. Durham, 1980

Parsons, C., Peachey, C., and **Pearson, G. R.**, *Slogan Postmarks of the United Kingdom* (2 vols and supplements). London, 1971–74; *Slogan Postmarks of the Seventies*. London, 1980

Pearson, George R., *Special Event Postmarks of the United Kingdom, 1851–1973*. London, 1973

Povey, A. and **Whitney, T. J.** *The Postal History of the Manx Electric Railway*. Hadleigh, n.d.

Robertson, Alan W., *The Maritime Postal History of the British Isles*. London, 1955–60

Scott-Archer, Michael, *Welsh Post Towns*. Chichester, 1969

Sedgwick, William A., *Postal History of Doncaster*. Sheffield, 1975 and **Ward, Ronald**, *Sheffield's Post Offices in the Wapentake of Strafforth and Tickhill*. Sheffield, 1979; *Postal History of Harrogate, Knaresborough and Ripon*. Sheffield, 1976; *Postal History of Goole, Howden and Selby*. Sheffield, 1981

Stitt-Dibden, William G., *Leicester and the Posts*. London, 1966

Trinder, Ivan F., *Postal History of the Tendring Hundred of Essex*. Clacton, 1971

Viner, Brig. G. A., *The Postal History of Chichester, 1635–1900*. Chichester, 1965

Ward, Ronald, *The Postal History of Upper Wharfdale, Ilkley and Otley*. Sheffield, 1976; *Temporary Handstamps of Yorkshire*. Sheffield, 1977; and **Leese, Brian**, *Manx Mail*. London, 1969
Warn, Ian M., *Bristol 5th Clause and Penny Posts*. Bristol, 1980
Willcocks, R. Martin, *England's Postal History*. London, 1975; *The Postal History of Great Britain and Ireland*. London, 1972; and **Jay, Barrie**, *British County Catalogues* (London, 1978–   )

Maps and topographical prints

Baynton-Williams, Roger, *Investing in Maps*. London, 1969
Crone, G. R., *Maps and their Makers*. London, 1962
Engen, Rodney K., *Dictionary of Victorian Engravers, Print Publishers and Their Work*. Cambridge, 1979
Fordham, Sir H. George, *Maps: Their History, Characteristics and Uses*. London
Lee, R. J., *English County Maps*. London, 1953
Lister, Raymond, *How to Identify Old Maps and Globes*. London, 1965; *Antique Maps and their Cartographers*. London, 1970
Lynham, Edward, *British Maps and Map-makers*. London, 1944
Radford, P. J., *Antique Maps*. Portsmouth, 1965
Robinson, A. H. W., *Marine Cartography in Britain*. London, 1962
Russell, Ronald, *Guide to British Topographical Prints*. Newton Abbot, 1979
Skelton, R. A., *Decorative Printed Maps of the Fifteenth to Eighteenth Centuries*. London, 1969; *County Atlases of the British Isles*. London, 1972
Tooley, R. V., *Maps and Mapmakers*. London, 1972; *Collecting Antique Maps*. London, 1976.

Coins and tokens

Bell, R. C., *Tradesmen's Tickets and Private Tokens*. London, 1966; *Unofficial Farthings, 1820–1870*. London, 1981
Berry, George, *Taverns and Tokens of Pepys' London*. London, 1980
Dalton, Richard, *The Silver Token Coinage, 1811–12*. London, 1972
Dalton, R. and **Hamer, S. H.**, *The Provincial Token Coinage of the Eighteenth Century*. London, 1910, reprinted 1975
Davis, W. J., *The Nineteenth Century Token Coinage*. London, 1969
Dolley, Michael, *Medieval Anglo-Irish Coins*. London, 1969
Finn, Patrick, *Coins of Ireland*. London, 1979
Hawkins, R. N. P., *Public House Checks of Birmingham and Smethwick*. Birmingham, 1978
Mack, R. P., *The Coinage of Ancient Britain*. London 1976
Mackay, James A., *The Pobjoy Encyclopaedia of Isle of Man Coins and Tokens*. Sutton, 1977
Mathias, P., *English Trade Tokens*. London, 1962
Purvey, P. Frank, *Coins and Tokens of Scotland*. London, 1973
Seaby, B. A., *Coins of England, 18th edition*. London, 1981
Seaby, Peter, *Coins and Tokens of Ireland*. London, 1965
Todd, Neil B., *Tavern Tokens in Wales*. Cardiff, 1982

Waters, A. W., *Notes on Eighteenth Century Tokens.* London, 1954; *Notes on Nineteenth Century Tokens.* London, 1957
Whitting, P. D., *Coins, Tokens and Medals of the East Riding of Yorkshire.* London, 1969

Commemorative and Prize Medals

British Museum, *Medallic Illustrations of the History of Great Britain and Ireland.* (2 vols). reprinted London, 1969
Brown, Laurence, *Historic Medals, 1760–1960.* London, 1981
Brown, M. D., *Catalogue of Medals relating to the History of Transport.* London, 1968
Cochran-Patrick, R. W., *Catalogue of the Medals of Scotland.* Edinburgh, 1888
Cresswell, Oliver D., *Irish Medals.* Belfast, 1961
Linecar, Howard W. A., *The Commemorative Medal.* Newton Abbot, 1974
Mackay, James A., *Commemorative Medals.* London, 1970
Welch, C., *Medals struck by the Corporation of London, 1831–1893.* London, 1894
Whiting, J. R. S., *Commemorative Medals.* Newton Abbot, 1972

Notaphily and Scripophily

Angus, Ian, *Paper Money.* London, 1974
Douglas, James, *A Collector's Guide to Bills of Exchange.* Carlisle, 1978; *Scottish Banknotes.* London, 1975; *Collecting British Cheques.* London, 1980
Duggleby, Vincent, *English Paper Money.* London, 1975
Hendy, Robin, *Collecting Old Bonds and Shares.* London, 1978
Le Marchant, R., *Paper Treasure of the Channel Islands.* Guernsey, n.d.
Narbeth, Colin, *Collect British Banknotes.* London, 1970; and **Lyon, David** and **Douglas, James**, *Successful Investing in Stamps and Banknotes with a Catalogue of Early English Banks.* London, 1975
Quarmby, Ernest, *Banknotes and Banking in the Isle of Man, 1788–1970.* London, 1971

Militaria

Abbott, P. G. and **Tamplin, J. M.**, *British Gallantry Awards.* London, 1971
Almack, Edward, *Regimental Badges Worn in the British Army One Hundred Years Ago.* London, 1900; reprinted, 1970
Anderson, D., *Scots in Uniform.* Edinburgh, 1972
Bloomer, W. H. and **K. D.**, *Scottish Regimental Badges, 1793–1971.* London, 1973
Bowling, A. H., *Scottish Regiments, 1660–1914.* London, 1970
Carman, W. Y., *Headdress of the British Army* – **Cavalry.** Sandhurst, 1968; *Yeomanry.* London, 1970; *Glengarry Badges of the British Line Regiments.* London, 1973
Chichester, H. M. and **Burgess-Short, G.**, *Records and Badges of the British Army.* London, 1970
Cole, H. N., *Badges on Battledress.* Aldershot, 1953

Edwards T. J., *Regimental Badges*. London, 1968
Farmer, J. S., *Regimental Records*. London, 1901
Gordon, L. L.*British Battles and Medals*. London, 1971
Harris, R. G., *Fifty Years of Yeomanry Uniform*. London, 1972
Higham, R., *A Guide to the Sources of British Military History*. London, 1972
Kipling, A and **King, H.**, *Headdress Badges of the British Army*. London, 1973
May, W. and **Carman, W. Y.**, *Badges and Insignia of the British Armed Services*. London, 1974
Parkyn, H. G,, *Shoulder-belt Plates and Buttons*. Aldershot, 1956
Peacock, Primrose, *Buttons for the Collector*. Newton Abbot, 1972
Purves, Alex, *Collecting Medals and Decorations*. London, 1968
Ripley, H., *Buttons of the British Army, 1855–1970*. London, 1971
Simkin, R. and Archer, L., *British Yeomanry Uniforms*. London, 1971
Squire, Gwen, *Buttons: A Guide for Collectors*. London, 1972
Taprell-Dorling, T., *Ribbons and Medals*. London, 1974
Wilkinson, Frederick, *Badges of the British Army, 1820–1960*. London, 1971
Wise, T. *A Guide to Military Museums*. Hemel Hempstead, 1971
Wright, R. J., *Collecting Volunteer Militaria*. Newton Abbot, 1974

Glass

Bedford, John, *Bristol and other Coloured Glass*. London, 1964
Crompton, Sidney (ed.), *English Glass*. London, 1967
Davis, Derek C., *English and Irish Antique Glass*. London, 1965
Elville, E. M., *English and Irish Cut Glass*. London, 1953; *Paperweights and other Glass Curiosities*. London, 1954
Fleming, J. A., *Scottish and Jacobite Glass*. London, 1938
Fletcher, Edward, *Bottle Collecting*. Poole, 1975; *Digging up Antiques*. London, 1975
Hollister, Paul, Jr, *The Encyclopedia of Glass Paperweights*. New York, 1969.
Lloyd, Ward, *Investing in Georgian Glass*. London, 1969
Mackay, James A., *Glass Paperweights*. London, 1973
Ruggles-Brise, Lady Sheelah, *Sealed Glass Bottles*, London, 1949
Thorpe, W. A., *English Glass*. London, 1961
Warren, P., *Irish Glass*. London, 1970
Wills, Geoffrey, *English and Irish Glass*. London, 1968; *Antique Glass*. London, 1971; *The Bottle-Collector's Guide*. Edinburgh, 1977

Ceramics

Andrews, Sandy, *Crested China: The History of Heraldic Souvenir Ware*. Hayling Island, 1980
Ball, Abraham, *The Price Guide to Pot Lids*. Woodbridge, 1970; *The Price Guide to Underglaze Colour Printed Ware*. Woodbridge, 1979
Barnard, Julian, *Victorian Ceramic Tiles*. London, 1972
Barton, K. J., *Medieval Sussex Pottery*. Chichester, 1979
Bemrose, Geoffery, *19th Century English Pottery*.
Bell, R. C., *Tyneside Pottery*. London, 1971

Blunt, R., *Cheyne Book of Chelsea Porcelain*. London, 1924
Boney, Dr. Knowles, *Liverpool Porcelain*. London, 1957
Bryant, G. F., *Chelsea Porcelain Toys*. London, 1925
Clarke, Harold G., *The Pictorial Pot Lid Book*. London, 1960
Cushion, John P. and **Honey, W. B.**, *The Handbook of Pottery and Porcelain Marks*. London, 1965
Eyles, Desmond and **Dennis, Richard**, *Royal Doulton Figures Produced at Burslem, 1890–1978*. Burslem, 1978
Fleming, J. Arnold, *Scottish Pottery*. Wakefield, 1973
Garner, F. H. and **Archer, Michael**, *English Delftware*. London, 1972
Gilhespy, F. B., *Derby Porcelain*. Leigh-on-Sea, 1950
Godden, Geoffrey, *The Encyclopaedia of British Pottery and Porcelain Marks*. London, 1968; *Caughley and Worcester Porcelain, 1775–1800*. London, 1969; *Coalport and Coalbrookdale Porcelains*. London, 1970; *The Illustrated Guide to Lowestoft Porcelain*. London, 1969; *Minton Pottery and Porcelain of the First Period*. London, 1968
Grant, M. H., *The Makers of Black Basaltes*. London, 1967
Henderson, Ian T., *Pictorial Souvenirs of Britain*, London, 1974
Hurlbutt, F., *Bow Porcelain*, London, 1926; *Chelsea China*. London, 1937; *Old Derby Porcelain*. London, 1925; *Bristol Porcelain*. London, 1928
Imber, Diana, *Collecting Delft*, London, 1968
John, W. D., *Nantgarw Porcelain*. London, 1948
King, W., *Chelsea Porcelain*, London, 1922
Lewis, Griselda, *A Collector's History of English Pottery*. London, 1969
Lockett, Terence A., *Victorian Tiles*. Woodbridge, 1979
Mackay, James A., *Commemorative Pottery and Porcelain*. London, 1971
MacKenna, F. S., *Chelsea Porcelain* (3 vols). Leigh-on-Sea, 1948–52; *Champion's Bristol Porcelain*. Leigh-on-Sea, 1947; *Cookworthy's Plymouth and Bristol Porcelains*. Leigh-on-Sea, 1946; *Worcester Porcelain*. Leigh-on-Sea, 1950
McVeigh, Patrick, *Scottish East Coast Potteries*. Edinburgh, 1980
Mankovitz, Wolf, *Wedgwood*. London, 1968; and **Haggar, Reginald**, *Concise Encyclopaedia of English Pottery and Porcelain*. London, 1957
Meager, K. S., *Swansea and Nantgarw Potteries*. Swansea, 1949
Mountford, Arnold R., *Staffordshire Salt-glazed Stoneware*. London, 1971
Murton, A. E., *Lowestoft China*. Lowestoft, 1932
Nance, E. Morton, *The Pottery and Porcelain of Swansea and Nantgarw*. London, 1943
Oliver, Anthony, *The Victorian Staffordshire Figures: A Guide for Collectors*. London, 1971
Paul, I., *The Scottish Tradition in Pottery*. Edinburgh, 1948
Pountney, W. J., *Old Bristol Potteries*. Bristol, 1920
Pugh, P. D. Gordon, *Staffordshire Pottery Figures and Allied Subjects of the Victorian Era*. London, 1971
Rackham, Bernard, *Early Staffordshire Pottery*. London, 1951
Rice, David, *The Illustrated Guide to Rockingham Porcelain*. London, 1970
Rodgers, David, *Coronalism Souvenirs*. London, 1975
Sandon, Henry, *Worcester Porcelain, 1751–1793*. London, 1980
Savage, George, *The Story of Worcester Porcelain and the Dyson Perrins Museum*. London, 1969

Smith, Alan, *The Illustrated Guide to Liverpool Herculaneum Pottery, 1796–1840*. London 1970
Stringer, G. E., *New Hall Porcelain*. London, 1949
Towner, Donald, *The Handbook of Leeds Pottery*. Leeds, 1951; *English Cream-coloured Earthenware*. London, 1957
Ward, Roland, *The Price Guide to the Models of W. H. Goss*. London, 1975
Watney, Dr Bernard, *Longton Hall Porcelain*. London, 1957
Whiter, Leonard, *Spode*. London, 1970
Williams, I. J., *Guide to the Collection of Welsh Porcelain in the National Museum of Wales*; Cardiff, 1931
Williams-Wood, Cyril: *Staffordshire Pot Lids and their Potters*. London, 1972
York Castle Museum *The Long Collection of Delft and Creamware*. York, 1980

Metalware

Bury, Shirley, *Victorian Electroplate*. London, 1971
Frost, T. W., *Price Guide to Old Sheffield Plate*, Woodbridge, 1971
Hartfield, G., *Horse Brasses*. London, 1965
Hughes, G. Bernard, *Horse Brasses and other Small Items for the Collector*. London, 1962; *Antique Sheffield Plate*, London, 1970
Michaelis, Ronald, *British Pewter*; London, 1969
Peal, C. A., *British Pewter and Britannia Metal*. London, 1971
Perry, Evan, *Collecting Antique Metalware*, London, 1974
Richards, H. S., *All About Horse Brasses*. London, 1944
Wills, Geoffrey, *Collecting Copper and Brass*. London, 1962; *The Book of Copper and Brass*. London, 1969

Treen

Buist, John S., *Mauchline Ware*. Edinburgh, 1974
Pinto, Edward H., *Encyclopaedia and Social History of Treen and Other Wooden Bygones*. London, 1969
Pinto, Edward H. and **Eva R.**, *Tunbridge and Scottish Souvenir Woodware*; London, 1970

Textiles

Godden, Geoffrey A., *Stevengraphs and other Victorian Silk Pictures*. London, 1971
King, D., *Samplers*. London, 1960
Sprake, Austin, *The Price Guide to Stevengraphs*. Woodbridge, 1972

Index